Frontier Religion

Elder Daniel Parker, His Religious and Political Life

Dan B. Wimberly

EAKIN PRESS Fort Worth, Texas
www.EakinPress.com

Copyright © 2002
By Dan B. Wimberly
Published By Eakin Press
An Imprint of Wild Horse Media Group
P.O. Box 331779
Fort Worth, Texas 76163
1-817-344-7036
www.EakinPress.com
ALL RIGHTS RESERVED
1 2 3 4 5 6 7 8 9
ISBN-10: 1-68179-010-6
ISBN-13: 978-1-68179-010-7

Library of Congress Cataloging-in-Publication Data

Wimberly, Dan B.
   Frontier religion : Elder Daniel Parker : his religious and political life / by Dan B. Wimberly.
    p. cm.
   Includes bibliographical references and index.
   ISBN 1-68179-010-6
   1. Parker, Daniel, b. 1781. 2. Parker, Daniel, b. 1781—Political activity. 3. Baptists—United States—Biography. 4. Pioneers—United States—Biography. I. Title.
BX6495.P265W55   2000
286'.4
[B]--DC21
                                        99-30033
                                           CIP

Contents

Acknowledgments		v
Introduction		vii
Chapter 1	Georgia and Tennessee: The Formative Years	1
Chapter 2	The Illinois Years: Political Life	26
Chapter 3	The Illinois Years: Religious Controversy	56
Chapter 4	The Texas Years: Pioneer and Political Leader	91
Chapter 5	The Texas Ministry	126
Chapter 6	Conclusion: "A Man of War"	146
Endnotes		161
Bibliography		193

List of Figures

1 Modern Illinois Showing Population Density in 1820   29

2 Texas in 1834   96

3 Locations in which Daniel Parker Settled   110

4 Churches Organized by Parker   141

Acknowledgments

Several persons and archival sources have been vital to the preparation of this book. Professors Alwyn Barr, Benjamin Newcomb, and Paul Carlson of the Department of History at Texas Tech University offered significant comments and suggestions. Elder Robert Louis Webb, curator of the Primitive Baptist Library at Carthage, Illinois, and Elder Dwight Dyer, pastor of Testament Baptist Church near Lafayette, Tennessee, provided access to rare church records. The following institutions were especially helpful: American Baptist Historical Society, Southern Baptist Historical Commission, Illinois State Historical Library, Illinois State Archives, Chicago Historical Society, Lilly Library at Indiana University, Indiana State Library, Tennessee State Archives and Library, Sumner County (Tennessee) Archives, Arkansas State Library, Texas State Archives and Library, Center for American History at the University of Texas, Lewis Historical Library in Vincennes, Indiana, and Mahon Public Library in Lubbock, Texas. Several counties made available valuable manuscripts and documents. Among these were Crawford, Clark, Coles, and Edgar in Illinois and Dickson in Tennessee. Several members of the Parker family contributed genealogical information. Finally, my wife, LaMarsha Kay Wimberly, offered invaluable clerical aid and encouragement.

Introduction

Sometime around the War of 1812, farmer-preacher Daniel Parker, by then in his mid thirties, ascended the speaker's platform of a Nashville meeting house. The blossoming frontier city, the commercial hub of Middle Tennessee, evidenced increased settlement and commercial enterprise. Parker had been invited to preach by fellow Baptist and politically eminent Richard C. Foster. Seating soon became scarce as listeners crowded into the small structure to hear Parker. In the audience anticipation rose as the small-statured, dark-haired, and rather slovenly dressed preacher announced his text. Parker began his sermon but soon felt constrained by his neck tie. Removing this article of encumbrance, he continued to preach. As his animated oratory progressed, Parker took off his coat and vest. Apparently shocked at Parker's lack of pulpit decorum, scholarly Rev. Gideon Blackburn, perhaps the most eloquent Presbyterian minister in Tennessee, whispered to Foster: "Will he pull his shirt off?" After Parker had concluded, Foster asked Blackburn for an assessment of the sermon. The polished Blackburn, recognizing the homespun ability of Parker, replied: "It is a pity that man has not a good education, and some refinement. He might have made a right good preacher."[1]

The above episode examples the life of Daniel Parker. Born on the frontier without education or refinement, Parker drew large numbers of followers through spell-binding oratory and natural talent. Rising to prominence during the Market Revolution, the years which followed the War of 1812, he experienced the strains that an increasingly national economy placed on the frontier. Although aware of his educational and social limitations, Parker made a name for himself in the pulpit and statehouse. While doing so, he rubbed shoulders with commoners and men of prominence. Yet in his efforts to achieve recognition, many scorned Parker for his impetuous temperament and desire for advancement.

A product of the Second Great Awakening and Jeffersonian republicanism, Parker exuded the pioneer spirit of individualism and self-reliance. He first gained recognition in Tennessee as a backwoods Baptist preacher. His ministry spanned the first four decades of the nineteenth century. In those years he lived and preached in Georgia, Tennessee, Illinois, and Texas. Parker seemingly thrived on controversy. Political and religious strife often swirled about him. As a minister he drew criticism by opposing centralized missionary and benevolence societies. Furthermore, in 1826 he ignited a firestorm among western Baptists with his Two-Seed-in-the-Spirit doctrine. This self-conceived hyper-Calvinistic dualism attempted to harmonize the righteousness of God with the seemingly arbitrary nature of election.

Parker entered politics in 1822. His desire for public office earned him a seat in the Illinois Senate. There, he resisted the legalization of slavery. In 1833 Parker became a part of Texas history when he and members of his newly organized Pilgrim Predestinarian Baptist Church migrated en masse from Illinois to Texas. This congregation became the first Baptist church to exist on Texas soil. Less than two years after immigrating, Parker emerged in Texas politics. Serving as a member of the Consultation and later the Provisional Government of Texas, Parker drew on his previous legislative experience to provide leadership during the frenzied days of the Texas Revolution.

The religious and political activities of Parker categorize him as more than the average frontiersman. With virtually no education, he vaulted to religious and political prominence. Possessing a strong will, Parker attracted followers but also made enemies. Yet ironies and contradictions surrounded him. The preaching of Parker exalted the grace of God while vehemently condemning the dissemination of the gospel through missionary and benevolence societies. Parker claimed allegiance to republican ideals but zealously resisted the spiritual individualism of Arminianism. A champion of religious freedom, he defended the autonomy of local Baptist churches but also exhibited a despotic streak. Parker extolled free speech but flinched at criticism. He broadsided critics with withering accusations, at times labeling his opponents as the progeny of Satan. He staunchly opposed slavery in the Illinois Assembly but voiced no recorded opposition to slavery in Texas. The publications of Parker reveal a bias against wealth and class. But many of his conflicts pitted him against persons with social and economic backgrounds similar to his own. Although contemptuous of the perceived rank and privilege of easterners and the southern planter elite, his opponents usually did not come from the ranks of the wealthy. Rather, they most often emerged from backwood challenges to Parker's economic opportunities or positions of leadership. These rivalries impeded his hopes for social, economic, and political ascendancy. Finally, the quick mind and charismatic oratory of Parker propelled him to responsible positions of public trust. Yet on one occasion Parker promoted a visionary treasure-hunting scheme as a means to achieve governmental solvency.

Unfortunately, historians have treated Parker with little more than casual remarks or cursory sketches.[2] In 1902 Benajah Harvey Carroll laid the foundation for studies about Parker. His work, *The Genesis of American Anti-Missionism*, briefly touched on Two Seedism and the role of Parker in the missions controversy. Other books have focused on the role of Parker among Baptists in Indiana, Illinois, and Texas. Most noted among these are James Milton Carroll's *A History of Texas Baptists* (1923) and *The Origin and Development of the Missionary Baptist Church in Indiana* (1942) by John F. Cady. Basically narratives, these works have offered sparse historical research and analysis.

Parker also has been discussed in several unpublished dissertations and theses. The first of these, "Daniel Parker and the First Baptist Church in Texas," appeared in 1924. This dissertation, authored by Lorine Maud Scott at the University of Chicago, devotes two chapters to Parker. The remaining pages primarily survey social and religious life on the Texas frontier. Since then, other works of this type have dealt rather superficially with the role of Parker in the development of antimissions activity on the frontier. Unfortunately, most follow the initial research of Benajah Harvey Carroll and offer little in terms of fresh insight. These studies have relied on the records of the Pilgrim Predestinarian Baptist Church, only one of Parker's pastorates, and refer extensively to three works by Parker: *A Public Address, Views on the Two Seeds*, and a thirty-one page autobiography in a single issue of the *Church Advocate*, a paper published by Parker from 1829 through 1831. Yet his other publications, *The Author's Defence, Plain Truth, A Short Hint,* the remaining twenty-four issues of the *Church Advocate,* and personal correspondence have not been consulted. Neither have numerous church records and denominational publications been included.

A particularly glaring omission concerns the political involvement of Parker. While focusing on the religious activities of Parker, scholars have virtually ignored his place in light of political and economic developments on the frontier. In 1958 Donald F. Tingley published "Illinois Days of Daniel Parker, Texas Colonizer" in the winter issue of the Journal of the Illinois State Historical Society. Although Tingley consulted some court records relating to land transactions, his narrative lacked an in-depth analysis of the political activity of Parker in Illinois. Yet other county and state records in Tennessee, Illinois, and Texas documents, which illuminate the political and economic activities of Parker, have been overlooked. Most lamentable is that a considerable amount of untapped information in the journals of the Illinois Assembly and records of the Provisional Government of Texas has been neglected. Historians likewise have failed to analyze early Indiana and Illinois newspapers for valuable social, economic, and political information.

Without a comprehensive study, the casual reader might dismiss Daniel Parker as a frontier oddity, railing against the encroachments of benevolence societies and an educated professional ministry. A closer look, however, suggests a more complex figure. Parker mirrored the broad political, social, and economic developments that challenged frontiersmen in the Early National and Jacksonian periods. An ardent advocate of individual rights, he represents the expansion of Jeffersonian republicanism and serves as a transitional figure into the Jacksonian era. He admired the Jeffersonian ideals of liberty and opportunity for yeomen, but, comparable to Jackson, Parker championed the individualism of the common man. Certain traits reveal an affinity between Parker and Jackson. Having been born in poverty, Jackson strove to gain political recognition, wealth, and power. Contentious, given to dueling, and impatient with opponents, Jackson struggled to ascend. Parker likewise manifested a penchant for rancor. In religious and political realms he resisted alleged attempts by centralized missionary societies and privileged autocrats to impose their wills upon the people.

Entering politics, Parker became a scrappy contender, keenly aware of his personal economic and political interests.

Rooted in Revolutionary fervor, American republicanism contrasted with the aristocratic and autocratic regimes of Europe. Republicanism extolled the virtuous citizen and condemned the insidious usurpation of rights. But not all Americans agreed on the best manner in which a strong republic might be preserved. Shortly after the Revolution, two loosely structured political parties appeared on the American stage. The political philosophies of Alexander Hamilton and Thomas Jefferson polarized supporters into Federalists and Democratic-Republicans. Federalists, the followers of Alexander Hamilton, favored the commercial and industrial development of the young nation. They regarded protective tariffs and internal improvements in transportation as necessary to the economic growth of the Union. According to them, the best hope of accomplishing these nationalist goals lay in a strong centralized government. Hamiltonian political thought also distrusted the ability and intelligence of the common people. Hamilton felt that the education and experience of the well-born entitled the elite to rule the masses. Hence, Federalists based their political philosophy on a more class-oriented framework. Also, the conflicting philosophies partially took on a sectional nature. Federalism did not appear strictly in the northeastern states. Pockets of federalism also existed in the South. For example, John Marshall of Virginia allied with Federalists. Because federalism offered military protection, it also found advocates on the frontier. But perhaps more than other sections of the Union, New England, which served as the manufacturing hub of the nation, stood to profit from federalism. Federalism, with its emphasis on commercial development, promoted the interests of many New England merchants and shippers.

Thomas Jefferson felt that the best preservation of liberty lay in an agrarian society of virtuous citizens. According to him, the best republic would be composed of small landholders. Because these landed yeomen would have a vested interest in government, Jefferson believed that they would safeguard the Republic from corruption. Eschewing autocracy, he espoused a weak central government. Although Jefferson agreed that the wealthy elite should provide political leadership, he felt that landed commoners should vote and fill offices in the lower legislative assemblies. Because of the agrarian emphasis of Jeffersonian republicanism, it attracted a strong following in the southern and western frontier. Falling under the partisan designation of Democratic-Republicans, Jeffersonians resisted taxes which might accompany governmentally sponsored internal improvements. Jeffersonians, fearing the loss of local and state self-determination to a perceived autocratic national government, looked askance at a strong central government.

By the 1790s and first decade of the nineteenth century, Federalists and Republicans vied for power in the national government. New England remained the stronghold for federalism. Yet the victory of archrepublican Thomas Jefferson in the 1800 presidential election indicated serious weaknesses in Federalist circles. Another blow to federalism came as a result of the War of 1812. Having experienced interrupted sea commerce with Great Britain, New England shippers and merchants suffered economic reversals. In December 1814 Federalists from several northeastern states assembled at Hartford, Connecticut to attend a convention that opposed the war and discussed the secession of New England from the Union. Viewed by many Americans as paramount to treason, the Hartford Convention became the death knell of the Federalist faction.

New England Congregationalist ministers had special cause to resent the Republican ascendancy. Since early colonial days, Congregational churches in Massachusetts and Connecticut, constructed around the framework of Puritan oligarchy, had been funded by public tax revenues, and republicans objected to tax support for churches. The threatened loss of financial support and the anticlerical excesses of republicanism as evidenced by the French Revolution caused many New England Federalist clergy to recoil. Wishing to maintain some control over the moral development of the nation, they sought to carry their cultural hegemony to the West. Once in the Ohio and Mississippi River valleys, they clashed with independent-minded backwoodsmen such as Parker.

Known as the Market Revolution, the social and economic changes which transpired in the early nineteenth century strained the agrarian cords of Jeffersonianism. The expanding frontier resulted in a more geographically mobile society. Speculators competed for large tracts of land. Trade, industry, and improvements in transportation spurred the growth of towns and cities. Economic expansion after the War of 1812 presented new challenges to government. Unleashed nationalism called for improvements in the financial and transportational infrastructures. The Bank of the United States, established in 1791 and reinstituted in 1816, sought to stabilize the money supply and provide for a uniform currency. But the constitutionality and value of the Bank remained in question. The degree to which government should involve itself in the private economy remained unclear. Moreover, the fall in crop and land prices, which accompanied the Panic of 1819, wrought economic havoc on the frontier. Wishing to shore up a weakened financial structure, the Bank recalled loans and tightened credit. This abrupt change in policy, which had followed an expansionary boom, caught debtors off guard. In the West small merchants and yeomen farmers suffered foreclosures. Along with his neighbors, Daniel Parker experienced hard times. Because the Bank had been headquartered in the East, many financially troubled westerners viewed it as an extension of eastern hegemony. They seemed to think that small farmers had been victimized by the money lords of the East.

In 1829 General Andrew Jackson, the military hero of the West, became president. Jackson also doubted the constitutionality and worth of a national bank. He felt that the institution excessively empowered trustees, directors, and private shareholders. Jackson subsequently sought to kill the Bank. Large numbers of westerners applauded the war of Jackson against the eastern-controlled banking monopoly. Furthermore, many westerners felt that Jackson had been cheated out of the presidency in 1824, and although he lacked a necessary majority, he held more popular and electoral votes than any of the other three candidates. But contender Henry Clay virtually decided the election. Having been eliminated, Clay urged his supporters to vote for John Quincy Adams of Massachusetts. The influence of Clay secured the White House for the New Englander. The ensuing appointment of Clay as secretary of state by Adams irked many Jackson supporters. They complained that skulduggery had robbed their candidate of victory. Yet Jackson did not acquiesce to the will of his political foes. The Jacksonian triumph in 1828 ushered in the Tennessean to the White House. Westerners, including many Illinoisans, had seen their hero conquer the forces of corruption. From 1828 to 1846 Jackson and

Jacksonian ideology strongly influenced the United States. During the Jacksonian era, a renewed spirit of democracy exalted the commoner. Whereas Jeffersonianism had recognized the worth of yeomen, Jacksonian democracy extolled the average citizen. Newspapers and public gatherings lauded the virtue and wisdom of the people.

The political and social developments of the Jacksonian era have been the focus of a number of studies. *The Age of Jackson*, a seminal work published in 1945 by Arthur M. Schlesinger, Jr., and Robert V. Remini's *The Jacksonian Era*, published in 1972, have called attention to the impetus for popular democracy which appeared in the 1820s and 1830s. More recent books by Harry L. Watson and Charles Sellers have examined political and economic interactions of the Jacksonian period. Two contributions by Watson, *Jacksonian Politics and Community Conflict: The Emergence of the Second American Party System in Cumberland County, North Carolina* in 1981 and *Liberty and Power: The Politics of Jacksonian America* in 1990, underscore the dynamics of local and state politics in the emergence of a national pro-Jackson party. In *The Market Revolution: Jacksonian America, 1815-1846*, published in 1991, Sellers describes the effect of a burgeoning economy on capitalism, politics, and culture. Among other issues, Sellers illuminates the Panic of 1819, which affected political development on the frontier and the ensuing ascendancy of Andrew Jackson. The political and economic trends, as described by Watson and Sellers, also influenced Daniel Parker, whose primary political activities coincided with the beginnings of Jacksonian democracy.

The place of Parker in American Christianity also represents Jeffersonian and Jacksonian ideals. The 1820s and 1830s remain a watershed in American religious history. New denominations and sects blossomed on the frontier. Most of these groups shared a desire to restore in some manner the first-century Church, uncluttered by human and ecclesiastical trappings. In many cases the new sects had been spawned by charismatic leaders who realized an opportunity to carve a niche for themselves in American Protestantism. Of course, the methods of reformation varied. Marked by extreme departures from orthodox Protestantism, such groups as Mormons, Millerites, and Shakers espoused millennialism, charismata, and social and familial reorganization. Less radical reformers, as exampled by Reformation Christianity leader Alexander Campbell, discarded creeds, traditions, and ecclesiastical addenda that they saw as not basic to New Testament Christianity.

Gordon S. Wood and Nathan O. Hatch have focused on the religious fecundity of the 1820s and 1830s. An essay by Wood, "The Democratization of Mind in the American Revolution," in *Leadership in the American Revolution* (1974) and *The Democratization of American Christianity*, published by Hatch in 1989, consider the profuse developments in religion to be more than coincidental. Rather, they propose that the American Revolution encouraged popular democracy in political as well as ecclesiastical realms. Hatch contends that the popular religious movements of the early republic were democratic in three ways. First, they denied the time-honored tradition of learned professional theologians as clerics. Second, such movements catapulted ordinary people to places of spiritual leadership. Finally, these new leaders stressed millennialism. They looked forward to a rapidly approaching overthrow of coercive political and ecclesiastical powers. Once accomplished, a new age of social harmony would dawn. Wood likewise argues that the post eighteenth-century emergence of evangelical Christianity characterized a new-found emphasis on self-assertion. The Revolution had blurred class distinctions. Ordinary citizens saw their chance for a voice in government and the Church.

Primitivism, an interpretation partially incorporated by Wood and Hatch, emphasizes the desire in American Protestantism for a return to the spiritual and ecclesiastical characteristics of ancient Christianity. Paralleling the American Revolution's ideal of restoring republican political purity as an example, primitivism promulgated the revival of innocence and simplicity as found in the first-century Church. Richard T. Hughes and C. Leonard Allen in *Illusions of Innocence: Protestant Primitivism in America, 1630-1875*, published in 1988, examine the upheaval in American Christianity during Parker's era. They attribute primitivism to the efforts of seventeenth-century English Puritanism to restore genuine and uncorrupted religion.

In England and America seventeenth-century Puritans and Independents incorporated primitivism through, among other practices, congregational autonomy. Baptists, like Congregationalists and Puritans, made primitive claims. Pre-Revolutionary American

Baptists espoused a restoration of primitive practices. They exalted the ancient practices of Baptism, the Lord's Supper, and foot washing. Separate Baptists, a New Light group which had been strongly influenced by the Great Awakening, restored other ancient practices. Some of these included the laying on of hands, the right hand of fellowship, and the anointing of the sick. The desire to shed nonbiblical innovations remained strong among frontier Baptists.

An aspect of Parker's theology that coincided with the primitivist impulse of the 1820s and 1830s was Two-Seed dualism. Dualism is no stranger to Judaism and Christianity. During the eighth-century before the Christian era, the Hebrew prophet Amos revealed Yahweh as a righteous god. This unveiling challenged the previously held assumption that all developments, good and evil, had their origin in Yahweh. By the first century of the Christian era, the concept of separate forces of good and evil had entered Jewish theology. Over the next three centuries, a variety of dualisms challenged the Church. Gnosticism, Neoplatonism, and Manichaeanism competed with orthodox Christianity. Dualisms continued to appear in the Middle Ages. Bogomils in the Balkans and Cathars in southern Gaul maintained strongly dualistic heresies.

Although not directly influenced by earlier heterodoxies, Two Seedism represents a hybrid of dualism and hyper-Calvinism. According to Calvinism, the eternal fate of all mankind had been divinely sealed. Every human numbered among the elect or nonelect. But Two Seedism expanded on Calvinism. Using his dualism to justify the origin and fate of the nonelect, Parker preached that God had implanted the divine seed of the elect in Adam. Satan had supplied Eve with the propensity to sin. Not having the divine seed, the offspring of Eve fell victim to sin which condemned them to Hell. The archfiend thereby had implanted his seed in the offspring of Eve, the generation of the nonelect. Moreover, Parker insisted that all of Adam's seed composed the Church. This meant that the Church had existed from Creation. Thus, this homespun theology retraced the origin of the elect to the innocence of Eden and cradled them in the cosmic plan of God.

Because of a dwindling base of supporters, Two Seedism had become virtually extinct among Baptists by the middle of the twentieth century. Yet its place as a self-styled theology should not be ignored. Although convoluted and heterodox, Two Seedism reflected the Jeffersonian penchant for self-assertion. But the publication of Two Seedism also coincided with the Jacksonian emphasis on the common man. Similar to Joseph Smith and other innovative religious leaders in the Jacksonian era, Parker felt free to produce his own theology. Confident that his hermeneutic remained a valuable elucidation to holy writ, Parker adamantly defended Two Seedism.

Yet in denominational affairs Parker also mirrored Jacksonian individualism. Because the New Testament had not offered examples of missionary societies, Parker and many backwoods Baptists considered these organizations as nonscriptural corruptions. As in the case of Two Seedism, antimissionism recaptured something of the primitive nature of the Church. But in the contest against missionary societies, Parker exceeded the desire to keep Baptist principles pure. The intransigence of Parker took on a Jacksonian characteristic. The pioneer preacher incorporated the missions issue into a personal struggle for denominational power. As a result, coreligionists who differed with Parker became the objects of his suspicion and ostracism.

With the foregoing historical framework, this book focuses on the religious and public life of Daniel Parker. Molded by Jeffersonian republicanism and active during the Jacksonian period, Parker is seen as an example of the social and political forces which shaped the frontier. Faced with poverty and hardship, he appreciated the opportunities which Jeffersonianism held for the yeoman. But caught up in the political and economic changes which characterized the years following the War of 1812, Parker strove to benefit socially, politically, and economically from the triumph of the common man under Jacksonian democracy. In his effort to achieve, Parker became "a man of war."

The first chapter examines his early life in Tennessee. These formative years stiffened the resistance of Parker to missionary societies, slavery, and the hegemony of the planter elite. Chapter 2 concerns his political career in Illinois amid the social, political, and economic developments on that frontier. Especially important is the role of Assemblyman Parker in the struggle to keep slavery out of Illinois. The chapter also discusses factional politics and the failure of Parker to adapt to the newly developing system of Jacksonian partisanship. Chapter 3 uncovers the personal, political, and ecclesial circumstances which shaped his Illinois ministry. The remaining two chapters relate the Texas years. Chapter 4 encompasses his public life that included his brief service in the Consultation and Provisional Government and his friendship with Sam Houston. The interest of Parker in land speculation is cast against the economic downturn of the Republic of Texas in the late 1830s and early 1840s. Ironically, his reaction to slavery underwent a transition in light of the need for slave labor in Texas. Chapter 5 details Parker's Texas ministry, in which he continued the struggle against the perceived encroachments by centralized benevolence societies. Yet some of his sharpest criticism came from his antimissionary brethren. Finally, Chapter 6 summarizes the significance of Parker among Baptists and frontier democracy.

Chapter 1

Georgia and Tennessee: The Formative Years

AFTER THE DEFEAT of the British in 1783, the fledgling American nation struggled to establish itself politically and economically. Politicians and statesmen wrestled over the benefits of a loosely confederated nation as compared to a strong centralized government. Merchants, manufacturers, and planters sought to weld a healthy economy out of the disruption wrought by eight years of war. The vast Transappalachian frontier had been off limits to settlers under British rule. Following the end of the Revolution, this region attracted restless frontiersmen, ambitious politicians, and enterprising speculators. By 1803 three Transappalachian territories—Kentucky, Tennessee, and Ohio—had entered the Union. Settlers from the original thirteen colonies floated downriver on barges or carted their belongings through mountain passes to these new states. They also brought their social and cultural baggage that included varying degrees of concern about religion. The frontier bustled with activity as newcomers such as the John Parker family sought new land and opportunities.

Wagons creaked and jostled on June 23, 1803, along the crude Elbert County, Georgia, roads as the family of John Parker accompanied relatives and friends on a two-month migration to Middle Tennessee.[1] In 1784 Georgia had implemented the distribution of land bounty grants to Revolutionary War veterans. Shortly thereafter, Parker, a former Continental soldier in a Virginia unit, had moved from the Piedmont region of Culpeper County, Virginia, to Georgia.[2] After approximately seventeen years in northeastern Georgia, forty-four-year-old John Parker deemed it time to move farther westward. Tennessee had caught Parker's fancy. By 1796 the Indians in Tennessee had been defeated and statehood had been granted.[3] Settlers poured over the mountains, attracted to the rich bottom lands of the Cumberland and Harpeth rivers.

In 1803 the family of John and Sarah White Parker numbered at least ten children, eight sons and two daughters.[4] Daniel Parker, the eldest child of John and Sarah, traveled with them. Born April 6, 1781, Daniel had spent his youth on the Georgia frontier, where, he enjoyed the independence of frontier life.[5] Virtually self-taught, the extent of Daniel's education consisted of reading the New Testament and crude penmanship. When not obligated with farm labor, he participated in the boisterous mirth common to the backwoods. In his teen years he spent a substantial amount of time hunting, which afforded him the opportunity to develop self-reliance. In the uninhabited wilderness that adjoined the Parker home, Daniel "ranged the woods as a hunter, nearly as much in company with Indians as with the whites."[6] On March 11, 1802, he took on the responsibility of a wife. When the caravan departed, Daniel and Patsey Dickerson Parker, his wife of fifteen months, had become the parents of a six-month-old daughter.[7] The John Parkers, like most frontier families, lived without benefit of wealth, education, or refinement. But one trait assumed a particular saliency among the Parkers. They manifested a marked attachment to religious concerns.

In the 1740s the Great Awakening had profoundly influenced the religious life of the American colonies. In New England, Massachusetts, and Connecticut in particular, the preaching of George Whitefield and Jonathan Edwards had generated spiritual interest. Many had felt that the tedious sermons of Puritan divines failed to meet the needs of a changing society. Listeners had warmed to the emotional elocution of Whitefield. Instead of sterile Calvinism, the audiences of Whitefield had imbibed heart-felt religion and genuine repentance. Presbyterians, Baptists, and Congregationalists had divided into New Lights and Old Lights. The conservative Old Lights had scorned the emotional excess and lack of learning often exhibited by the ministers who supported the Awakening. New Lights, those who favored the Great Awakening, had heralded the event as an inspired movement of divine grace and found no fault in an uneducated ministry. Across the colonies the Awakening had stirred social repercussions. Offended by alleged Old Light pretentiousness, New Lights had questioned the authority of the established and seemingly unregenerate clergy. In the southern colonies the Awakening had sparked the evangelization of slaves.

Yet by the end of the Revolution, religion had languished throughout the former thirteen colonies. Perhaps no more than 10 percent of Americans claimed membership in a church.[8] The exigencies of war had resulted in societal and economic disruption. Soldiers, forced by military duty to forsake domestic life, returned to fallow farms and exhausted finances. To avail themselves of economic opportunities and government land grants, veterans joined the westward rush. As a result, eastern churches experienced the loss of membership. In the wake of this exodus, settlers placed less emphasis on cultural refinement, education, and religion. Southerners likewise seemed indifferent to spiritual concerns. A brief revival flared among Virginia Baptists in the late 1780s. Revival began around 1785 and had peaked by 1789. Baptist congregations in the central part of present Virginia, including Culpeper County, experienced spiritual renewal. Yet this short-lived stirring served primarily to accent the drab spiritual conditions. By the close of the eighteenth century, however, the frontier again appeared ripe for a profound spiritual stirring.[9]

In July 1800 the Great Revival, an event which marked the beginning of the Second Great Awakening, erupted on the Kentucky frontier. The Reverend James McGready, a Presbyterian, held open-air religious services at the Gasper River Presbyterian Church in Logan County, Kentucky. The popular enthusiasm which accompanied McGready's success encouraged Barton Warren Stone, a McGready convert from western North Carolina, to invite frontiersmen to a series of open-air preaching assemblies at Cane Ridge, Kentucky. The meetings began August 6, 1801, and continued for six or seven days. The rustic frontier surroundings belied the pivotal importance of the event. In terms of popular response and evangelical innovation, it remains crucial to American Christianity. Estimated attendance, dwarfing the populations of frontier towns, reached 10,000 to 25,000.[10]

4   FRONTIER RELIGION

The Great Revival touched off the Second Great Awakening, a spiritual stirring among evangelical Protestants which reached from Georgia to New York. While the immediate activity of the first Great Awakening had taken place in more settled New England, the Second Great Awakening became associated with the frontier. Backwoods Protestant churches surged with vitality. In the North, aftershocks reverberated in western New York as late as the 1820s. The Awakening also established the camp meeting as a means of church growth. In the process, it initiated schism and conflict. For example, in the South traditional Presbyterians and most Baptists remained committed to the five principles of Calvinism. Not only did Calvinists preach the total depravity of man and unmerited grace of God, but they also taught the perseverance of the saints, unconditional election, and a limited atonement. On the other hand, Methodists, a denomination of more recent origin, challenged Calvinism. Opponents of predestination, they proclaimed the Arminian tenets of universal atonement and free will.[11]

On the Georgia frontier Baptists and the more Arminian-inclined Methodists felt the effects of revival. Methodist minister Moses Black reported from Georgia in December 1802 that revival raced across the frontier "like fire in dry stubble."[12] According to Black, camp meetings occurred most frequently in Elbert County, the home of Daniel Parker. In 1803 Jesse Mercer, a frontier Georgia Baptist minister, wrote of the "glorious Revival of the Religion of Jesus" which Georgia Baptists had experienced the previous year.[13] Mercer estimated that 4,400 new converts entered the Georgia Baptist fold between 1802 and 1803.

The Revival also affected Parker. In the midst of this outpouring, he anguished over the claims of Arminianism and limited atonement. Reared on a steady diet of election, Daniel tried to sort out the perceived mass movement of God on the hearts of men. This seemed to differ with his view of conversion. For how could men claim conversion without the spiritual assurance that they numbered among the elect? He evidently felt that proof of election manifested itself only after intense and personal introspection. Moreover, the apparently indiscriminate working of grace with little consideration for election appeared incompatible with limited atonement. Daniel's doubts persisted until a pivotal event. Under the preaching of Elder William Denmon, he sensed a marked serenity. Following the evening worship, Daniel began the five-mile walk to his home. Before his arrival, alone on a rural path, he assessed the events of the evening. In so doing, he became convinced that God had brought him to repentance. Satisfied that he numbered among the elect, he related his conversion to Nail's Creek Baptist Church in Franklin County, Georgia. On January 19, 1802, Daniel received baptism and joined that congregation. Shortly thereafter, unable to resist what he believed to be a divine calling, Daniel "engaged in the ministry."[14]

John Parker also had been impressed with the workings of divine grace as well as certain Baptist ministers. In 1804 he named Silas, his sixth son, after Silas Mercer, an eminent Baptist minister and brother to Jesse Mercer. Like son Daniel, John expressed an interest in the ministry. Other kindred Parkers besides Daniel and John had confessed the call to preach. In 1791 William's Creek Baptist Church in neighboring Wilkes County reported Aaron Parker, a kinsman if not a brother of John Parker, as a candidate for the ministry.[15] Before the Parkers departed for Tennessee, the Nail's Creek Church had licensed, but not ordained, John Parker as a preacher.[16]

Customarily, the licensing congregation assessed the pulpit skills and devotion of licentiates. After rendering its approbation, the licensing congregation recommended licentiates to other congregations. The licensing of unlearned preachers occurred quite often among frontier Baptist churches. The authenticity of a man's call, rather than educational requirements, qualified a minister in the eyes of backwoodsmen.[17] On the frontier, mystical experiences such as irresistible mental impressions validified the ministerial call. Unencumbered by educational requirements and financially self-supporting, frontier Baptist preachers proved more mobile than clergy from established liturgical denominations. Baptist farmer-preachers tended their fields during the week and preached on Saturdays and Sundays. They neither sought nor expected remuneration for their ministerial labors. These preachers often moved with their potential congregations to new areas. Once at the new location, the preacher might receive an invitation to assume the pastoral care of a newly organized church. If unordained, the preacher submitted to an ordination service arranged by his would-be congregation. Sometimes the ordaining congregation would be one which the licentiate had personally gathered. This seems to have been the case with John Parker.

In August 1803 Daniel Parker settled on Turnbull Creek, approximately twenty miles southwest of Nashville. The following August the state legislature incorporated this area in the organization of Dickson County.[18] The new county soon exhibited signs of numerical growth and prosperity. The May 24, 1806, edition of the *Nashville Impartial Review* advertised for construction bids on a courthouse to be built "in an elegant manner" in the county seat of Charlotte. In July of the following year, the same paper announced the opening of a cotton gin in Dickson County.[19] Coincident with the increasing local population, John and son Daniel began to interest area settlers in the formation of a church. In April 1806 fourteen prospective members met at the house of John Parker on Turnbull Creek to organize Turnbull Baptist Church. At least ten of the fourteen charter members belonged, through blood or marriage, to the Parker clan.[20]

For at least the next six months the membership of Turnbull Church continued to meet at the home of John Parker. During this period several notable events occurred. On the twenty-eighth of May the church ordained Daniel Parker, listed on the minutes as "Daniel Parker, Jr.," and a close relative if not uncle, Daniel Parker, Sr., to the gospel ministry.[21] The church specified the two as "itinerant" ministers. This designation implied that they were free to preach to other congregations and administer the sacramental ordinances.[22] In June Patsey Parker, now the wife of an ordained minister, presented herself for baptism. In September, pending the search for a permanent pastor, the church chose Daniel Parker, Jr. as interim shepherd.[23] In July events developed which augured the nature of Daniel's lifelong ministry. In October John involved his preacher son in a dispute concerning John's preaching credentials. For the next thirty-seven years controversy swirled around Daniel Parker, Jr.

With the church meeting at his home and his son temporarily at the pastoral helm, John Parker made good use of this congregational leverage. Previous to October, John had requested of the Nail's Creek Church official recommendation concerning his preaching qualifications. Perhaps he hoped that this would result in ordination and the eventual pastorate of Turnbull or a neighboring church. The Georgia church provided John with a written recommendation which he presented to the Turnbull congregation. In the communique Nail's Creek gave its approbation but not without reservation. It required that John rectify existing transgressions against a certain Tennessee congregation.

John had held, or possibly still claimed, membership in the Buffalo Creek Baptist Church, a congregation in the western section of Dickson County. Yet all was not well between John and the membership of Buffalo Creek. Queries by the Turnbull church revealed that John, guilty of some alleged offense against the Buffalo membership, remained under ecclesiastical censure by that church. The Turnbull minutes did not specify the impropriety but did disclose that Parker possessed an inordinate proclivity for bellicosity and spirits. In order to avoid usurping the disciplinary authority of Buffalo Church, Turnbull members requested an arbitrational council. Ordained pastors from Mill Creek, near Nashville and neighboring Yellow Creek and Buffalo Creek churches, served as an informal council. This inquest, scheduled for April 20, 1807, accomplished little. John Parker simply failed to appear.[24] Perhaps John anticipated an unfavorable ruling. It seems more than coincidental that Sally Parker, a three year member of the Mill Creek Church and possibly a relative or the wife of John, attended the Mill Creek conference on April 18, 1807. This somewhat regularly held monthly congregational business meeting convened two days before the appointed date for the John Parker examination. During the conference, Mill Creek approved the participation of pastor James Whitsitt as a councilman. Immediately following this action, Sally abruptly requested a letter of dismission from the church.[25]

Entries concerning John Parker's standing continued to appear in the Turnbull minutes. On April 7, 1809, the Turnbull congregation placed him under observation, a form of congregational probation, after he acknowledged his "sin of drunkedness [sic]."[26] In spite of attempted reform, John lost favor with Turnbull. Apparently, his efforts at repentance proved unconvincing. Furthermore, John's intercongregational political leverage weakened. By May 1807, the month following the abortive inquest for John Parker, Daniel's brief pastoral interim had ended. The church called another supply pastor.[27] The Parkers also lost a congregational voting majority. Baptist churches typically followed democratic practice regarding church polity. A majority vote of the membership in each local church determined congregational policy. Over the course of two years, the membership of Turnbull had enlarged. No longer did a Parker familial core dominate congregational voting. New members included those either unrelated or not as closely connected to the Parkers. Finally, on July 9, 1809, Turnbull excommunicated John Parker.[28]

By 1809 Daniel no longer resided in Dickson County. After "particular impressions of mind, and remarkable turns of providence," events which Daniel never completely detailed, he exited Dickson County in 1807.[29] Perhaps his father's debacle with Turnbull influenced his decision. More likely, however, economic opportunities and the presence of kindred Parkers in Sumner County induced his departure. By October 1807 he had moved to Sumner County, thirty miles northeast of Nashville.[30] Becoming a man of his own, he deleted "junior" from his name and became known as Daniel Parker. He and Patsey, with their three small children, settled approximately ten miles north of the Cumberland River port town of Cairo.

In the early 1800s the Cumberland River, the primary commercial artery of Sumner County, served as an important link between backwoods tobacco farmers and the New Orleans market. As early as 1789, a New Orleans-bound flatboat had been built on Bledsoe's Creek, a Sumner County tributary of the Cumberland.[31] Cairo began developing around 1800. An influx of settlers quickly populated the land along the river. After 1805, the flatlands already taken, newcomers located on the hilly terrain known as the Ridge. This geological elevation paralleled the northern bank of the Cumberland River. Although its steep slopes prohibited extensive cultivation, this area seemed ideal for small farms. Soil in the Ridge valley-basins yielded abundant harvests of corn, tobacco, and hemp. With the combined toil of wife and children, yeoman farmers, too poor to own slaves, might nevertheless profit from cash crops grown on a limited amount of land.

Opportunities for economic advancement did not remove financial hardships. During these early years, Tennesseans experienced serious economic woes. Because of the national devaluation of gold, few gold coins had been minted since 1805. Of these fewer still remained in circulation.[32] As the first decade of the nineteenth century progressed, United States commercial shipping fell victim to Anglo-French conflicts. In December 1807, desiring to insulate America from the possibility of war, Congress imposed a trade embargo. This act bottled up exports of southern grain, cotton, and tobacco. Consequently, Tennessee farmers found it difficult to market their crops. The elimination of the National Bank in 1811 only exacerbated the matter. As a result, numerous state banks, some floating inflated currency, mushroomed. In the wake of reams of worthless currency, New England merchants and manufacturers demanded payment in hard money.[33] The resultant drain on specie reserves gave rise to a serious lack of specie throughout middle and southern states. Deprived of income from tobacco and short on hard money, Sumner County farmers resorted to a barter economy. In such an uncertain economy those who incurred extensive debts risked the loss of land and property.

In 1831 Daniel Parker described his early Sumner County years in terms of virtual destitution. He only had one horse and "little or no money."[34] Because Parker feared indebtedness, his only horse went unshod for two years. Rather than ride the animal over rocky terrain, Parker often walked fifteen to twenty miles to preaching appointments. Luxuries remained rare. Coffee sold for forty-four cents per pound in Cairo.[35] Parker felt that he could ill-afford this amount. He instead chose to ration his family's coffee consumption to a pound per year.

But the penury of Parker did not result entirely from circumstances beyond his control. He remained shrewdly aware of opportunities for self-advancement. Instead of expenditures on simple luxuries, he had invested available money in land. On October 8, 1807, perhaps six to eight months after moving to Sumner County, he paid $320 for 640 acres in Dickson County.[36] He evidently used the profits from the sale of portions of this tract to bankroll land purchases in Sumner County. In November 1809 he received $420 from the sale of 200 acres in Dickson County.[37] Fourteen months later, Parker purchased 215 acres for $425 near his Sumner County residence.[38] Parker's so-called destitution therefore partially resulted from self-imposed frugality. While waiting for buyers in Dickson County, he avoided indebtedness. He thus wisely managed his profits and invested them in Sumner County property.

Daniel Parker implied that his exodus to Sumner County had been divinely and mysteriously directed. Accordingly, he went "to a strange part, where I knew not man woman nor child."[39] Yet the circumstances surrounding his exodus suggest more evidence of earthly rather than heavenly causes. The hope of economic advancement and presence of kindred Parkers in Sumner County more likely influenced Daniel. He first settled in Sumner County near present day Bethpage, the home of the Nathaniel Parkers. It appears that kinship linked Daniel to the family of Nathaniel Parker. Nathaniel had lived in Sumner County since the early 1790s.[40] Besides being well established, Nathaniel had gained additional prominence by marrying the widow of Colonel Anthony Bledsoe, prominent Sumner County pioneer and Indian fighter.

The signposts along the road to Sumner County may not have thundered angelic voices nor beamed heavenly visions, but the ten-year sojourn of Daniel Parker in Sumner County proved nonetheless propitious. During this period, he became an effective orator and recognized leader among Tennessee Baptists. Although ordained in 1806, his lack of education and polish engendered feelings of inferiority. This sentiment exacerbated self-doubt concerning his ministerial abilities and calling. Shortly after settling in Sumner County, Parker joined the newly organized Hopewell Baptist Church, nine miles east of Gallatin on Bledsoe's Creek.[41] On July 25, 1807, Hopewell invited Parker to accept the pastoral leadership. Parker accepted the call and pastored the church for the next ten years.[42] During this decade, he launched a virtual vendetta against Arminianism, the archfoe of predestinarian Baptists.

During the first two decades of the nineteenth century, Methodist and Baptist congregations made significant gains in Sumner County. But the Methodist influx exceeded Baptist converts. As the nineteenth century advanced, Sumner County and surrounding areas became a virtual Methodist stronghold.[43] The Methodist success shaded Baptists and consequently threatened to undermine the ministerial leadership of Parker.

Several reasons explain the Methodist surge. One concerns the fear of God which entered backwoodsmen as a result of the New Madrid earthquake. Between December 1811 and January 1812 the earth quivered throughout the Mississippi Valley. By January 7, 1812, Nashville had recorded at least fifty tremors.[44] Coincident with the 1812 earthquake, frontier churches of various denominations experienced an influx of terrified converts.[45] The Concord

Association, composed of Baptist congregations northeast of Nashville, witnessed a phenomenal number of conversions. Between 1811 and September 1812, baptisms totaled 866, an increase of 807 over the 1811 immersions.[46] In spite of the baptismal boom, Middle Tennessee Baptists fell far short of Methodist gains. In 1812 Methodist churches in the Cumberland District, roughly encompassing the same area as the Concord Association, reported 4,472 communicants.[47] The same year the Concord Association reported only 2,031 members.[48] Marked Methodist expansion created the need for a new conference. On November 12, 1812, Methodist bishops Francis Asbury and William McKendree organized the Tennessee Methodist Conference at Fountain Head in northwestern Sumner County.[49]

Other factors besides a geological phenomenon also aided Methodism, Parker's denominational rival. Another reason was Methodism's use of camp-meeting evangelism. Sumner County lay diagonally southeast of the state line from Logan County, Kentucky, the birthplace of the Great Revival. In the summer and fall of 1800, the Logan County revival, cresting on manifestations of enthusiasm, overflowed into Sumner County. As in Logan County, Sumner County revivals drew thousands. One observer reported that "people fell before the word like corn before a storm."[50] Support for the Sumner County revival came mostly from Methodist and Arminian-inclinded Presbyterian ministers. While these preachers jointly promoted camp meetings, Baptists shunned the revivalistic gatherings as a perceived Arminian innovation.[51] With frontier religion characterized by a keen competition for converts, the Methodist-Presbyterian impetus meant that these denominations, rather than Baptists, benefited numerically.

The organizational and administrative structure of Methodism provided an additional advantage over Baptists. Methodism, an outgrowth of the Anglican church, retained elements of Anglican polity. Methodist churches, under episcopal administration, fell under a fairly rigid organizational framework of conferences and supervisory clergy. The Baptist Church, on the other hand, maintained a rather loose denominational organization. Historically influenced by seventeenth-century English Congregationalism, Baptists touted congregational self-government.[52] Baptist denominational organization likewise allowed autonomy. Churches within the same geographical bounds voluntarily supported the Baptist cause through quasi-formal bodies known as associations. Because individual Baptist churches acted autonomously, associational membership carried little extraecclesiastical control. Independent of one another and officially nonhierarchical, associations convened once annually. These meetings often lasted three days, beginning on Saturday and concluding on Monday. Representatives met in order to report membership totals, discuss matters of common interest, exchange information with official visitors from other associations, and hear sermons. Baptists, harboring vivid memories of persecution in Massachusetts and Virginia, venerated local church and associational autonomy. Yet such extended freedom proved detrimental to the Baptist cause. A loosely federated denomination encouraged the appearance of schisms, internal heresies, and doctrinal aberrations. Furthermore, the more organizationally structured evangelistic denominations exercised a more unified effort in seeking souls. With such an advantage, the Methodists edged out the Baptists in the battle for converts.

Arminian Methodism also presented a doctrinal challenge to Daniel Parker and Middle Tennessee Baptists. Free will, a product of Arminianism, challenged the Calvinistic tenets of irresistible grace and limited atonement. Most Middle Tennessee Baptist churches traced their doctrinal heritage to Particular Baptist churches in Virginia. Particular Baptists in America espoused the limited atonement of their English Particular Baptists antecedents. Unfortunately for American Particular Baptists, their battle with Arminianism focused on more than theological differences.

The controversy resonated political, social, and psychological overtones. Many freedom-minded backwoodsmen responded favorably to Arminianism. Perceiving the God of Calvinism as inexorably arbitrary and autocratic, they viewed free will as a spiritual parallel to the political freedom achieved by the Revolution.[53] Ironically, the Revolution also galvanized the Calvinism of Particular Baptists such as Parker. The persecution of Virginia Baptists had been mainly at the hands of the established, Arminian-disposed, Anglican church. Baptists in the Piedmont and Tidewater regions of Virginia remained aware of the imprisonment and verbal abuse dealt out to their coreligionists. To Particular Baptists, Arminianism therefore smacked of aristocracy. Virginia Baptists emerged from the ranks of the poor and unlearned. Their voiced opposition to aristocratic ostentation annoyed the gentry. While Baptists targeted cock fights, dancing, and horse racing as examples of vanity, the elite did not view such displays as vices. Rather, they considered such activities as essential confirmation of political and social dominance by the gentry. In turn the gentry ridiculed Baptists as ignorant levelers and Bible quoters.[54]

On the other hand, Particular Baptists found solace in unconditional election and limited atonement. They held dear the biblical doctrines as revealed in the five principles of Calvinism. Their advocacy of full-blown Calvinism fulfilled scriptural admonition. Thus, they obediently contended "for the faith which was once delivered unto the saints."[55] Yet the commitment to limited atonement also carried sectional and social overtones.

Separate Baptists had entered Virginia and the Carolinas in the mid-eighteenth century. The Separate Baptist church, with links to the Congregational Church, had developed in New England. Although Calvinistic in doctrine, Separate Baptists presented a more evangelical thrust. Moreover, the ministerial leadership of Separate Baptists had come from New England. Although Particular Baptists predated the Separates in Virginia, the Particulars had been weak. Arriving in the 1750s and 1760s, the evangelistic Separate Baptists harvested an influx of converts. Soon Separate Baptist congregations outnumbered those of their Particular Baptist brethren.[56] Although Separates and Particulars occupied the lower rungs of society, Separate Baptists had enjoyed more numerical gains. Overshadowed numerically and battered by feelings of social inferiority, Particular Baptists felt vulnerable.[57] Unconditional election therefore sheltered hard-pressed Particulars. In their minds redemption lay entirely outside of human effort. Election elevated the chosen in the eternal plan of God. Hence, the uneducated farmer, if one of the elect, enjoyed divine recognition and approval. The nonelect, no matter how wealthy and genteel, would never experience such a divine promotion. For this reason, strict Calvinism appealed to many Particular Baptists.

Methodists had organized a fellowship near Hopewell Church as early as 1792.[58] Because of a dearth of Baptist ministers in Sumner County, Hopewell Church had allowed visiting Methodists to preach prior to Parker becoming pastor. This practice was not unusual. Methodist and Presbyterian ministers frequently exchanged pulpits in this area.[59] After Parker accepted Hopewell, Methodist ministers, accustomed to mixed denominational services, anticipated continued pulpit sharing. This disturbed Parker. Lashed by feelings of inadequacy, he perceived Methodist preachers as a threat to his self-worth, pastoral leadership, and the Baptist faith.

> I had until this time, been altogether raised and traditionized [sic] to the backwoods . . . having no learning, and being rough and course in my language and manners, I made but a poor appearance as a preacher, and those Methodists at first appeared as if they thought me hardly worth notice, but . . . by their conduct seemed to think it might be better to put me out of their way, before I did them much harm, and so they engaged in war against me.[60]

Armed with the Bible, his self-styled "Jerusalem Blade," Parker became a "man of war."[61] Accordingly, he figuratively marched forth to smite Methodism and Arminianism hip and thigh. In 1808, shortly after acceptance of the Hopewell pastorate, he engaged the Reverend Valentine Cook, a ranking Methodist, in public debate. Ten years earlier, Cook—who had a reputation as an experienced debater and scholarly preacher—had served as presiding elder over the Cumberland District. The two opponents squared off near Gallatin. The contest consisted of a sermon by each preacher on baptism. According to Parker, Cook provided no scriptural defense for pedobaptism. Parker used this alleged weakness to apparently best Cook on the subject of pedobaptism.[62] As a result, Parker gained fame as a Baptist champion.

Having experienced the exhilaration of public debate, Parker accepted another verbal duel. In July or September 1812, Rev. Samuel King, according to Parker a well-known Methodist minister, publicly disputed Parker at Testament Baptist Church, another of Parker's pastorates in northeastern Sumner County.[63] After Parker had finished preaching, King publicly accused him of "preaching the Devil's Doctrines," and challenged Parker to debate.[64] In a series of five encounters, one of which according to a Parker family member was quite vindictive on the part of King, Parker stood his ground. Although the exact verbal contents of the contests have not been recorded, the two exhorters argued the differences between Arminian and Particular Baptist doctrines of baptism and election. Evidently, Parker either proved his mettle or his Arminian opponents focused on more important goals. For after the King encounters, Parker claimed that the Methodists had ceased to challenge him.[65]

During the second decade of the century, Parker's reputation as an able pulpiteer and Baptist leader expanded throughout Middle Tennessee and Southwestern Kentucky. He pastored Hopewell and Testament churches, preaching once monthly at Hopewell on the fourth Sunday and at Testament on the first Sunday. The Concord Association, composed of twenty-two churches with thirty-one ministers, met at his Hopewell pastorate on September 26, 27, and 28, 1812.[66] At the 1814 associational meeting, held at Concord Meeting House in Williamson County, Tennessee, Parker preached the annual sermon. The following year he served the Concord Association as moderator.[67] In 1816 and 1817 he accepted requests to preach at the neighboring Red River Association. At these meetings, attended by churches in Kentucky and northwestern Tennessee, Parker encountered some of the leading Baptist ministers in Kentucky and Tennessee.[68]

Parker's appearance and lack of refinement belied his remarkable oratorical ability. At times he apparently became quite absorbed in his sermons. While in Sumner County, he once had a preaching appointment approximately five miles from his residence. Near sundown, after finishing tillage, he departed for his appointment without washing. He arrived at the destination and began preaching. Well into his message, he noticed his pants still rolled up and his legs caked with dirt.[69] Reuben Ross, a well-known Kentucky Baptist minister, had heard Parker preach in 1817 and 1820. Ross described Parker's physical features and oratory.

> He was a small, dry-looking man, of the gipsy [sic] type, with black eyes and hair and dark complexion.
> On rising in the pulpit to speak, he soon gave us to understand that he meant business,—pulled off his coat and vest, laid them deliberately on the pulpit near him, and unbuttoned his shirt collar. After this preparation it is almost incredible with what ease and fluency he spoke.[70]

Baptist missionary John Mason Peck, a polished New Englander and future rival of Parker in Illinois, witnessed Parker's pulpit skills in 1822. Peck conceded that Parker spoke "with such brilliancy of thought, force, and correctness of language, as would astonish men of education and talents."⁷¹

Although he claimed victory against the Methodist barrage, Parker remained troubled about Arminian inroads among Baptists. Not all Baptists upheld Calvinistic tenets as strongly as Particular Baptists. Separate Baptists represented a doctrinal variation. Separate Baptists had originated in eighteenth-century New England as a result of the Great Awakening. Questioning the scriptural foundation of pedobaptism and the arid Calvinism of Old Light Congregationalism, many New Light dissenters withdrew from Old Light Congregational churches. These bolters organized separated congregations or united with anti-Calvinistic Baptists in New England. The new churches became known as Separate Baptists. More evangelistic than Particular Baptists, Separate Baptists became less ardent in their attitude toward unconditional election. By the 1750s Separate Baptists had moved into Virginia and presented a doctrinal challenge to Particular congregations.⁷²

Many Baptist ministers such as Parker, who clung to Particular Baptist orthodoxy, held strong reservations concerning the Separates. Because Separate Baptists did not stress Calvinism as strongly as Particulars, Particular Baptist churches remained reluctant to recognize their Separate brethren. Wishing to distance themselves from the Separates, Particular Baptists adopted the name of Regular Baptists to distinguish themselves from Arminian-proned Separate Baptists. But as Baptists continued to meet persecution in Virginia, a move toward unification occurred among Separates and Regulars as early as 1767. Yet not all Baptists favored union. Not until 1787 did Regular and Separate Baptists in the Carolinas and Virginia unite. Participants in the merger called themselves United Baptists. In 1801 Separates and Regulars also fused in Kentucky.⁷³ Parker evidently remained concerned that Arminianism, either through Methodists or Separate Baptists, might corrupt the true Baptist faith. In his farewell sermon to Testament Church, taken from Nehemiah 12:23, Parker evidently implored the church to remain untainted from Arminian dross.⁷⁴ In this exhortation Parker focused on Nehemiah's prohibition of Jewish intermarriage with pagans. In later sermons and publications he allegorized this prohibition as a warning against Arminianism and the missions system.⁷⁵

Besides the perceived Arminian advance evidenced by the

Regular-Separate union, another ecclesiastical innovation entered Tennessee. In 1814 the Baptist Triennial Convention, the national coordinating body for Baptist missionary societies, organized in Philadelphia. In one sense the missions effort represented an extension of the Old Light-New Light tension which had appeared during the Great Awakening. Regular Baptists, more aligned with Old Light Calvinism, held firm against ecclesiastical or theological novelties, especially ideas which they deemed tainted by Arminianism. But the missions system manifested an organizational challenge as well. Centralized missionary organizations had become relatively recent innovations among American Protestants. Missionary societies engaged in Bible distribution, tract publication, benevolence, and evangelism. These bodies also provided the framework for soliciting pecuniary support from individual churches and benefactors. The impetus for Protestant missionary societies in the United States lay with New England Congregationalists. In the late 1790s missionary societies had been formed by Connecticut and Massachusetts Congregationalists.[76] Massachusetts Baptists had formed a missionary society in 1802, but its influence among American Baptists was not widespread.[77]

The primary initiative for Baptist missions originated with former Congregationalists Luther Rice and Adoniram Judson. In 1812 the American Board of Commissioners for Foreign Missions, composed primarily of Massachusetts and Connecticut Congregationalist ministers, sponsored Rice and Judson as missionaries to India. The two set sail, but while underway Judson engaged in discussions with English Baptists concerning immersion. He subsequently accepted the Baptist view of immersion. After arriving in India, Rice reached the same conclusion. The two resigned as Congregational missionaries and became Baptists. Judson later labored in Burma as a Baptist missionary. Rice returned to the United States on September 7, 1813. That fall he visited Baptist churches and associations in Philadelphia, Baltimore, Washington, Richmond, and Charleston on behalf of missions. Rice envisioned an overarching Baptist society, which would be organizationally similar to the American Board. On May 18, 1814, his efforts materialized in the formation of The General Missionary Convention of the Baptist Denomination in the United States for Foreign Missions. Soon the Convention, meeting triennially, became known as the Triennial

Convention. Its constitution restricted each missionary society and religious group which annually contributed at least $100 to two delegates. The administrative board, composed of twenty-one Convention-elected members, formed The Baptist Board of Foreign Missions for the United States.[78]

The year of 1815 proved momentous for Rice and Parker. Rice, by then an official agent of the Baptist Board of Foreign Missions, solicited support from Baptist groups throughout the United States. At the 1815 meeting of the Concord Association, messengers heard Rice's communique. Parker also had achieved some degree of prominence. The previous year he had preached the annual sermon of the Concord Association and held the Baptist banner in the debates with King. As moderator of the 1815 association, Parker occupied a position of respect.

At first the appeal of Rice favorably impressed Parker, but other messengers expressed their indecision. After a lengthy discussion, representatives failed to reach accord regarding support. Referring the matter to member churches, they postponed a final decision until 1816. In the interim individual laymen and ministers, without official associational sanction, formed a separate missionary society. This agency appointed Concord Association ministers John Wiseman and Cantrel Bethel as their missionaries and Elder Jeremiah Burns as societal general agent. In one year the two missionaries preached as far south as Alabama and collected $100.[79]

By the 1816 associational meeting, opposition to the missions system had hardened. Elder George Tilman, pastor of Arrington's Creek Baptist Church, opened the meeting with a sermon critical of missionary societies. Taking his text from Luke 24:46–47, Tilman urged the preaching of the gospel solely in the name of Christ.[80] In 1815 Parker had favored the Baptist Board and its missionary endeavors. He later compared his initial sentiments to a youth infatuated with the beauty of a maid. As such, he "was taken in" by its merits and lofty purpose.[81] Parker refrained from any official comment, however, until the September 1816 meeting of the Concord Association. By then his opinion had completely reversed. He regarded the missions innovation as "a speculative plan of man's invention" and "the work of Satan."[82]

Convinced of the malevolence of the missions system, Parker attempted to prevent any links to the Baptist Board. To suppress support, he used his influence as an associational power broker in an attempt to bring promissionary advocates under rein. John Bond, present at the 1816 association, recorded that Parker circulated outspoken personal opposition to the missions system. According to Bond, Parker revealed intentions to rupture the association if the body continued missionary operations and correspondence with the Baptist Board.[83] Apparently, messengers took Parker's threat seriously. On September 9, the last day of the conference, the Concord Association officially voted to withdraw "Missionary business" and sever any official correspondence with the Baptist Board.[84] Furthermore, in what may have been a conciliatory gesture, the association elected Parker as the alternate speaker for the honorary 1817 introductory sermon.

If Parker and the antimissionary faction had been victorious, their triumph soon vanished. At the 1817 Concord Association events transpired that disturbed Parker. Following the introductory sermon, messengers elected exmissionary Wiseman to the moderatorship and promissionary advocate Whitsitt to the position of clerk. Furthermore, none other than Luther Rice, official field representative of the Baptist Board, attended. Rice had been touring the West in an attempt to establish goodwill with local associations. Six days before, he had visited the Green River Association in Barren County, Kentucky.[85] At its opening session, Saturday, August 2, the Concord Association officially recognized Rice and allowed him the opportunity to speak. The tall and eloquent New Englander desired to reopen communications between the Concord Association and the Baptist Board.[86] Rice made copies of the Baptist Board's third report available to the attending messengers of representative churches. In exchange Rice requested that Robert C. Foster, the associational clerk, direct a copy of the forthcoming 1817 Concord Minutes to the Board. Parker considered this action as a ploy by Rice to force correspondence with the association.[87] On Sunday, at the request of the association, Rice and two other ministers preached. Following the sermon by Rice, listeners had the opportunity to voluntarily contribute to foreign missions on an individual basis.[88] When asked if he had contributed, Parker gave an unequivocal response. He quipped. "No, he had no counterfeit half-dollars; if he had he would have thrown in, but as he had none he would not throw away good money for such an object."[89]

A superficial assessment of Parker's opposition may suggest

solely ecclesiastical and personal convictions. The mission impinged on the autonomous domain of local churches and associations. But outside religious organizations rivaled preachers such as Parker who remained sensitive to ministerial and denominational competition. This assessment partially explains the rather abrupt volte-face by Parker. Closer scrutiny of the Concord Association from 1815 to 1817 points to the development of intraassociational factions and personal rivalries.

The thirty-four-year-old Parker had been elected to the associational moderatorship in 1815. Elected annually by messenger vote, moderators served during the two-to-three day annual conferences. Although the moderatorship required some degree of aplomb and rudimentary parliamentary knowledge, the office was largely honorary. Election signified associational approbation of electees as leading pulpiteers or pastors. The Concord constitution barred any individual from two consecutive terms as moderator.[90] Yet promissionary advocates Whitsitt, Wiseman, and Bethel early on surfaced as associational stellars. From Concord's first assembly in 1811 through 1813 Whitsitt and Wiseman had served as associational clerk and moderator.[91] They also alternatively stood at the helm during the crucial 1816 and 1817 associations. In 1816 Whitsitt served as moderator. The next year Wiseman held that position and Whitsitt sat in the clerk's chair.[92] In 1824 Parker alluded to the existence of a faction which aimed at his destruction. According to Parker, antimissions champion Tilman, able and prepared to thwart the promissionary forces, suffered an unexplained exclusion between 1816 and 1817.[93] Although neither Parker nor the Concord minutes detail the censure of Tilman, Parker implied that it resulted from Tilman's stand against missionary societies.[94]

Two factors may explain the allegations by Parker regarding the perceived promissions intrigue. One concerns the organization of a missions society by some of the leading ministers in the Concord Association. The other involves possible jealousies and personal rivalries with some of Concord's foremost ministers. Most of the preachers with longer records of associational service apparently had supported the short-lived local missionary society.[95] The esteemed older ministers of Concord included Whitsitt, Wiseman, and Bethel. Wiseman and Bethel, besides serving as exofficio Concord missionaries, maintained a close friendship.[96] Bethel pastored

Salem Baptist Church, one of the largest churches in the association. Wiseman, in Sumner County since 1805, pastored Dixon's Creek, located in the general vicinity of Parker's Sumner County home. Following Parker's resignation of Testament in 1814, the Testament congregation had extended a call to Wiseman.[97]

In reputation and respect, Whitsitt seemed the preeminent Baptist in Tennessee. Whitsitt, pastor of Mill Creek, had joined that congregation in 1794 and later received ordination there. He participated at the organization of the Mero District Association, the first association in Middle Tennessee. He also received national recognition as a Baptist stalwart. In 1810 the Baptist historian David Benedict lodged in the home of Whitsitt while on tour of Tennessee. In 1811 Benedict, contemplating publication of a Baptist history, acknowledged Whitsitt as a source of information in a letter to the *Nashville Democratic Clarion* and *Tennessee Gazette*.[98] Because of his involvement and influence, Whitsitt's ministry reflected a virtual history of the Baptist denomination in the Cumberland Valley.[99] Furthermore, Whitsitt later favored the associational support of missions. In 1833 Whitsitt hosted a meeting at Mill Creek which established a promissions convention.[100]

In 1816 Mill Creek, with 156 members, had become one of the two largest churches in the Concord Association.[101] In terms of eminence, however, it ranked as the leading Baptist Church in the Cumberland Valley. Located on the southeastern outskirts of fast-growing Nashville, Mill Creek's membership boasted the wealthy and politically active Robert C. Foster. A wealthy planter and preeminent member of the Tennessee Senate, Foster became a gubernatorial candidate in 1817.[102] In addition to Mill Creek, pastor Whitsitt simultaneously shepherded at least three other churches in the Concord Association. In a day of many small churches and few preachers, simultaneous pastorates were common. Besides one principal church, a minister might tend as many as three or four other flocks. This practice also invested prominent ministers with ad hoc political significance. In matters which required the approval of associations, each church typically had an equal voice. But ministers with plural pastorates, assuming that they could influence each congregation, exercised a greater voice in associational voting.[103]

Not only did Whitsitt, Wiseman, and Bethel, who were respected and influential, support missionary societies, but they also had been involved in ecclesiastical inquests concerning John Parker. In 1807 Whitsitt had been requested to arbitrate a fellowship grievance between Turnbull Church and John Parker. The absence of the elder Parker spared Whitsitt the responsibility of a formal decision. He nonetheless participated in the proceeding.[104] Six years later, Wiseman, the pastor of Dixon's Creek, and Bethel, the pastor of Salem, also became entwined in errant John Parker's fellowship status. By February 6, 1813, Daniel Parker had pastored Testament Baptist Church for almost a year. On that day John Parker and two of Daniel's younger brothers, Joseph and James, presented themselves as candidates for membership in Testament. The church accepted Joseph and James but declined John's request. John evidently still remained under censure by the Turnbull Church.[105] The previous October he had sought restoration but had been denied. Sidestepping his excommunication, father Parker apparently hoped to ease himself into his son's pastoral care.

In accordance with the prevailing custom, Testament, like Turnbull, sought to settle John Parker's membership request by petitioning a meeting of ministers from neighboring churches. On May 1, 1813, an informal council, composed of ministers from Salem, Dixon's Creek, and Puncheon Camp churches, met to investigate Parker. Although the Testament minutes omit the names of the councilmen, it was common practice for the pastor of each solicited church to serve as a councilman. In this case, two of the three invited pastors would have been Bethel and Wiseman. After reviewing the issue, the inquest ruled against Daniel's father. The council recommended that Testament reject John Parker until he reconciled himself to the Cumberland Association, the association to which Turnbull belonged.

Within two years councilmen Bethel and Wiseman would enter missionary ranks. The participation of Bethel and Wiseman in the John Parker inquest did not spark the resistance of Daniel Parker to missions. Yet it may have helped to solidify his sentiments against the two men. By 1816 Parker had sided against Bethel and Wiseman in the missions issue.

John Parker shortly reconciled with the offended Cumberland Association churches. Although Testament received him as a member, his sojourn proved brief. On March 5, 1814, the Testament congregation approved his request for a letter of recommendation "as he was going to move out of our bounds."[106] The elder Parker, like many others from Kentucky and Tennessee, had heard of the fertile lands along the Wabash River. By 1814 the Indians along the Wabash, a barrier to American settlement during the War of 1812, had been subjugated. Virtually free from Indian resistance and land speculators, the Illinois territory lured land-hungry southern yeomen farmers. Thousands of Kentuckians and Tennesseans trekked north along the Vincennes Trace through western Kentucky and southwestern Indiana to Illinois. In October 1814 John Parker authorized son Daniel to settle pending lawsuits and then he hastened to Illinois.[107]

Over the next three years Daniel Parker made several excursions to the new environs of his father. By 1816 he contemplated joining the elder Parker. In a brief autobiography, published in 1831, Parker attributed his wanderlust to spiritual and material impulses. He later claimed divine unction as the primary motivation. After the "war" with the Methodists in Tennessee, he confessed that his "mind was roving in the defence of the truth against error."[108] He accordingly felt impressed to go to Illinois where the alleged missions society and Arminian heresies prevailed most against the truth. Actually, it seems that Parker exaggerated the scope of missionary activity in Illinois in 1816. For almost no missions society presence existed on the Illinois frontier in that year. On the contrary, western Indiana and Illinois, noted for spiritual destitution, remained virtually unchurched by any denomination.[109] At the time of writing, Parker evidently had in mind the controversies with promissionary advocates which he encountered between 1817 and 1831. On October 3, 1816, less than a month after the triumph of the antimissionary faction in the Concord Association, Parker purchased 160 acres of government land northeast of present Palestine, Illinois.[110]

The second persuasive factor concerned economic advancement. Parker thought that he "could do better for my family by going to a new country."[111] Abundant land offered the enterprising immigrant possibilities of speculative profits on the resale of land to latecomers. By April 21, 1817, Parker had entered 776 acres of government land in Crawford County, Illinois.[112] On Saturday, the twenty-second of the following November, Parker resigned the pastorate of Hopewell.[113] The following day, Hopewell's membership assembled for Sunday worship. Very likely Parker preached his farewell sermon on this day.[114] Within the next few days, Daniel Parker and family set out for Illinois. They arrived at some date in December 1817.[115]

The formative years of Daniel Parker in Georgia and Tennessee shaped perceptions which would influence his ensuing religious and political controversies. In 1803 Parker had entered Dickson County as a backward and undersized Georgia youth. Fourteen years later, he had gained recognition as one of the most powerful pulpiteers in Middle Tennessee and Southern Kentucky. During this self-elevation, he also had observed the social and economic disparities which juxtaposed the wealthy genteel planter class against poor backwoodsmen. Slavery exacerbated this inequity. The majority of slaveholders in Middle Tennessee owned one to four slaves. Yet farmers who owned a few slaves maintained an advantage over farmers without any slave laborers. Slaveowners, large and small, reaped far greater harvests than those without slaves. Hence, while nonslaveholders scratched out a living through their own exertion, slaveholders banked hopes of success on human bondage. Slavery also tended to deprive free mechanics and yeoman farmers of opportunities for economic advancement. Planters often hired out skilled slaves.[116] This practice reduced the wages for white craftsmen and laborers already hard-pressed for specie.

In Tennessee Parker first experienced the political, cultural, and economic clash between the commercial and industrial East and the agricultural West. Frontiersmen, more favorable to republicanism, resented New England's attempts at political and economic hegemony. Although waning by 1812, New England federalism had espoused a centralized government. New England—the mercantile, banking, and manufacturing center of the Union—held strings which reached to remote frontier hamlets. In terms of refinement, backwoodsmen viewed Eastern culture as vain and pretentious. On the other hand, easterners disdained the perceived uncouth naivete, immorality, and squalor of frontier society.[117]

Finally, Parker allowed the bias against centralized control to influence his theology and ecclesial polity. Parker had entered Tennessee as a poor unknown. Election, a cardinal tenet of Calvinism, convinced him of his worth before the Almighty. Yet Arminianism, with its conditional atonement, challenged Parker's spiritual *raison d'etre*. The possibility of overwhelming numbers of people sweeping into the heavenly kingdom without the spiritual confirmation of election challenged the Calvinist's position before God. In this conflict Parker felt threatened by powerful foes. Moreover, Parker felt certain that his adversaries, some of whom were ministerial associates, sought to destroy him. In 1824, harboring paranoic inclinations, he wrote: "From that time to this, I do not hesitate to say my life has been sought, perhaps as close as Saul persued [sic] David."[118] In 1816 Parker had been able to stall the inroads of missionism. But by the following year, it appeared to him that the centralized Baptist Board, through the efforts of New Englander Luther Rice, once again wanted to wrap its tentacles around the Concord Association. This intensified Parker's opposition and sense of betrayal. He evidently hoped that he could prevent a similar occurrence in Illinois. With this in mind, he began erecting ecclesiastical and doctrinal bulwarks along the Wabash.

Chapter 2

The Illinois Years: Political Life

WHEN DANIEL PARKER moved to Illinois in 1817, he had no inkling of his impending political life and resultant controversies. From 1822 to 1826 he would serve in the Assembly and experience the rough-and-tumble nature of backwoods politics. During these years, he became involved in the struggle against slavery. The 1820s also witnessed a political development in Illinois and most of the Union. Loosely confederated partisan factions would coalesce into national political parties. All of these challenges affected Parker.

The immigration of Parker to Illinois virtually coincided with the entry of Illinois into the Union in 1818. When Parker moved to Illinois in December 1817, he entered a state that had been part of the Indiana Territory, which had been carved out of the Northwest Territory by Congress in 1800. The vast Indiana Territory encompassed the modern states of Illinois, Indiana, Wisconsin, most of Michigan, and part of Minnesota. On February 3, 1809, Congress divided Illinois and Indiana into separate territories. Territorial Illinois only endured nine years. With the pacification of the Wabash Valley following the War of 1812, Illinois experienced an influx of settlers. The availability of cheap land coupled with relaxed payment obligations encouraged immigration.

The bulk of Illinois land became available on credit. Such an arrangement proved attractive to settlers like Daniel Parker. Deeds in Tennessee reveal that Parker had paid lump sums for land transactions in Dickson and Sumner counties. But land west of the Wabash proved easier to purchase. In Illinois most tracts sold for $2.00 per acre. In 1817 Congressional legislation reduced the minimal acreage requirement for the purchase of government land from 160 to 80 acres. Furthermore, a mere five percent deposit held land for forty days. At the end of forty days purchasers delivered an additional 20 percent. The balance, paid in three annual installments, was interest free.[1] As a result, thousands flocked to Illinois. Between 1815 and 1818 the population leaped from 15,000 to near 40,000.[2] In 1818 Illinois entered the Union as the twenty-first state.

From its territorial days Illinois had received large numbers of southern immigrants. The more populous southern third part of the state had been settled largely by southerners like Parker from Tennessee and Kentucky. Abraham Lincoln numbered among the new settlers. After seven years in Indiana, Kentucky-born Abraham followed his father, Thomas, to Illinois in 1823.[3] In 1820 the census listed nineteen counties and a state population of 55,000. Of this number, perhaps seventy-five percent came from western or southern states.[4]

Most of the immigrants in southern Ohio, Indiana, and Illinois had come from the South. For several reasons southern Illinoisans did not typify the wealth and refinement of the Southern aristocracy. Rather, limited funds and education characterized the average southern Prairie Stater. The transplanted family, often large in number, farmed small to medium-sized tracts. In many cases every family member of sufficient age contributed labor. Because of economic and social factors, few owned slaves. Most lacked the financial means to afford servants. The high price for slaves virtually precluded ownership for yeomen. In Tennessee yeomen like Parker had to pay between $500 and $700 for adult slaves.[5] Rather than purchasing slaves, farmers of limited means invested their resources in land, housing, improvements, and farming implements. These farmers also feared the social, political, and economic threats which the southern plantation system posed to them. They resented the perceived snobbery of elite southern planters. Many farmers had immigrated for land and economic opportunities. The class and political hegemony which planters might impose held little attraction for yeomen.[6] Furthermore, small farmers took seriously the possibility that cheap slave labor and agricultural overproduction might lower wages and crop prices.[7]

Attitudes concerning race also governed the opinions of many southern immigrants. Some took the high moral ground and considered slavery to be a base violation of human rights. Racial bigotry molded the sentiments of others. Yeomen southerners remained uneasy at the marked increase in the free black population in the Old Northwest. Between 1800 and 1820 the numbers of free African-Americans in Ohio, Indiana, and Illinois had climbed from 500 to 6,459.[8] In the minds of southern yeomen, slavery, either through immigration, births, or manumissions, resulted in an unwelcome population of free blacks.[9] They regarded African-Americans, free or bound, as a menace to their property, wives, and daughters.[10] White southerners feared increased criminal activity and miscegenation at the hands of African-Americans. Even Edward Coles, the antislavery governor of Illinois during Parker's term as a legislator, opposed the immigration of free blacks. Coles, who had emancipated his slaves in 1819, referred to African-Americans as "a kind of population not to be desired."[11]

Climatic, topographical, economic, and legal aspects also discouraged the development of the plantation system. Cotton production, traveling in tandem with plantation slavery in the Lower South, never flourished in the Wabash country. Similar to the Upper South, southeastern Illinois produced tobacco and grain. The limited amount of cotton production along the Wabash aimed at satisfying domestic demand for cloth rather than a cash crop.[12] Moreover, large slaveholders remained reluctant to import their human property into Illinois. Although de facto bondage existed in Illinois under the guise of indentured servitude, some slaveholders feared that future state laws or a United States Supreme Court decision might abolish any form of slavery in Illinois.[13] Large slaveholders opted instead to take their slaves to neighboring Kentucky and Missouri where their investments in human flesh remained protected by law.

In 1818 Crawford County, the largest in the state at that time, encompassed much of the eastern part of Illinois. As shown in **Figure 1**, Parker settled in the most populous section of the county. This area, a ten-mile wide strip in the extreme southeastern part of the state, roughly paralleled the Wabash River. Palestine, the

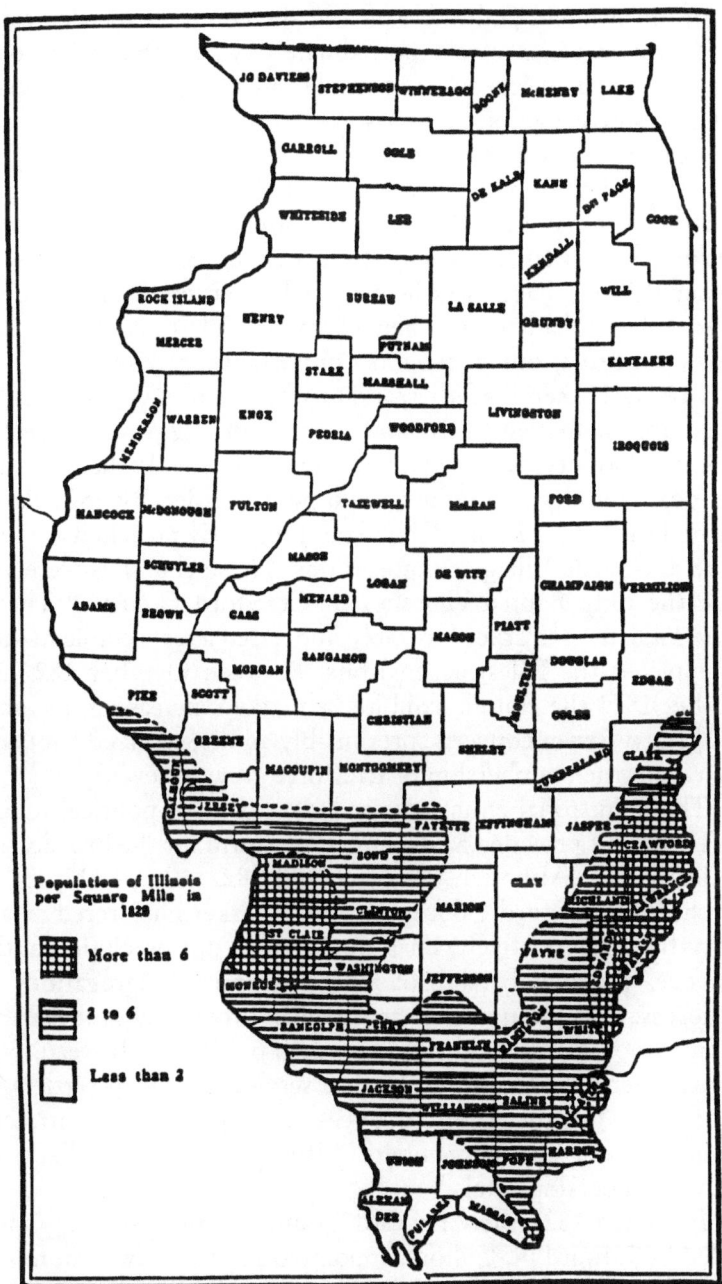

Figure 1. Modern Illinois showing population density in 1820. From The Frontier State, 1818-1848 *by Theodore Calvin Pease.*

seat of government and only town in the county, had been established near Fort La Motte. Approximately twenty-five miles northwest of Vincennes, Indiana, and a mile and a half from the Wabash, Fort La Motte had been garrisoned by a small detachment of American Rangers during the War of 1812. In 1816, following the evacuation of the post, settlers laid off Palestine a short distance from the fort. At first Palestine exhibited little growth, but the location of a United States land office there in 1820 boosted the significance of the village. All who acquired government land in southeastern Illinois had to file their claims in Palestine. By the mid-1820s it ranked as one of the most important towns in the state.[14]

In 1817 Parker, his father, and brothers James W. and Isaac had settled approximately twelve miles north of Palestine in present-day Clark County. In a matter of months Daniel Parker began to gain local visibility as a minister and public leader. By 1821 Parker pastored the Grand Prairie Church and regularly preached at the La Motte and Little Village congregations. These churches were very likely the only Baptist churches in Crawford County.[15] The La Motte ministry of Parker favorably impressed a respectable number of people in the Palestine environs. Between October 1822 and October 1823 the church exhibited a marked increase in membership.[16] Forty-seven converts, presumably adults, received baptism.[17] As a result, the membership of La Motte grew to seventy.[18]

This ministerial eminence seeded a potential political following. The pulpit provided a convenient platform for the broadcast of political issues. Although the combined 1822 membership of the churches in Crawford County to which Parker ministered totaled ninety-five, this relatively small number did not preclude political influence. The membership of frontier Baptist congregations did not necessarily indicate actual attendance. Frontier churches of any denomination rarely held weekly worship services. Instead, worshippers met once monthly. Because services provided settlers the opportunity for socialization, once-monthly preaching attracted nonmembers as well as members. Attendance therefore likely exceeded membership totals.[19]

In March 1822 the Crawford County Commissioners Court, headed by Edward N. Cullom, appointed Parker to two county offices. The Court designated Parker and fellow church member William Ryan to oversee the public care of paupers in the Palestine

Township. The second appointment entrusted Parker with the supervisory maintenance of certain county roads.[20] Yet these duties did not satiate his desire for public office. Sometime in the spring of 1822 Parker entered the race for the Third General Assembly as a senatorial candidate from Crawford and Clark counties.

Except for a previous acquaintance with Tennessee legislator and gubernatorial candidate Robert C. Foster, Parker lacked any experience in state politics or legislative procedures. Yet neither the absence of experience nor involvement in the ministry barred legislative participation in early Illinois. In 1818 twelve out of forty-two members in the First Assembly gained office without any prior experience as appointive or elected officials.[21] The participation of preachers as candidates in Illinois, including frontier Crawford County, did not prove uncommon. From the southern part of the state, Baptist minister and merchant William Kinney, who had been taught to read by his wife, held several high-level state political and legislative positions in the 1820s.[22] Thomas Young, a Baptist minister and candidate from the White and Jefferson counties district, suffered defeat in the 1820 race for the Illinois House of Representatives. In Crawford County, New Light preacher David McGahey emerged victorious in 1822 and 1824 bids for the Illinois House.[23] Rather than hinder officer seekers, homiletical elocution often proved beneficial. Politicians and lawyers often incorporated the rousing pulpit-style oratory common to backwoods preachers.[24] Fortunately for Parker, his ministerial eloquence appealed to the electorate.

In 1822 the Illinois political scene which Parker entered lacked definite partisan parameters. In the wake of the War of 1812 the Federalist Party, mostly rooted in New England, had unraveled. The economic lifeline of New England merchants, shippers, and manufacturers had been knotted by the British navy. The opposition of New England Federalists to the war had stained their party with an unpatriotic cast. Moreover, Republicans had incorporated the demand of the Federalists for nationalism and internal improvements into the Republican agenda. With the demise of the Federalist Party during the presidency of James Monroe, partisan politics temporarily waned. In local, state, and presidential elections, voters rallied around individuals, issues, or loosely organized factions.

In the early 1820s, local and state politics reflected concern over the national economy. Along the Wabash and across the United States, the Panic of 1819 had jolted the financial pyramid. Small farmers, laborers, mechanics, merchants, manufacturers, and bankers had been pinched by high debts, falling prices, and a sluggish economy. The postwar opening of the West to settlement had crested on a wave of speculative investment. Settlers needed credit for land improvement. Feeding on this frenzy, eastern manufacturers tried to meet the western demand for supplies. Western creditors, anticipating continued prosperity, made low collateral loans. An insufficient supply of specie resulted in a shortage of hard money. Entrepreneurs responded with an increased shift of transactions to paper instruments. Bank notes and bills of exchange, often from wildcat banks, replaced sound money. Inflation spiraled as the value of bank notes fell. While banks scrambled to stave off collapse, requests for the redemption of notes mounted. In the autumn of 1818 the bubble burst. The Bank of the United States called in loans and required state banks to redeem their own notes. In 1819 the hard-strapped economy quaked from a worldwide fall in commodity prices. Borrowers who had contracted high-interest loans sank in debt. Unable to repay loans, farmers and merchants suffered foreclosure. In the Northeast, shops closed or reduced labor forces.[25] In frontier Illinois, a virtual economic microcosm of the nation, Parker witnessed the hardships of debt-strapped neighbors and foundered businesses.

The basis for factional organization in Illinois, accented by the Panic of 1819, revolved around antipathy or support for United States Senator and former Illinois territorial governor Ninian Beal Edwards. Prior to his appointment as territorial governor in 1809, Edwards had been an aristocratic Kentucky judge. At times kindly and charitable, he also manifested a pompous and affected demeanor.[26] After coming to Illinois, he became involved heavily in land speculation and banking. At the national level Edwards supported the presidential aspirations of John C. Calhoun while many backwoodsmen favored William Harris Crawford.[27] The Edwards coterie included some of the most influential figures in the state. Foremost were Nathaniel Pope, Daniel Pope Cook, and Thomas C. Browne. Pope held office as a federal judge. Cook, the son-in-law of Edwards, had served in the United State House of Representatives since 1819. Thomas C. Browne occupied a seat on the Illinois Supreme Court. The anti-Edwards forces grouped around United States Senator Jessie Burgess Thomas, a political nemesis of Edwards and ally of William Harris Crawford. Luminaries in this constellation included Governor Shadrach Bond, Secretary of State Elias Kent Kane, Illinois Supreme Court justice Joseph B. Phillips, and United States Representative John McLean.[28]

The 1822 legislative and gubernatorial contest, the election that Parker entered, focused on economic issues and slavery. Because of the specie shortage, a barter economy had developed throughout Illinois and western Indiana. Merchants accepted wheat, bees wax, honey, pelts, butter, hides, and whiskey in exchange for merchandise.[29] By 1820 the Bank of Illinois at Shawneetown and the Bank of Edwardsville, both undercapitalized, had flooded the country with bloated bank notes. In 1821 the Bank of Edwardsville closed. The legislature attempted to rectify the troubled currency and specie shortage. Determined that citizens should have sound money, the Assembly chartered the State Bank of Illinois in 1821. Unfortunately, the institution, suffering from poor management and insufficient capitalization, soon entered stormy waters. Instead of alleviating money problems, the bank only pumped more worthless notes into the economy.[30] Illinois and Indiana newspapers carried notices of failed businesses and warnings against counterfeiters. Accusations of counterfeiting even plagued Daniel Parker.

The foremost economic issue in the election of 1822 concerned internal improvements. Economic development necessitated improvements in transportation. State government saddled counties with the construction and maintenance of roads. County commissioners' courts appointed highway supervisors who assessed citizens for labor or money.[31] Having served as a Crawford County supervisor, Parker remained aware of the poor roads and the difficulties that maintenance incurred.

Residents of Palestine and Crawford County such as Parker also had an interest in water traffic. La Motte Creek near Palestine, which emptied into the Wabash River above Vincennes, served as the first artery for produce-laden keelboats on the long journey to New Orleans. But river traffic, the lifeline of the Illinois economy, presented financial difficulties. Merchants and farmers marketed their goods in New Orleans but received manufactured goods from the East. The circuitous shipping routes, from Philadelphia and Baltimore to New Orleans and from upriver down to the Ohio from Pittsburgh, increased freight charges and exacerbated the money shortage. Instead of waiting on counting houses from New Orleans to New England to process interest costly credit transactions, eastern manufacturers preferred payment in sound money. Low water levels on the Mississippi, Wabash, Ohio, and inland rivers interfered with shipping and held the Illinois economy hostage. While keelboats and barges, the most convenient and cost-efficient form of downriver conveyance, maneuvered best during the high water season, southbound shipping posed hazards. In 1828 Daniel Parker and two of his brothers suffered financial loss when their keelboat sank near the confluence of the Ohio and Tennessee rivers.[32] But even safe voyages did not always guarantee profits. Inundated with produce, prices on the New Orleans market dipped. Furthermore, shippers of perishable goods—such as flour, pork, and beef—risked weather-related spoilage in the heat and humidity of southern Louisiana. To remedy this impasse, many Illinoisans favored the construction of an Illinois-Michigan canal.[33] Once completed, they anticipated that the canal would make eastern markets more accessible and plug the specie drain.

Along with economic issues, Parker felt particular concern about slavery, another issue in the election of 1822. The controversy over bondage involved constitutional, social, and economic aspects. The military exploits of George Rogers Clark had brought the Illinois territory under the domain of Virginia. In 1784 Virginia ceded this area to the Confederation Congress. But the cession guaranteed property rights, including human chattel, to French inhabitants who professed Virginia citizenship.[34] Although the Northwest Ordinance had banned slavery north of the Ohio River, slavery advocates argued that the guarantee of property rights by the Virginia cession established a precedent for slavery in Illinois.

An 1807 Indiana territorial statute had outlawed involuntary servitude. Yet the proscription took on an ambivalent quality. Immigrant slaveholders merely registered their slaves as indentured servants. This practice remained in force in territorial Illinois and accompanied the state into the Union. By 1819 Illinois had passed a comprehensive Black Code. This law, which placed severe restrictions on all African-Americans, aimed at preventing the emancipation of slaves in Illinois and the immigration of refugee slaves. Although the law incorporated provisions which protected African-Americans, enforcement varied. For example, a double standard applied to white and black indentures. While contracts usually obligated white servants for seven years, excessively long indentures for black servants virtually bound them for life. Furthermore, the act sanctioned the purchase of the contracts of indentured African-Americans.[35] Although freedom remained possible, it was not easily obtained nor maintained. Once liberated, free blacks had to file evidence of emancipation before circuit courts. This process required the deposit of a $1,000 security bond for each imported slave who received manumission in Illinois. Even under these restrictions, legal claims to freedom often proved illusory. Free blacks, apprehended and hauled before magistrates as slaves or indentured runaways, stood in peril of being sold into slavery.[36]

For some Illinoisans economic considerations provided strong incentives for human bondage. Slavery, open or de facto, provided socially mobile professionals, lawyers, merchants, and entrepreneurs with servants. In 1820 black servants in Illinois accounted for 917 out of a total African-American population of 1,512.[37] State law also permitted a certain degree of legally sanctioned slavery. The Illinois constitution allowed the leasing of out-of-state slaves for salt production at the Shawneetown salines. Located on United States government land across the Mississippi River from Kentucky, the salines provided a lucrative source of income for lessees.[38] From 1,000 to 2,000 bondsmen, many leased from Tennessee and Kentucky owners, labored at the salt works. Finally, the Panic of 1819 contributed to the demand for slavery. Prices for crops, livestock and real estate plummeted.[39] Mired in economic distress, Prairie Staters looked on as slaves trooped across Illinois behind southern planters on their way to Missouri. Between 1810 and 1820 the Missouri slave population had swelled from 3,011 to 10,222. Hard-pressed Illinoisans speculated that the legalization of slavery might induce wealthy southerners to bring their dollars to Illinois. If so, southern capital would boost land values. Illinois, rather than Missouri, would prosper.[40] With this in mind, many landowners in the southern tip of Illinois shelved moral opposition to slavery.

Influenced by the clamor for slavery, some ambitious Illinois politicians began to propose legalized slavery. Politicians who endorsed slavery included six future United States senators, a former governor, two future governors, and a host of minor officials.[41] Yet crafty politicians sidestepped direct support of slavery. Instead, they hypocritically veiled proslavery sentiment under the mantle of a constitutional convention. Office seekers argued that only the fiat of a constitutional convention could finally abolish all forms of slavery abuse. They simultaneously realized that hopes for the genuine legalization of slavery lay in a constitutional convention. For if such an event made slavery an unassailable part of state law, human bondage would become entrenched.

With the above issues capturing the attention of the electorate, the 1822 gubernatorial election featured three main contenders. The Edwards faction backed Thomas C. Browne. Distancing himself from controversy, Browne endorsed popular positions such as education, business, and internal improvements. Joseph B. Phillips, chief justice of the Illinois high court, represented the anti-Edwards camp. Phillips opposed the canal but backed a constitutional convention.[42] Neither Phillips nor Browne openly advocated slavery. Yet the proconvention stance of Phillips indicated a proclivity for slavery. The third contestant, Virginia aristocrat Edward Coles, ran as an independent.

A three-year resident of Illinois, Coles lacked the political base which characterized Phillips and Thomas. But Coles was no stranger to politics. An ambassadorship to Russia in the administration of James Madison had provided him with the aura of international experience. Unlike his opponents, Coles publicly denounced slavery. On a flatboat in the Ohio River, while en route to Illinois from Virginia in April 1819, Coles had dramatically emancipated his twenty incredulous slave families.[43] In a hard-fought campaign, amply supplied with stump oratory and free whiskey, Coles emerged the victor. With 33 percent of the votes, Coles squeaked by second-runner Phillips with a meager statewide plurality of 167 ballots.[44]

In Crawford and Clark counties, the district which sent Parker to the statehouse, evidence of an anti-Edwards sentiment emerged. Leading county political leaders Edward H. Piper, Edward N. Cullom, David McGahey, Joseph Kitchell, and Wickliff Kitchell fell under the patronage of Elias Kent Kane or Jessie Burgess Thomas.[45]

Moreover, the electorate in Crawford and Clark counties only cast a small margin of the ballots for Browne, the favorite of Edwards.[46] Parker did not leave any record which might have indicated a gubernatorial preference. For him to have favored the faction of the aristocratic landholding, Edwards certainly seems out of character with the populist-proned Parker. Rather, it is possible that he, like many state politicians of the era, publicly remained noncommital. Such a posture would have prevented him from making initial political enemies and allowed him more maneuverability.[47]

The 1822 Crawford and Clark counties senatorial race pitted Parker against three candidates. Edward N. Cullom, the most formidable, ranked among the foremost political and civic leaders in Crawford County. Cullom and associates Joseph and Wickliff Kitchell, future political rivals of Parker, soon emerged as perhaps the most powerful county faction. A Kentucky immigrant, Cullom had settled in Palestine in 1814. He and Joseph Kitchell had represented the county in the territorial government and during the 1818 constitutional convention.[48] During the convention, they opposed the total abolition of slavery and voted to retain indentured servitude.[49] In 1818 Cullom and Joseph Kitchell had donated much of the land for the town of Palestine. Their benevolence also led to some personal aggrandizement. In return for their generosity, Palestine—which hosted the county seat—became the logical choice for the location of a public land office.[50] Cullom likewise occupied a salient position on the county commissioners' court. From February 1817 until the construction of a court house in 1819, the Crawford County court convened in the Cullom home. Cullom remained on the court through March 1822.[51]

Joseph Kitchell and his brother Wickliff had familial roots in colonial New Jersey. The brothers had moved from Cincinnati, Ohio, to Indiana and then to territorial Illinois.[52] Early on Joseph became involved in land speculation in Crawford County. From September 1816 through October 1818 he acquired 1,645 acres.[53] After serving in the constitutional convention, Joseph returned to the statehouse as senator from Crawford County. In the legislative election for United States senator, he worked to defeat Ninian Edwards. Daniel Pope Cook warned Edwards of the political opposition of senators Joseph Kitchell and Willis Hargrave. Cook opined that Kitchell and Hargrave had proven to be the most "ignorant and corrupt" of all men.[54]

Wickliff and Joseph Kitchell were not novice politicians. The brothers had been accustomed to political cliques at the county level. In 1816 Joseph had served as an associate judge of the circuit court in Jackson County, Indiana. At the same time Wickliff served that county as sheriff. Lamed by an accidental ax blow, Wickliff read enough law to pass the bar. Around 1817 he joined Joseph in Illinois and established the first law practice in Crawford County. Like his brother, Wickliff quickly gained prominence in county politics. By the end of 1819 he held the positions of county treasurer, county commissioner, and notary public.[55]

Firmly in the anti-Edwards camp, the Kitchells became political patrons of proslavery advocates Elias Kent Kane and Jessie Burgess Thomas.[56] Joseph Kitchell took an ambivalent attitude toward African-Americans. He officially denounced slavery as a political and moral evil, but in practice he supported de facto slavery in the form of indentured servitude.[57] In 1830 Joseph remained one of nine Crawford County residents who kept African-American indentured servants.[58] In 1821 the political patronage of Joseph did not go unrewarded. Thomas used his friendship with Secretary of the Treasury Crawford in order to secure the appointment of Joseph as registrar of the Palestine Land Office.[59]

After appointment to the land office on July 23, 1821, Kitchell chose not to seek reelection.[60] With Kitchell bowing out, Cullom entered the race. Cullom soon discovered that the politically inexperienced Parker presented a serious challenge. By mid-June the Baptist minister already had concluded a two-to-three week electioneering tour.[61] On election day, August 5, 1822, Palestine echoed political rhetoric. At 8:00 A.M. Thomas C. Browne had mounted the stump within earshot of the poll.[62] Browne, the pro-Edwards candidate, accomplished little in Crawford County. Voters favored him with a mere thirty-seven ballots. Phillips collected 122. Coles won with 165.[63] In the senatorial contest the pioneer preacher bested the experienced politician. Out of 364 votes in Crawford and Clark counties, Parker garnered 134 to 104 for Cullom. In Crawford County, the base of Cullom's political strength, Parker outstripped him 113 to 83.[64]

Parker served in the Senate from 1822 to 1826. His legislative activities during the Third and Fourth Assemblies indicate that he supported populist issues and sound fiscal government. Although inflation had reduced the real value of the $2.00 per diem allotted to assemblymen, he voted against pay increases for legislators. On the frontier wolves posed a threat to valuable livestock. Territorial law had allowed $2.00 for each wolf scalp. Backwoodsmen availed themselves of this source of income. In 1818 James Parker, the brother of Daniel, had collected $12.00 in bounty money.[65] Senator Parker nevertheless opposed increasing the $2.00 state bounty on wolf scalps. An advocate of internal improvements and former road supervisor, Daniel Parker became convinced that the method of maintaining county roads needed reform. Because local road construction and maintenance fell under the responsibility of the county commissioners' courts, these bodies annually appointed highway supervisors and called on citizens for labor or money commutation.[66] The difficulty of levying labor no doubt presented problems. Parker recognized the need for change and supported a more equitable method of road maintenance.

At the statewide level, Parker devoted much of his legislative energy to bills which concerned internal improvements, debt relief, and the shortage of specie. Aware of the need to facilitate market transportation, Parker introduced or supported construction bills for at least four roads in the central and eastern parts of the state. He also favored the improvement of navigation and the construction of a canal from Lake Michigan to the Illinois River. Parker sought to alleviate the specie shortage by repealing an act which restricted the circulation of unauthorized currency. In terms of relief, he supported the reduction of taxes on town lots and relief for debtors who resided on public lands. His legislative career also encompassed the mundane. On November 20, 1824, Parker moved that the stationary committee provide each desk in the senate chamber with one ink stand, a lock and key, six candlesticks, and six copies of the statute laws. By his legislative record Parker seems to have exhibited a genuine interest in the public good and his constituency. For example, he remained sympathetic to the needs of the Quaker constituency in Crawford County. The Baptist minister introduced a resolution which exempted pacifist Quakers and Dunkers from hiring substitutes for the militia.[67] Yet his foremost contribution concerned the bitter struggle against slavery.

On December 2, 1822, the Third Assembly convened in Vandalia. Parker and sixteen fellow senators took their seats. Three days later Governor Coles delivered his inaugural address to a joint session of the Assembly. Coles appealed to the legislature for sound money, a canal connecting the Wabash to Lake Erie, and the establishment of a state penitentiary. No part of his proposed legislative agenda raised more controversy than the proposed revision of laws relative to African-Americans. In the "cause of humanity," Coles implored the Assembly to relax the strict slavery codes and enact laws which would prevent the kidnapping of free blacks. The governor argued that slavery had indeed existed in Illinois but should not continue. Because few, if any, of the mature slaves owned by French masters still lived, time had invalidated the guarantees of the Virginia cession. He reasoned that the framers of the Virginia ordinance had not intended to establish perpetual slavery in Illinois. The governor therefore called for the "abrogation of slavery in the State."[68]

The proposed abolition of slavery faced a bitter struggle in the Assembly. Both houses conceded that abrogation lay outside the bounds of legislative authority. The Senate proposed that only a constitutional convention could abolish slavery. Furthermore, only a referendum would authorize the calling of a convention. Proslavery advocates clamored for a convention. If the Assembly approved the proposed referendum, the legalization of slavery seemed likely. After all, strong proslavery sentiment existed among the electorate as well as in the statehouse. Had the proslavery Phillips and Browne factions united in 1822, Coles would not have been victorious. Adolphus Frederick Hubbard, the lieutenant governor and president of the Senate, openly advocated slavery. Furthermore, a proslavery majority sat in the Assembly.[69]

Although Parker had published little about slavery, he entered the struggle against human bondage. The opposition of Parker grew out of concerns about class, economics, and his political constituency. He also stood to gain politically by taking an antislavery stance. Although a religious minority in Crawford County, the Quaker inhabitants resisted slavery as a moral evil. Broader opposition came from the nonslaveholding yeomen who composed the great majority of his constituency. Out of 683 households in Crawford and Clark counties, only eleven possessed slaves.[70] Beset by hard times, yeomen looked askance at possible attempts to legalize slavery. If large planters immigrated with their slaves to southeastern Illinois, hard-pressed farmers and mechanics would have difficulty competing against slave labor. In 1820 he published *A Public Address*. This essay against missionary societies briefly condemned slavery and indicates the reservations of Parker about wealthy slaveholders.

> It is a stubborn fact that through the United States that hold slaves, where the mission spirit prevails very considerably, that there are numbers engaged in the mission plan who do not labor one day in a year, and yet possess great wealth.... Their slaves by intense labor have accumulated this wealth. Now I ask a candid public whether this is the religion of Christ? Let us take a glance at the situation of the Negro. Neither money nor time are given even to teach him to read the Bible. Go to his hut which he built in the night. It is not fit for a work horse to stand in; his lodging is a scaffold with some straw on it; his diet is at best the scraps which fall from his master's table; perhaps not so good. And as to his clothes, decency and modesty cannot look at him without blushing. All this he endures besides the abuse he meets with from a hard master.[71]

Many of the Methodists and Baptists in the subsistence culture of the Upper South voiced opposition to the perceived opulence and cultural arrogance of the slaveholding plantation elite. The issue of slavery had surfaced among Kentucky Baptists as early as 1792. In 1807 antislavery Baptists in Kentucky had separated from their brethren and formed "The baptized Licking Locust Association Friends to Humanity."[72] Antislavery sentiment also produced a rift among Illinois Baptists. In 1808 certain antislavery Baptists in Illinois, dissatisfied with the slow progress against slavery, had withdrawn from the Illinois Association. As in Kentucky, these schismatics called their fellowship The Friends of Humanity.[73] Although he did not go to this extreme, Parker struck out at slavery through the auspices of the Wabash District Association. Parker dominated the southeastern Illinois churches which composed the association. In 1824 his La Motte pastorate condemned slavery in the minutes of the Wabash District Association as contrary to the principles of free government, Christianity, and God.[74]

On Friday, December 6, 1822, the convention struggle crystalized in the Senate. The upper house agreed to elect a five-man Committee on the Abrogation of Slavery and the Kidnapping of Free Blacks. From the initial balloting it became apparent that Parker and fellow antislavery senators composed a definite minority. Out of eighty votes cast on the first ballot for committeemen, Parker and three other anticonvention senators received a total of eight.[75] All five electees represented strong proslavery counties near Missouri and Kentucky. The following Thursday, the Committee recommended to the Senate a convention referendum. Accordingly, voters would decide the issue at the 1824 election for assemblymen. Yet before the recommendation began official, it had to gain passage in the Senate and the House.

During the next sixty days, the Senate deliberated the convention. Although proconvention senators held the majority, their success was not guaranteed. The law required a two-thirds majority for passage, but out of eighteen members of the Senate only seventeen answered roll. Parker and five other solons took the minority position. The proconvention faction lacked the crucial vote of proconventionist senator John Grammer, who had been detained in his district. Because the minority had enough votes to block but not defeat passage, their stratagem revolved around delay. For if Grammer failed to appear, Senate approval would not be forthcoming. And without passage of the recommendation, the Senate would have no bill to present to the House. On December 12, 1822, the Senate committee on slavery recommended no change in existing laws other than "the redoubled diligence of our grand jurors and our magistrates."[76] Not content with this sop, Parker introduced a bill five days later to inflict a penalty for failure to enter names and ages of children of indentured servants. Unfortunately, his proposed legislation remained stillborn.[77] Whisked off to a committee, the bill failed to emerge in time for passage. In the midst of these weighty deliberations Parker moved on January 7 to have daily Senate sessions opened with prayer. Opposed to any motion which might divert debate over slavery, the Senate tabled the motion.[78]

In spite of these obstacles, minority senators maintained their vigilance. On January 24 proconvention solon Theophilus W. Smith offered a motion concerning the immediate restoration of freedom to African-Americans in Illinois. Smith moved that a special committee examine the necessity, if any, of legislation designed to free "every negro, mulatto, or person of color."[79] If passed, the legislation would have emancipated slaves. Yet this did not seem to be the purpose of Smith. Rather, by raising the issue, he merely wanted to put the issue to a parliamentary death. By a vote of 9 to 8 the Senate delayed action on Smith's motion until March 1.[80] This delay sealed the defeat of the resolution. The Senate had concurred with the House on January 22 that no new business would be introduced after February 1.[81] Unhappy with this dodge, Parker sought permission the next day to revive discussion by repealing "several sections" of the proposed legislation.[82] The Senate denied his request. On January 27 the Senate again tabled the resolution until March 1, 1823.[83] This delay silenced attempts to completely outlaw slavery through legislation.

Although the anticonvention senators resisted passage of the convention resolution, their efforts met with defeat. On Friday, February 7, proconvention senator Grammer arrived and took his seat. The presence of Grammer meant that the proconvention faction had the necessary twelve votes for a two-thirds majority.[84] On February 10, 1823, the Senate, in a twelve-to-six decision, narrowly passed the resolution for a convention referendum.

In the House the convention debate produced greater turmoil. On January 27, 1823, the House fell short of the required majority by two votes. By February 11 the gap had narrowed to one. Proconvention forces resorted to intimidation and legislative acrobatics in an effort to gain the necessary single ballot. That night an indignant mob burned dissenter Representative Nicholas Hansen, a convention opponent, in effigy. In the course of the demonstration they marched defiantly past the lodgings of the minority. The crowd shouted "The Convention or Deathm," the proslavery potto.[85] The following day, February 12, the House challenged the credentials of Hansen and ousted him. On February 12, six days prior to adjournment, the House then seated proslavery John Shaw. The single vote secured, the House hastened to pass the convention resolution the same day.[86]

On the evening following adjournment, the minority met in order to plan their course of action. Five senators, including Parker, and ten representatives quietly gathered in a Vandalia boarding house. Hamstrung in the Assembly, the antislavery legislators sought public support through the publication of an antislavery manifesto. Their declaration condemned slavery as a violation of the will of God as well as the Northwest Ordinance. They further argued that the human degradation brought on by slavery would discourage immigration to Illinois.[87] The conclave also formulated plans to fund an antislavery campaign in the *Edwardsville Spectator*. This decision became crucial to the success of the minority. With the exception of the *Spectator*, the remaining four Illinois newspapers supported slavery.[88]

At this meeting Parker contributed fifty dollars to defray the expense of printing. The surreptitious meeting proceeded without incident, but his contribution drew public criticism. The proslavery *Illinois Intelligencer* soon publicized the meeting and names of the participants. The following June a proslavery lobbyist published a letter to Parker in the *Illinois Intelligencer*. The lobbyist, familiar with the conviction which Parker held toward salaried preachers, badgered the Crawford County senator. He accused Parker of using public funds, meaning the seven dollar per diem then allotted to each assemblyman, for "bribing" a printer to publish anticonvention material.[89]

From February 1823 to August 1824 the convention issue divided communities and families. The question stirred such intense controversy that the possibility of civil war ensued.[90] The chief strength of the anticonventionists lay among their gifted writers and organizers. Proslavery advocates could not match the originality and logic of antislavery writers such as English immigrant Morris Birkbeck. The pulpit likewise rendered invaluable service to the anticonventionists. Methodist and Baptist ministers thundered against slavery. Baptist minister John Mason Peck, a supporter of the Baptist Board of Foreign Missions and missionary nemesis of Parker, found rare common ground with Parker on the convention issue. Peck used his position as Bible distributor to circulate antislavery literature.[91]

The Third Assembly had scheduled the election on a proposed convention to coincide with the August 1824 general election. The delay allowed both parties an opportunity to canvass for support. On August 2, 1824, voters went to the polls to decide the convention question. Interest had peaked in the near eighteen-month interval since the adjournment of the Third Assembly. In his district

Parker earnestly campaigned against the convention. He allegedly left the bedside of his dying mother to rally the anticonvention vote.[92] No riots occurred, but across the state voters turned out in record numbers. The 1824 ballot count exceeded the 1822 total by 3,006.[93] John Reynolds, a candidate for the Assembly from St. Clair County, later wrote that the "aged and crippled were carried to the polls, and men voted on this occasion that had not seen the ballot-box in twenty years."[94] Out of a total of 11,612 ballots, voters statewide rejected the convention by a modest 1,668 majority. Parker's district, which included newly created Edgar County, overwhelmingly rejected the proposal.[95]

After the convention defeat, Parker continued to provide exemplary representation in the Fourth Assembly. The senator from Crawford County sat on committees which dealt with internal improvements, state salines, petitions, and elections. These appointments carried significant political weight. A seat on the internal improvements committee allowed Parker to tailor road and waterway construction. As a member of the Committee on Petitions he helped to determine legislative consideration for special requests and the relief of individual debtors. In a display of virtual unity, Parker joined fourteen other solons in blocking an attempted coup by Lieutenant Governor Adolphus Frederick Hubbard. In the absence of Governor Coles, Hubbard had openly claimed the governorship for himself. On January 2, 1826, the Senate refused to legally condone the action of Hubbard.[96]

During the final session of the Fourth Assembly—January 21, 1826—Senator Thomas Sloo moved that the Reverend Daniel Parker dismiss the Senate in prayer. The Senate concurred. Immediately following "an extemporaneous address to the Throne of Grace, by the Rev. Mr. Parker," the Senate adjourned.[97] This was the last official act of Senator Parker. Developments in his senatorial district already had transpired which eventually toppled Parker and ended his legislative career in Illinois.

In 1822 the electoral base in Crawford and Clark counties had been small. Only 364 voters had participated in the election. During his first term, Parker had been able to use the political inbreeding which often characterized frontier Illinois county administrations to his advantage. In newer counties the same officials often held several elected or appointive positions.[98] In the early 1820s Parker and several of his associates had gained elective or appointive positions in Crawford and Clark counties. On December 28, 1822, the Senate confirmed the appointment of eleven Crawford County justices of the peace. Three of these, Baptist minister Ziba H. Woolcott, Elisha Dodson, and James Parker, belonged to churches in which Daniel Parker ministered.[99] The following January the Senate confirmed the appointment of William P. Bennett, another church associate of Parker, as a Clark County justice of the peace.[100] The jurisdiction of justices extended to civil matters not exceeding $100. Justices also had general powers in criminal cases. The Assembly had empowered them with the authority to jail on all offenses and to free in minor cases. Because fees remained small, the primary motivation for holding county positions concerned their political significance.[101] Thomas Kennedy, pastor of the La Motte Baptist Church, had served as the treasurer of Crawford County since 1819. In February 1823 the Senate confirmed Kennedy as a judge of probate for that county. Charles Neely, a member of Parker's Grand Prairie pastorate, received a similar confirmation for Clark County.[102] Moreover, in 1824 Asa Norton, a deacon in the Little Village Church, had been elected to the House of Representatives from neighboring Lawrence County. In 1820 Parker and Kennedy had composed the presbytry which had ordained Norton.[103]

The Cullom-Kitchell clique, with strong ties to legal and mercantile interests, did not ignore the development of a rival faction. In 1826 Wickliff Kitchell challenged the incumbent Parker for his Senate seat. On January 8, 1825, Kitchell baited the Crawford County senator with a request for an explanation regarding some alleged remarks by Parker. Kitchell maligned Parker for lacking the moral qualifications for office. He demanded that Parker respond to allegations of counterfeiting, spinning tales about a treasure hunt in Tennessee, and demagoguery.

In the eyes of the public, the primary responsibility of a republican officeholder remained the untarnished service of the people and state. The most effective manner of attacking an elected official centered on impugning his reputation.[104] Kitchell timed his letter to correspond with the adjournment of the first session of the Fourth Assembly on January 18, 1825. Through this means Kitchell designed to cast aspersion on the integrity of Parker. Having returned from the statehouse, Parker could not use senatorial duties as an excuse for not responding. Parker read the letter with detachment. At first he regarded the accusations as "unworthy of notise."[105] But on second thought, Parker realized that Kitchell had political ambitions. Only six months prior Kitchell had lost a bid for the Illinois House of Representatives by fifty-three votes.[106] Kitchell threatened to address Parker "through another medium," presumably the press, if Parker failed to respond.[107] If not squelched, the allegations imperiled the reelection of Parker. Moreover, Parker dared not take lightly the accusation of counterfeiting. Counterfeiting carried serious consequences for convicted public officials. The 1816 territorial laws had barred from public office those who knowingly circulated forged specie.[108] If substantiated, the allegations could have resulted in the removal of Parker from the Assembly.

Lawyer Kitchell had carefully selected his accusations on the hearsay of Joseph Kitchell and Thomas Kennedy. Parker allegedly had complained to Joseph Kitchell that Cullom and James Shaw, political enemies of Parker, had leveled charges of counterfeiting at the preacher-senator.[109] The allegations of counterfeiting evidently had circulated throughout the community previous to the 1824 assembly election and convention referendum. By April 1824 the rumors had attracted so much attention that Parker sought the aid of the La Motte congregation. At the request of Parker, the church appointed a committee of seven to investigate the matter. On August 7, five days after the convention election, the committee exonerated Parker at the monthly church conference.[110]

Joseph Kitchell also had related that Parker had boasted about a dubious treasure-expedition. According to Daniel Parker, he and his brother, Joseph, had returned to Tennessee in order to search for Spanish gold. Wickliff challenged Senator Parker to verify the story with details. Unless Parker could justify the money-hunting excursion, such a venture might support charges concerning the importation and circulation of bogus money. If proven false, the story cast Parker as an irresponsible tale-teller, unworthy of public trust.

Joseph Kitchell had received the third accusation from Thomas Kennedy. Kennedy reported that prior to the 1822 election Parker had trumpeted a presumed God-ordained call to serve in the Assembly.[111] Although Parker later denied this charge, it is possible that he inserted religious issues into the campaign.[112] David Mc-

Gahey, an 1822 candidate for the Illinois House of Representatives, and Cullom belonged to religious groups which espoused Arminianism. In the mind of Parker, the missions system had been an offspring of Arminianism. Moreover, some viewed nineteenth-century manifestations of progress, such as banks and corporations as well as missionary and benevolent societies, as departures from the purity of republican tradition. As early as 1820 Parker had complained that the missions system threatened "republican government."[113] Wickliff attacked the alleged God-ordained clamor of Parker as demagoguery. By raising this issue Wickliff meant to impugn Parker as a power-obsessed official. Such an insinuation cast doubt on the republican principles of Parker. Jeffersonianism decried the abuse of popular trust. The accusation of Wickliff therefore implied that Parker lacked moral integrity and the necessary commitment to republican government.[114]

Parker answered Wickliff Kitchell in a letter written February 15, 1825. Parker verified the circumstances of the treasure-hunting expedition. Although he did not offer a specific refutation of demagoguery and counterfeiting, Parker summarily dismissed all of the allegations as false. Moreover, he attacked Wickliff Kitchell for purposely engendering strife in order to reap personal political gain.[115] In a riddlelike narrative Parker chided Kitchell for undeserved criticism.[116] Five days later, Kitchell fired back with an insulting five-page epistolary. He hurled charges of apostasy and tyranny against Parker. With more personal barbs, Kitchell referred to the "disordered mind" of Parker and also insinuated possible sexual improprieties. In addition, the lawyer accused the preacher-politician of crying persecution in order to distract attention from an "unquenchable desire for worldly riches."[117]

Parker took no immediate legal action against Kitchell. But the rumors failed to subside. In April and May 1825 one of Parker's church members allegedly defamed Parker in Palestine. Elijah Dodson, a member of the Grand Prairie Church, accused his pastor of manufacturing counterfeit money in Tennessee. The retort which Parker had made at the 1817 Concord Association regarding a collection for missions had returned to haunt him. Dodson recommended that Parker stand trial in Tennessee.[118] Parker felt impelled to redeem his reputation in advance of the August 1826 election. On August 5, 1825, he filed a $10,000 suit against Wickliff Kitchell for trespass of character. In regard to Dodson, Parker ignored the scriptural injunction against taking a fellow Christian to court. Three weeks later he entered a $2,000 slander suit against Dodson.[119]

The case against Kitchell went to court on November 15, 1825. Because Robert Gill, a crucial Parker witness, failed to appear, Parker withdrew his suit. Whereupon, the court required Parker to pay the cost of Kitchell's defense. But Parker did not intend to allow his money and reputation to depart so easily. Shortly after the dismissal of the first case, Parker entered a second suit against Kitchell for $12,000. The next circuit court convened on May 8, 1826. The second *Parker v. Kitchell* trial occupied the entire week. The defending attorney maintained the innocence of Kitchell. He argued that Kitchell had merely repeated, but not contrived, the prevailing allegations of demagoguery, counterfeiting, and deception. On Saturday, May 16, the jury, one of whom belonged to Parker's Little Village pastorate, declared Wickliff Kitchell not guilty.[120]

The legal defeat of Parker foreshadowed his political decline. In the August 7, 1826, election Parker faced Wickliff Kitchell and William B. Archer in the senatorial contest. Parker and Archer had known each other for several years. As late as 1823 Archer had owned a farm less than a mile from a mill operated by Parker in Clark County.[121] Archer had relatives in Ohio but had moved from Kentucky to Illinois in 1817. Tall and resolute of character, he took a commanding position in civic affairs. Although a former slave state resident, Archer championed the antislavery cause.[122] Early on he rose to political prominence when he served as the first clerk of Clark County. In 1824 Clark Countians elected him to the state House of Representatives. Two years later he replaced Parker in the Senate.

The ensuing defeat of Parker by Archer mixed politics with issues of personality, reputation, and demographics. Since 1822 Parker's senatorial district had been enlarged by the addition of Edgar, Vermillion, and Lawrence counties. These additions had resulted in an electoral increase of 984. Moreover, publication and legal costs had depleted his financial reserves.[123] By 1826 it had become more difficult for him to conduct a campaign over a broader area. In spite of the adverse publicity surrounding the Kitchell case, Parker apparently retained most of his 1822 electoral support in Crawford and Clark counties. In 1826 the Parker total among the

Crawford and Clark electorate fell only eleven votes shy of his 1822 tally. He also did well in Edgar County. Having familial and church connections there, Parker captured 119 out of 275 ballots. Yet his dismal showing in Vermillion and Lawrence counties spelled defeat. Even second runner Kitchell far outstripped Parker. Kitchell ran well in Crawford, Lawrence, and Vermillion counties. In Crawford County he received 205 votes. Throughout the district he trailed Archer by a scant twenty-nine votes.[124]

In Lawrence County Parker only received 36 out of 362 ballots while the congenial Archer collected almost 54 percent.[125] At first glance, it may seem that the anticonvention stance of Parker should have benefited his candidacy in Lawrence County. The county remained a stronghold for emancipated African-Americans. The 1830 Census listed more free blacks in Lawrence County than any other county in the 1826 senatorial district of Parker. Out of 173 African-Americans, only twenty-two remained in slavery or under indenture.[126] With such a marked number of emancipated slaves, it is possible to surmise that white Americans might have allowed racial prejudice and fear of increased economic competition by African-American laborers to influence the rejection of the convention. An anticonvention stance meant a voice against more African-Americans in southeastern Illinois. In the 1824 convention election 66 percent of the Lawrence County electorate, 261 out of 419 voters, rejected the convention proposal.[127] Voters in Crawford, Clark, and Edgar counties also had overwhelmingly voted against the convention. Furthermore, Parker had stood openly with the legislative minority against slavery. If the position of Parker on slavery had been the salient issue, the electorate in his district should have approved of his noted opposition to the convention. While Archer opposed slavery, he had not been an assemblyman in 1824. Moreover, Archer had not risked, as Parker had, his political future over slavery.

In light of this factor it seems that other developments worked against Parker. By 1826 Parker had been involved in rancorous conflicts over church leadership and support of missionary societies. This discord had marked Parker as a contentious and authoritarian leader. Such a reputation, real or alleged, did not conform to the principles of Jeffersonian republicanism. The *Parker v. Kitchell* litigations had done little to build the exemplary reputation of Parker as a virtuous public servant. The more polished and personable Kitchell and Archer, less vulnerable to accusations of immorality and rancor, appealed to a broader spectrum of the electorate than Parker.

Parker did not completely abandon political aspirations. In August 1832 his name appeared on the ballot from Crawford County as a candidate for the Illinois House of Representatives. He received 132 votes, the approximate total as in 1822 and 1826. William Highsmith, the victor, collected 164. The defeat of Parker by Highsmith implied more than political rejection. It indicated Parker's inability to broaden voter support. During the summer of 1832, Highsmith had commanded a company of Crawford County volunteers in the Blackhawk War.[128] Highsmith seems to have used this favorable exposure to his advantage. Popular officers often parlayed militia commands into political office.[129] Another blow to Parker concerned the church affiliation of Highsmith. Until February 1832 Highsmith had belonged to Parker's Little Village flock. Prior to the election, Highsmith moved his membership to North Fork Baptist Church in Jasper County, Illinois.[130]

The decline of Parker also reflected evolving national and state partisan frameworks. The presidential election of 1824 had incorporated the use of local nominating groups in the support of national contenders. By 1832 the supporters of Andrew Jackson and Henry Clay had coalesced into national political parties. Jacksonians formed the Democratic Party. In the South and West the Democratic Party attracted small farmers. Kentuckian Henry Clay had disappointed many of these yeomen in the election of 1824. In that contest Jackson led in electoral and popular votes. Yet Clay had committed the thirty-seven electoral votes cast for Clay to John Quincy Adams. This insured the victory of Adams at the expense of Jackson. Many southerners and westerners considered the shift of Clay to be a betrayal of republicanism. These yeomen also viewed Jackson as the champion of republican purity. In 1832 Jackson had vetoed the rechartering of the Bank of the United States. Small farmers and mechanics who deemed the Bank as a hegemony of eastern wealth and influence applauded Jackson. The followers of Adams and Clay rallied around the Whig banner. Whigs tended to support national internal improvements that would benefit transportation and commerce. Merchants, professionals, townsmen, and some planters often composed the ranks of southern and western Whigs. On a broad scope both Whigs and Democrats claimed to espouse pure republican principles such as egalitarianism and property rights. Local politicians molded this commitment to republicanism around local issues. Often this fine tuning determined the membership and support of parties at the local level.

In the 1824 presidential race, Crawford County equally divided 74 percent of the ballots between the electors of Andrew Jackson and Henry Clay. The John Quincy Adams electors received 27 percent. By 1828 Crawford County favored Andrew Jackson with almost a 70 percent majority. Across the state Jackson carried Illinois with 67 percent. By 1832 the Jackson standard had been even more firmly planted in Crawford County. In 1832 David McGahey wrote to United States Senator Elias Kent Kane concerning political developments in Crawford County. McGahey mentioned the increasing popularity of Jackson and the waning of Clay support.[131] In 1832 Jackson received 76 percent in the county as compared to 24 percent for Clay. Statewide totals gave Jackson 68 percent and Clay 32 percent.[132]

By 1832 party affiliation had become clearly important to local political campaigns. Increasingly, the lower tiers of office seekers identified local and state issues with national platforms and candidates. Wickliff Kitchell and Henry Eddy, Kitchell's attorney in the first *Parker v. Kitchell* case, rose to prominence in Democratic ranks. In 1824 Eddy had served as a Jackson elector. Eight years later, Archer represented Whigs as a Clay elector.[133] The national political alliance of Parker is unknown, for he omitted references to a partisan preference in his private and public writings. Had he remained in Illinois it is likely that he would have favored the Democrat Party. In 1836 his brother, Nathaniel, represented Coles and Clark counties in the Illinois Senate as a Democrat.[134] In addition, Crawford County became a Jackson stronghold.

If Parker took a partisan stand, however, he certainly failed to rise to prominence. On the other hand, he may have purposely shed partisan labels. Born during the Revolution, Parker had reached adulthood during the halcyon years of Jeffersonian republicanism. To Parker, the American Republic, righteously maintained and committed to egalitarian principles, remained the political hope and defense of the common man. In the early 1820s the public generally took a dim view of political parties. Partisan politics smacked of power-craving cabals. Only mean and disreputable office seekers joined or organized parties.[135] On the contrary, virtuous public officials repudiated parties. They sought to serve openly and preserve their integrity. It is therefore possible that Parker, already damaged by charges of moral turpitude and obsessive lust for power, chose to campaign as an independent.

Yet Parker evidenced characteristics that did not conform to Jeffersonianism. The formation of a pro-Parker group of kinsmen and church acquaintances in Crawford and Clark counties pointed at non-Jeffersonian factional alignment. Moreover, the juristic exoneration of Wickliff Kitchell seemed to have given credence to the rumors concerning Parker's desire for power. In terms of legislative activity, a close scrutiny of Parker indicates a desire for self-advancement.

Parker provided effective leadership during his brief tenure in Illinois politics. His antislavery stance provided the minority with much-needed political support. But for an electee without previous office holding experience, he quickly became a student of the wily craft of politics. A lobbyist described the Crawford County senator as "a man that would converse freely on all subjects that were introduced by any person in company where you might chance to be."[136] He remained attentive to legislation that enhanced his opportunities for reelection. Because of a high rate of illiteracy and the expense of printing ballots, the Illinois election process used the viva voce method.[137] Voters orally delivered their choices of candidates to an authorized panel of election clerks at official polls. In September 1822 defeated opponents Cullom and Samuel Prevo had challenged the returns of the Parker victory the previous month. Their allegations were partially related to so-called improprieties in the viva voce process which had favored Parker.[138] On December 28, 1822, less than a month after he entered the Assembly, Parker demonstrated his desire to prevent political opponents from robbing him of victory on the basis of a voting technicality. Parker supported a bill which changed the viva voce process to the ballot method.[139]

On January 13, 1826, during the last week of the Fourth Assembly, Parker introduced a petition from Vermillion County citizens. The request solicited the construction of a road through Vermillion County to the eastern border of Illinois.[140] Officially created January 18, 1826, Vermillion County recently had been added to the senatorial district of Parker.[141] Doubtless, such a favor to the Vermillion electorate would have garnered reciprocal political rewards to Parker in the approaching August campaign.

The hard-fought campaign against slavery also involved political and economic implications. Parker genuinely opposed slavery. Part of his resistance stemmed from the religious and moral principles espoused by many Evangelicals in the Upper South. Yet these principles likely did not form the wellspring of Parker's antislavery position. More probably, the racial prejudice of his southern yeomen environment negatively molded Parker's sentiments toward blacks. African-Americans and the plantation system presented economic, political, and social threats to southern yeomen like Parker. Furthermore, the few references which Parker offered to human injustice toward African-Americans served purposes other than humanitarian concerns. Parker conveniently used antislavery as shot and powder in his fusillades against religious adversaries. His senatorial attempts to guard the freedoms of free blacks did not necessarily indicate a magnanimous interest in the rights of African-Americans. Eleven years after the defeat of the convention, Daniel Parker—then a Texas resident—seems to have favored the reenslavement of unauthorized free blacks in Texas. Thus, the efforts by Parker in Illinois to restore liberty to illegally held blacks may have been a tongue-in-cheek measure against African-Americans. If Parker and others could have hindered the reenslavement of free blacks, the future of slavery would have become more tenuous. Consequently, any roadblocks to slavery meant fewer African-Americans in Illinois.

By 1832 Parker had not changed, but Illinois had. He retained virtually the same vote tallies as he had received in 1822. Yet he proved unable to broaden his political base. Furthermore, he lost the support of some of his closest and most influential associates. As in the missions controversy in Tennessee, Parker had opposed the aggrandizement of power and influence by a few. He defeated the Cullom-Kitchell faction in 1822 but lacked the political acumen and strength to emerge victorious in 1826 and 1832. The era of independent candidates had given way to a more tightly organized system. Instead of independent republican candidates, voters gathered around Whig or Democratic banners. The beginnings of Whig and Democratic partisan formation had begun to take root in 1824. Local nominating organizations with links to national candidates evidenced this trend. But the convention issue distracted voters and delayed the appearance of firm partisan parameters. As the decade waned, however, partisan lines hardened. Familiar political names such as Edward Coles, Ninian Edwards, and Daniel Cook faded from view. A new group of leaders, more adaptable to the party system, took the place of the old guard. [142] Moreover, popular distaste for the party system weakened. Instead, voters came to see that the public benefited from partisan competition. The party system helped to define issues and rally the electorate.[143] Yet bogged in personal and religious controversies, Daniel Parker lacked the political appeal to be successful in the changing political environment.

Chapter 3

The Illinois Years: Religious Controversy

A GROUP OF barefooted youths gathered on a Sunday morning outside a rural Crawford County meeting house. Garbed in typical frontier fashion, the young men wore leather breeches and tow-linen shirts. The backcountry belles crowned their rustic attire with sunbonnets. Exchanging bashful glances, the youths patiently anticipated the arrival of Daniel Parker. The preacher did not disappoint them. Upon arriving, he walked straight into the meeting house and threw his leather coat on the floor. After singing a hymn and offering a prayer, Parker readied himself to preach. For the next two hours he "poured hot shot into the world, the flesh and the devil."[1]

Such intensity not only characterized the pulpit style of Parker but also his ministerial career. From 1818 until 1833, he maintained a vigilant campaign along the Wabash against missionary societies, organized benevolence, salaried preachers, and the Christian Reformation movement of Alexander Campbell. The activities of Parker against the missions system became one of the primary causes for the eventual division among Baptists throughout the Wabash and Ohio River valleys into antimissions and promissionary congregations. In a theological fortification of antimissionism, Parker propagated the hyper-Calvinistic Two-Seed doctrine. Unfortunately for Parker, some of his closest associates rejected Two Seedism as heresy. The ensuing acrimony sparked division in the La Motte Baptist Church, the congregation in which he held membership. The rancor also diminished his influence among some Wabash Baptists.

When Parker first moved to the Wabash in 1817, he found little competition from other denominations. During its territorial status, first as part of the Indiana and later Illinois territories, southeastern Illinois manifested scant evidence of organized religion. A Roman Catholic church, founded in Vincennes during 1749, ministered mostly to French trappers and traders.[2] Around the turn of the nineteenth century, Anglo settlers, many with Protestant backgrounds, began to trickle into the Wabash Valley. Coincident with the movement of settlers into the soon-to-be-created Indiana Territory, the Second Great Awakening stirred evangelical fervor along the Ohio Valley and throughout the South. With renewed interest in evangelism, Methodists, Presbyterians, and competing Baptists saw an opportunity to plant churches in predominantly Anglo settlements northwest of the Ohio River. Methodist itinerants first held services in 1805 near Vincennes in what became southwestern Indiana. The same year a Presbyterian minister conducted a preaching tour of the southern Indiana Territory. In 1806 Presbyterians established a congregation in Vincennes. By 1815 the Methodist church had organized far-flung preaching stations in the Vincennes circuit along the Wabash River that separated Indiana and Illinois.[3] On May 20, 1809, thirteen Baptists became the organizational nucleus of the Maria Creek Baptist Church about ten to fifteen miles north of Vincennes.[4] The same year, the Maria Creek congregation joined with eight other churches in the lower Wabash Valley and formed the Wabash District Association.

The Maria Creek Church, albeit small in membership, provided the impetus for church planting. Within seven years the Maria Creek Church had sponsored three new congregations. In June 1811 licensed minister Thomas Kennedy, a member of Maria Creek since 1810, began holding services for Baptists at La Motte Prairie, twenty-five miles northwest of Vincennes.[5] The La Motte Baptist Church organized in 1812.[6] Besides gathering the nucleus of La Motte, Kennedy early on provided this church with pastoral leadership. At the request of the La Motte congregation, Kennedy received ordination on Saturday, August 16, 1817, at the Maria Creek Church.[7] His pastoral tenure continued well into the late 1820s. In the summer of 1816 other members of the Maria Creek congregation who resided west of the Wabash began to hold separate services. In February 1817 these Baptists, meeting near a deserted Indian village in Crawford County, Illinois, became charter members of the Little Village Baptist Church. A third extension of Maria Creek emerged in the spring of 1818 when several members of Maria Creek Church moved north of Vincennes to present-day Vigo County, Indiana, where they formed the Prairie Creek Baptist Church.[8]

Besides aiding in the organization of neighboring churches, the Maria Creek congregation had as its pastor the widely respected Isaac McCoy. McCoy would become one of the chief rivals of Daniel Parker. During the second decade of the nineteenth century, McCoy ranked as perhaps the preeminent Baptist minister in the Wabash Valley. Born in Fayette County, Pennsylvania, on June 13, 1784, McCoy had moved with his family to Kentucky around 1790. In 1801 he joined the Buck Creek Baptist Church, a Regular Baptist congregation in Shelby County, Kentucky. Although the more Arminian-inclined Separate Baptists had entered Kentucky, Buck Creek held Calvinistic tenets.[9] In 1803 McCoy married Christiana Polke, the sister of William Polke. William would later become an eminent Baptist layman and future Knox County, Indiana, judge. Peck also would join McCoy in resisting Parker. The next year Isaac and Christiana settled in Indiana, across the Ohio River from Louisville. In 1809 the young couple moved to Knox County, Indiana, where they joined the Maria Creek Church in June 1810. The following October, the Maria Creek congregation ordained Isaac and called him pastor.

Like most frontier Baptist preachers Isaac endured hardships. His pastoral labors went without financial recompense. He earned his living as a farmer and blacksmith. When hostilities erupted between settlers and Indians around 1811, Isaac led expeditions against the Indians. At times the threat of Indian attack forced the cancelation of congregational worship. Determined to maintain worship services, Isaac shouldered his musket and rode from blockhouse to blockhouse.[10]

After peace came to the Wabash, Isaac McCoy became concerned about his limited ministry. He evidently had been moved by the degradation and sufferings of the Indians around Vincennes.[11] In March 1817 McCoy corresponded with the Baptist Board of

Foreign Missions and requested an appointment as missionary. The following October, McCoy received a one-year assignment. The Board instructed McCoy to labor among a number of counties in Indiana and Illinois but failed to specify any ministry to Indians. McCoy completed his appointment but felt disappointed at the lack of missionary emphasis among Indians. At his request, the Board granted McCoy a second appointment. With authorization in hand, McCoy began plans to launch an Indian mission. In July 1818 McCoy circulated a request for support among Baptist churches in Illinois, Indiana, and Kentucky. By September 1818 McCoy had prepared to move to an Indian mission on Raccoon Creek, several miles north of Terre Haute, Indiana. The night before he and his family departed, Joseph Chambers and other members of Maria Creek gathered at the house of McCoy for prayer. After a three-day journey, McCoy and his family arrived at the mission station on October 27, 1818.[12]

The extent to which Daniel Parker and Isaac McCoy previously had been involved is unknown. No doubt Parker had heard about McCoy during visits to the Wabash in 1816. McCoy had been acquainted with members of the John Parker family. On Sunday, July 14, 1816, McCoy had officiated at the wedding of James W. Parker and Martha Duty at La Motte Prairie.[13] The arrival of Daniel Parker in Illinois during December 1817 coincided with the focus of McCoy on Indian missions. With McCoy exiting the Maria Creek Church in 1818, the newly arrived Parker soon began to rival McCoy for preeminence among Wabash Baptists.

In July or August 1818 McCoy visited the Little Village Church in an effort to garner support for missionary endeavors.[14] Parker did not belong to Little Village but lived in the area and conducted services for its members.[15] After hearing the former Maria Creek pastor, some of the Little Village congregation pondered the scriptural basis for conducing mission work through such an avenue. Because of the lack of consensus, the church agreed to allow its eighteen members to use their own discretion concerning contributions.[16] Parker received word of the contention which had befallen Little Village as a result of the visit to McCoy. Desiring to be "an instrument in bringing about peace," Parker visited Little Village "in her distress."[17]

Parker determined to mount a stubborn resistance to what he

perceived as the unscriptural solicitation of McCoy. A few weeks later, probably in September or October 1818, McCoy visited the La Motte Church and a heated but unrecorded discussion ensued between Parker and McCoy concerning the missions system. For McCoy this discussion took place against the backdrop of personal tragedy—the recent loss of his eldest child. While away from his family in the interest of missions, his fourteen-year-old daughter had died on August 31, 1818.[18]

Supported by Parker and not content to let the missions controversy go unchallenged, the Little Village Church voted September 26, 1818, to seek the counsel of the churches which belonged to the Wabash District Association.[19] Accordingly, messengers of Little Village queried the Wabash District Association at the October 1818 session. The messengers from Little Village questioned the scriptural authority of the Baptist Board. After hearing the matter, the association chose to postpone a decision until the 1819 meeting. This delay allowed individual congregations to address the matter before the next associational conference. During the interim, it also gave opportunity for antimissions sentiment to develop.

William Polke, the moderator of the Maria Creek Church, sensed potential difficulties. In January 1819 Polke notified the Baptist Board of the antimissions faction in the Wabash District Association.[20] By the following month, Parker and Kennedy had announced plans to organize a new church, no doubt antimissionary, in Vincennes.[21] Because of the influence of the Maria Creek Church on the east bank of the Wabash, an antimissions congregation near Vincennes would fortify antimissionism in southwestern Indiana and increase the number of pro-Parker congregations. Along the Wabash, ministers and churches began to take sides.

Meanwhile, the ministry of Parker at Little Village had taken on a degree of formal countenance. Because of its small membership, the congregation had no designated pastor. Parker filled the pulpit but did not possess official pastoral authority. Seven weeks prior to the associational meeting, Little Village had elected Parker as its official congregational moderator.[22] The selection of Parker meant that the church entrusted Parker with the supervision of congregational conferences. This action implied congregational confidence in the ministerial and leadership abilities of Parker.

The 1819 association convened Saturday, October 2 at the Black River meeting house in Posey County, Indiana. McCoy, the primary advocate of missions in the association, did not attend. His ministry at the Indian mission prevented participation. The attending messengers took up the tabled question regarding missions. It ruled that the "principle and practice" of the Baptist Board of Foreign Missions did not conform to "gospel order."[23] As a consequence, the association voted to drop correspondence with the Board.

Parker soon noted that the cessation of correspondence had disturbed some Baptists in Illinois, Indiana, Kentucky, and Tennessee. Some associations had taken a dim view of the antimissions stance of the Wabash District Association. According to Parker, the Red River Association in southwest Kentucky had suspended communication with the Wabash District Association.[24] In light of this development, Parker felt compelled to publish an explanation concerning his stand against the Baptist Board.

By June 1820 he had written a pamphlet of about forty pages which criticized the Baptist Board and its missionary enterprises. He entitled his essay *A Public Address*. Parker delivered his work to a Vincennes printer and ordered, no doubt at considerable personal expense, 2,000 copies. He evidently intended to have his publication ready for circulation in advance of associational meetings which customarily met in the late summer or early fall. In his treatise Parker raised four primary criticisms of the Baptist Board. First, Parker argued that the Bible did not example missionary societies. Second, mission organizations violated and usurped the authority of local churches. Third, missionary societies enrolled contributing non-Christians as members.[25] Finally, because the missions system remained an unscriptural precedent, it seemed to reek of the overarching "abomination spoken of by Daniel," the apocalyptic "anti-christian spirit."[26] At the convention of the Red River Association on Saturday, August 12, 1820, Parker personally distributed his pamphlet. The following Friday, Sugg Fort, one of the foremost proponents of missionary endeavors in the Red River Association, notified McCoy of the visit by Parker.[27]

The activities of Parker against the missions system did not go unnoticed in the Wabash District Association. William Polke had corresponded with Isaac McCoy in June and July 1820 concerning the essay. After reading *A Public Address*, McCoy wrote "Three Letters to Daniel Parker." In this carefully crafted rebuttal of August 1820, McCoy vented his spleen against Parker. McCoy accused Parker of being ignorant, vain, and tyrannical.[28] Although it is not certain that Parker received the epistolary, the refutation by McCoy crystalized the promissions argument against the antimissionism of Parker.

For the next four years the missions controversy pitted the La Motte and Maria Creek churches against each other. The issue involved personal reputations as well as congregational accord. In his essay, Parker had accused mission proponents of fraud.[29] William Polke and Joseph Chambers, moderator and clerk respectively of Maria Creek, regarded the essay *A Public Address* as a personal affront. The prominent Polke felt especially wounded before the eyes of his Baptist brethren as well as the general public. Polke early on had supported interdenominational cooperation on behalf of benevolent organizations. On August 12, 1817, he had become a charter member of the Vincennes Bible Society.[30] Polke and Chambers had personally contributed to the McCoy mission. Moreover, Polke had spearheaded collections for the mission in the Wabash District Association.[31]

Yet for Polke the remarks in *A Public Address* involved more than religion. Polke stood to lose political and social eminence if the insinuations of fraud went unchallenged. Polke, the son of an Indian trader, had moved with his parents from Maryland to Kentucky around 1780. In 1782 seven-year-old William Polke had been held captive for two months by Indians. By 1808 he had settled fifteen miles north of Vincennes. The following year he became the first justice of the peace in the Vincennes Township. In 1811 Polke had served under General William Henry Harrison during the Battle of Tippecanoe. Polke soon achieved prominence in Knox County. By 1817 he ranked among the leading stockholders in the Bank of Vincennes. As a political aspirant, he occupied a salient position. Along with fellow Maria Creek members William Bruce and Charles Polke, William Polke quickly rose to leadership in county politics. In 1816 William Polke and brother Charles represented Knox County at the Indiana constitutional convention. The next year, Bruce hosted a meeting at his home for the purpose of nominating county officials. In 1818 and 1821 William Polke took advantage of personal prominence and made bids for the Indiana Senate.[32]

From November 18, 1820, to July 13, 1821, letters and committees from La Motte and Maria Creek traversed the Wabash. Influenced by William Polke and Chambers, the Maria Creek congregation requested that La Motte censure Parker. In turn, the La Motte congregation charged Maria Creek with violating the will of the Wabash District Association by harboring supporters of the Baptist Board. Furthermore, Parker contended that Maria Creek had violated New Testament directives in calling for his censure. Parker protested that Polke and Chambers had bypassed the initial reconciliatory procedure as stated in Matthew 18:15-17. These verses required offended individuals to attempt private reconciliation before seeking congregational intervention.

Representatives from both churches met July 13, 1821. The following day, after extensive debate, the opposing parties arrived at a temporary compromise. They agreed that advocates of missionary endeavors in Maria Creek should continue support of missionaries, in this case Isaac McCoy, until the "Baptist union" handed down a final decision. Presumably, the expected edict would justify or condemn missionary societies once and for all. Both parties expressed satisfaction. In spite of an apparent breakthrough, the issue remained unresolved. An important detail had not been addressed—neither side had defined the parameters of the Baptist union.

Parker felt that the union consisted strictly of the churches in the Wabash District Association. Able to influence the association, he felt confident of victory. By 1821 Parker had a strong following in at least four out of the twelve churches which composed the association. Parker either consistently preached to these congregations or had close relatives in their memberships. With McCoy away from the scene and Maria Creek pastorless, Parker reasoned that the union would reach a final decision in the forthcoming October 1821 associational conference.[33] On the other hand, the Maria Creek leaders opined that Baptist churches throughout the United States constituted the union. The Triennial Convention remained the closest body comparable to a national Baptist assembly, and the next meeting of the Convention would not convene until 1823. Because the Convention did not mandate local church participation, a ruling on the missions issue by a national quorum of Baptist churches might never transpire.

The October 1821 annual session of the Wabash District Association appeared promising for antimissionary forces. If the association assumed the role of the Baptist union, the Parker faction would emerge victorious. The association convened at the La Motte Church, the stronghold of antimissions sentiment. Yet the conference did not reach a decision concerning the missions controversy. Instead, attention turned to a constitutional technicality.

At the opening session the La Motte Church introduced charges against the Maria Creek congregation for supporting the Baptist Board. If carried, this action meant the possible expulsion of Maria Creek from the association. In a nineteen to eighteen vote, the association upheld the charges by La Motte against Maria Creek. The association agreed to pronounce disciplinary action at the 1822 association. The debate then turned to the interim voting status of Maria Creek. Parker suggested that the association allow Maria Creek voting privileges until the final resolution of the issue. The Maria Creek messengers countered with a shrewd observation. They commented that the associational vote already had ruled Maria Creek at fault. Hence, Maria Creek had lost voting privileges.

The association "appeared thunderstruck."[34] The ineligibility of Maria Creek threatened to hamstring future disciplinary proceedings. For the association to move against Maria Creek the next October, the constitution required the official vote of all churches present. If Maria Creek did not vote, the constitutionality of any future action remained in doubt. On the other hand, a concessionary withdrawal of charges by La Motte would have defeated the aims of the Parker faction.

The association immediately sought to remove any possible constitutional obstacle. The messengers appointed a committee of seven to recommend necessary constitutional amendments. After meeting at the home of Parker on Saturday evening, October 6, the committee recommended the alteration of "the manner of dealing with churches."[35] Such a change would mean that the association as a single entity, rather than individual churches, would investigate and charge transgressing congregations. In order to install any constitutional changes before the next annual meeting, the committee proposed a special conference of the Wabash District Association for the purpose of amending its constitution. The messengers scheduled the conference for June 8-10, 1822. Not everyone felt relieved. Maria Creek members viewed the proposed amendment as a ploy by Parker partisans to finally oust Maria Creek.[36]

By June 1822 both sides had girded themselves for a potentially rancorous assembly. The two groups realized that the future of missionary work along the Wabash hinged on this meeting. In an effort to rally support, Parker had conducted a two-to-three week tour of southern Indiana in May 1822.[37] The promissions faction likewise went on the offensive. Desiring moral support, William Polke solicited the presence of influential spokesmen. Sugg Fort from Kentucky announced plans to attend.[38] In a letter to McCoy, Polke urged the missionary to appear for the purpose of "amazements."[39] Polke and other promissions advocates from Indiana had also "earnestly" requested the presence of Rev. John Mason Peck.[40] Peck remained perhaps the most formidable champion of Baptist missions in the West. As early as February 1822 Polke had received confirmation of the intended visit by Peck.[41]

Contemporaries would have been challenged to find two Baptist ministers more opposite in appearance and background than John Mason Peck and Daniel Parker. Parker possessed a diminutive build and virtually no education. Peck had descended from sturdy New England stock. He embodied a powerful frame and robust constitution. Over six feet tall, he weighed over one hundred and eighty pounds. Peck became the foremost defender of missionary societies, theological education, Bible distribution, and Sabbath schools in Illinois and Missouri.

A meeting with Luther Rice in June 1815 had solidified the interest of Peck toward missions. The following year, Peck prepared for missionary service. He studied Greek, Latin, and Hebrew and attended lectures on botany and medicine. On May 14, 1817, the Baptist Board commissioned Peck and James E. Welch as missionaries to St. Louis. After a four-month journey from Litchfield, Connecticut, Peck and his family arrived in St. Louis on December 1, 1817. The Baptist Board funded Peck for the next two-and-one-half years. But in July 1820 the Board, experiencing a decrease in contributions, discontinued support. One of the primary reasons for the cessation of funding involved the opposition of Parker and other antimissions Baptists in the West. The Board requested that

Peck transfer to Fort Wayne, Indiana, and aid the recently relocated McCoy in a second Indian mission station. Peck declined. Instead, he felt impelled to continue his mission activities near St. Louis. He resigned from the Baptist Board and in March 1822 secured an appointment with the Massachusetts Missionary Society.[42]

The called meeting of the Wabash District Association assembled at Patoka Church, near present-day Princeton, Indiana, on Saturday, June 8. McCoy did not attend. After a five-day journey, the influential Peck arrived by horseback.[43] At the three-day conference, the association failed to amend its constitution. Delegates postponed a decision until the forthcoming October session. Instead, the missions controversy dominated the agenda.

Parker and Polke vied for control. The meeting involved more than religion. Both had their political futures at stake. Parker had been stumping for election to the Illinois Senate. Polke had entered the Indiana lieutenant gubernatorial contest. Parker preached on Sunday and Peck on Monday. Three days after the meeting adjourned, Peck recounted to McCoy the resistance of Parker.

> The subject [missions] was discussed in the most ample manner for more than five hours & Parker exerted every talent in ingenuity & intrigue to carry his point but had the mortification to find an overwhelming majority with elected hearts, vocies [sic], & hands decide against him. I never before met with an adversary in missions that so boldly & determinately opposed the subject as P[arker] did. . . .
>
> Though Parker was completely foiled in every attempt he made through the whole Association, he has not surrendered his weapons, but I hope the mode he has hurried will effectually open the eyes of many of his former adherents. Indeed this appears to be the case already for they begin to see the selfish and wicked motives that influence his conduct.[44]

For the promissions faction the meeting proved propitious. Not only did Parker encounter stiff opposition, but Peck galvanized support for missionary endeavors in western Indiana. He even urged William Polke to enter the ministry. Polke declined the entreaty but the following year gathered provisions and herded donated livestock to McCoy.[45] On Monday evening, June 10, following the adjournment of the association, Peck collected a generous offering from an audience at the Gibson County, Indiana, courthouse. By the following Thursday, Peck had ridden approximately sixty miles and preached seven sermons.[46]

Four months later, the regular session of the 1822 Wabash District Association assembled under circumstances which intensified division. The meeting convened October 5 at the decidedly promissions Prairie Creek Baptist Church in Vigo County, Indiana. The core membership of Prairie Creek had belonged to Maria Creek. Only five years old and with 106 members, Prairie Creek reported the largest membership in the association. The associational officers proved sympathetic to the promissions faction. William Polke served as clerk and Elder Tyre Harris moderated the conference.[47] In terms of congregations, the two factions remained equally divided. With only one exception, the division occurred along state lines. The Parker faction consisted of six churches: La Motte, Little Village, Grand Prairie, Mill Creek, and Glady Fork, all located in or near Crawford County, Illinois. Turman's Creek, the only pro-Parker church east of the Wabash, met in Sullivan County, Indiana. These congregations had a combined membership of 146. The six promissions churches, Maria Creek, Wabash, Prairie Creek, Little Flock, Busseron, and Union, lay in Indiana. Their memberships totaled 242.

Although the promissionary churches maintained a membership majority, membership meant little in terms of associational voting power. The constitution allowed each church, regardless of membership, three messengers. With seventeen representatives, the Parker faction held a thin majority. With the exception of the Little Village Church, all of the pro-Parker churches had been careful to send the maximum number of allowable messengers.[48] Three of these messengers belonged to the Parker family.[49] The promissions congregations mustered fourteen messengers but their number fell four shy of the allocable eighteen.[50]

Parker and Polke girded themselves for battle. Parker preached the introductory sermon from John 18:36: *"And Jesus answered, My kingdom is not of this world. . . ."* In his sermon, Parker alluded to the reconstruction of the temple and walls of Jerusalem without the aid of Gentiles. He deemed the human-devised missions system analogous to the extension of popery through Roman Catholic missionary orders. Parker kept his audience spellbound. Some had never heard anything to compare with such zealous preaching.

After the conclusion of the meeting, some of the attendees remarked: "Is not that a great man?"[51] But not everyone responded favorably. The sermon by Parker infuriated Polke. According to Corbly Martin, an associate of McCoy, Polke blushed with anger when talking about the actions of Parker.[52] After discussing the proposed constitutional amendment, the messengers postponed a decision until the 1823 meeting. Furthermore, the body referred the La Motte and Maria Creek dispute to the twelve member churches for their individual deliberation.[53]

The delay allowed the controversy to fester for another year. Parker did not remain content to entrust the churches with such a weighty matter. The missionary society forces had influential adherents in Palestine, the political and ecclesiastical base of Parker. George W. Lindsay, a son-in-law of William Polke, lived near Edward N. Cullom and Joseph Kitchell, two of the principal political foes of Parker. In 1821 Lindsay had donated an 175-pound hog to the McCoy mission station.[54] In December 1822 Polke wrote to McCoy concerning Crawford County Clerk of Court Edward H. Piper. A key political figure, Piper had requested that Polke invite McCoy to visit Palestine. Piper maintained support for missions and became a member of the Maria Creek Church.[55] Polke wrote that Piper "would arrange appointments for you [McCoy] in that Neighbourhood and he thought he could make some collections for the Fort Wayne mission."[56]

Once again Parker endeavored to gain support by arguing his case in print. In late 1822 and January 1823 Parker published two letters critical of theological schools in the *Illinois Intelligencer.* Parker viewed theological institutions as human infringements on divine authority. He contended that the proponents of theological education trusted educational institutions rather than the call of God for the preparation of ministers.[57] A few months later Parker again wielded the pen. On May 16, 1823, the La Motte Church approved an apologetic written by Parker to the churches of the Wabash District Association. Parker published his essay under the title of the *Plain Truth.*

The *Plain Truth* traced the controversy between Maria Creek and La Motte and warned against the dangers of an alliance between church and state. Moreover, Parker charged the Baptist Board with a gross encroachment of power. From 1818 to 1821 Dr. William

Staughton, corresponding secretary of the Baptist Board of Foreign Missions, had conducted an embryonic institution for the training of young ministers in Philadelphia. In 1821 a plot of land in Washington, D.C., had been donated to the Triennial Convention for the purpose of enlarging the school and moving it to the national capital. Known as Columbian College, the school opened its doors in the District of Columbia but soon encountered financial difficulties. Faced with possible collapse, the trustees of the college appealed to Congress for aid. They requested a congressional loan of $50,000, repayable at six percent interest over ten years. Congress debated the request but failed to act. Without having approved the loan request, Congress ceased discussion of the matter on March 3, 1824.[58] Although the measure met defeat, Parker protested that the missions system had established itself in the heart of government. According to Parker, this move confirmed the insidious bent of the missions system toward "money and power."[59] By making "long strides in our government," the Baptist Board had sought to influence national government.[60] While the Columbian College affair brewed, McCoy had endeavored to arrange for the services of support personnel at the Fort Wayne mission. In January 1822 he had visited Philadelphia in an attempt to gain funding for a blacksmith and teacher.[61] Parker viewed the hiring of such auxiliary personnel as a blending of "the matters of religion and the things of the world."[62]

Having circulated his case through the press, Parker attended the 1823 Wabash District Association. Messengers from twelve churches convened at the Maria Creek Church on Friday, October 3. The following Monday, ten member churches rendered their decisions concerning the La Motte and Maria Creek controversy. Each church cast one vote. Five supported the charges against Maria Creek while four found no fault. One church remained neutral. La Motte and Maria Creek, the aggrieved parties, did not cast ballots. The decision reopened the issue of a constitutional majority. The previous Friday, delegates had amended the constitution, and according to their decision, only those churches which voted determined the tabulation of a true majority. Had the constitutional changes been in place, this provision would have given leverage to the Parker faction. But formal approbation of the amendment required the sanction of individual congregations. If approved, it would not become effectual until the following year. The proposed amendment therefore did little to resolve the matter.

But the potential roadblock did not deter Parker. Because one congregation had remained neutral, Parker argued that the five-church decision against Maria Creek composed a true majority. The Maria Creek messengers, William Bruce, Joseph Chambers, and William Polke, stubbornly resisted. Parker thoroughly exasperated Polke. After heated debate, Polke finally yielded. He preferred exclusion to a seat in the association. Yet Bruce and Chambers refused to accede. Affairs had finally reached an impasse. Weary of five years of contention and unable to break the logjam, the thirty messengers appointed a committee to divide the association. Five messengers composed the committee. Daniel Parker, John Parker, and Asa Norton represented the antimissionary faction. Robert Elliot and Thomas Pound spoke for the promissions side.[63]

The 1823 meeting marked a watershed in the Illinois ministry of Parker. The following year, Baptist congregations throughout the Ohio Valley began to take sides on the missions issue. In September 1824 eight dissenting promissionary churches of the Wabash District Association formed the Union Association. These eight included five churches in the Maria Creek faction plus three recent enrollees. At least seven of the Union Association congregations were in Indiana.[64] As a result of the rupture, the Wabash District Association immediately declined from fifteen churches and 489 members to seven congregations with 203 total communicants.[65] Furthermore, only three ordained ministers—Parker, Richard Newport, and Thomas Kennedy—remained in the Wabash District Association. In October 1824 representatives from the Union Association visited the Wabash District Association and petitioned for formal recognition and fellowship. Because the Union Association harbored Maria Creek, the Wabash District Association virtually anathematized the Union Association. The messengers of the Wabash District Association bluntly refused to recognize the visiting delegation.[66]

By 1825 contention between the Wabash District and Union associations had overflown the Wabash Valley. Associations in Indiana, Kentucky, and other parts of Illinois carefully weighed the exclusionary action of the Wabash District Association. Promissions and antimissionary factions used the issue to vie for the allegiance of Baptist associations. Peck and Parker, champions of their separate causes, visited the 1825 White River Association in southwestern Indiana. On August 14 both antagonists shared the pulpit.[67] The following day, the White River Association deliberated the exclusion of the Union Association by the Wabash District Association. At the request of the White River messengers, Peck presented the view of the promissions faction. Parker countered. The Peck-Parker debate occupied several hours. The efforts by Parker proved futile. The White River messengers sided with Peck by a large majority. The White River Association recognized and opened official correspondence with the Union Association. In what must have been a personal affront to Parker, the White River Association severed relations with the Wabash District Association. The decision utterly dismayed Parker. Later, he attributed the opposition of the White River delegates to nothing other than satanic-induced spiritual blindness.[68]

By 1825 Parker had lost favor among many Baptists in the Ohio Valley. In 1824 and 1825 Baptist associations in Indiana, Illinois, and Kentucky dropped correspondence with the Wabash District Association. The Illinois Association broke formal ties in August 1824. The Highland Association in Kentucky had suspended correspondence because of "distance."[69] In October 1825 the Wabash District Association severed relations with the Baptist associations which had opened correspondence with the Union Association. Among the excluded were the White River, Blue River, and Salem associations in Indiana. As a crowning insult, in 1826 the Little Pigeon Association refused Parker the honor of addressing the assembly.[70]

By the late fall of 1825, forty-four-year-old Daniel Parker had experienced a tumultuous year. The 1824 convention referendum in Illinois had triumphed the cause of antislavery. Yet, for Parker, losses outweighed gains. His mother had died in July 1824. Moreover, political and denominational challenges imperilled his standing. Throughout 1825 his character had been sullied by accusations of counterfeiting and moral deficiency.

The litigation against Wickliff Kitchell had showcased allegations against Parker. Although these charges had not been proven, they encouraged gossip. Moreover, the proceedings involved close associates of Parker as well and members of his household. Stephen

Cryst, the husband of Parker's eldest daughter, had been summoned to testify on behalf of Kitchell.⁷¹ The case wounded the reputation of Parker as well as his pocketbook. Because of insufficient evidence, Parker had been forced to withdraw his first libel suit against Kitchell. In December 1825 the court had ordered Parker to pay the court fees of Kitchell. Shortly after the conclusion of the trial, Parker sold three tracts of land consisting of 137 acres. In one of these transactions, Robert Polke, the youngest brother of William Polke, purchased eighty acres.⁷² Parker suffered the ignominy of paying for the court costs of Kitchell with land sold to the brother of his chief rival among Wabash Baptists.

In the eyes of Parker the case also breached the loyalty of some of his Baptist brethren. Elijah Dodson, a member of Parker's Grand Prairie pastorate, had leveled charges of counterfeiting against Parker. Lewis Little, William Ryan, and Thomas Kennedy, all members of La Motte Baptist Church, had testified on behalf of Kitchell in November 1825.⁷³ In 1824 the membership of La Motte Church had investigated the accusation of counterfeiting but had found Parker innocent. Yet the official minute book of the church evidently recorded the charges and circumstances that surrounded them. The attorney for Kitchell had requested that these records become evidence for the defense. Whereupon, pastor Kennedy and Ryan, official clerk of La Motte, presented the church records and testified in court. These developments certainly did not enhance the ministry or reputation of Parker. In light of the legal embarrassment of Parker in 1825 and the shriveling of the Wabash District Association, Parker needed to bolster support.

Around January 1826 Parker published *Views on the Two Seeds*. This essay coincided with preparations by Parker for another law suit against Kitchell and the forthcoming August 1826 senatorial election. Facing these challenges, Parker needed to validate his righteousness and good character. Moreover, the promissionary element had made gains. The Union Association had succeeded in drawing away some of the former churches of the Wabash District Association. As a final affront, Peck, the champion of missions, had taken a collection for Sabbath schools in the state capital on November 13, 1825. Seven weeks later, on Sunday, January 1, 1826, Peck preached two sermons in the statehouse.⁷⁴ Faced with the gaining momentum of promissionary forces and encountering personal humiliation from his Baptist brethren in Indiana, Parker therefore felt impelled to respond. In *Views on the Two Seeds* Parker lashed out against missionary societies and Arminianism, the perceived enemies of predestinarian Baptists. He hinged his hermeneutic on Genesis 3:15: *"And I will put enmity between thee and the woman, and between thy seed and her seed."* The two cardinal tenets of Two Seedism concerned the origin of the elect and the pre-Creation union of Christ with the Church. Armed with Two Seedism, Parker attempted to bolster election. He maintained that "God never created a set of beings, neither directly nor indirectly, that he suffered to be taken from him, and made the subject of his eternal wrath and indignation. . . ."[75]

Parker did not claim total responsibility for the doctrine. It seems likely that Two Seedism emerged from an amalgam of Parker's personal theological reflections, doctrinal challenges concerning the deity of Christ, and the thoughts of Richard M. Newport. Parker confessed that he had first heard elements of the Two-Seed theology around 1812 from an "old brother" in Tennessee.[76] Questions regarding the deity of Christ had circulated in Tennessee during the second decade of the nineteenth century. Tennessee Baptist ministers had voiced alarm over the introduction of unorthodox Trinitarian views. In the last quarter of the eighteenth century, New England Congregationalists and Episcopalians had felt the inroads of Unitarianism. This doctrine emphasized reason, divine benevolence, the unity of the godhead, and the humanity of Jesus. According to Unitarianism, Jesus had been bestowed with divine goodness but had not preexisted as a member of the Trinity. By 1803 Unitarianism had appeared in Kentucky.[77] In an effort to halt the advance of Unitarianism, the Cumberland Association in Tennessee had issued a treatise. Published in 1816, this work attempted to harmonize the humanity of Christ, as part of the seed of Adam and Eve but adorned with the divine nature.[78] Elder Newport, a close associate of Parker in the Wabash District Association, claimed credit for launching the tenet which dealt with the eternal union of Christ and the Church. Newport noted that this second linchpin of Two Seedism had not been original with Parker but had been his "particular theme."[79]

Full-blown Two Seedism emerged as a convoluted attempt to refute Arminian free will. Parker traced the elect to the creation of

Adam. Accordingly, God had implanted the divine seed of Christ in Adam. As the progenitor of mankind, Adam had transmitted the divine seed to the elect. In a departure from traditional Christology, Parker held that the incarnate Christ also had received this implant at birth. As recipients of the shared seed, Parker reasoned that only the elect composed the Church, the body of Christ. Moreover, Christ reigned as head of the Church. Parker contended that the pre-Creation existence of Christ implied that the elect, those who composed the organ which Christ headed, also had existed in eternity. Hence, Christ had been eternally united with his Church.[80]

Not only did the doctrine of the Two Seeds defend limited atonement, it also justified opposition to missionary societies. According to Parker, only the Baptist Church could claim authority as the true apostolic Church. If the elect composed the Church, the Baptist Church therefore consisted of those who had been implanted with the divine seed. All other societies and churches had been crafted by man. These organizations perverted truth and imitated the genuine Church. He trumpeted that "all other sects but the Baptists are the daughters of the old mother Rome, or antichristian churches or sects, ..."[81] As such, other sects, denominations, or societies remained separate from the true Church. Hence, the formulation and support of religious institutions and churches outside the Baptist church manifested a gross error.[82] Missionary societies had accordingly "set themselves up in separate bodies, claiming the name, word, and authority which Christ gave to his church, ..."[83] They remained ecclesiastical frauds and the product of satanic guile.

In spite of his vehemence, Parker never completely resolved the presence of the elect in non-Baptist churches. Even Parker acknowledged that there "may be saints who are not Baptists."[84] Yet Parker distinguished the non-Baptist elect as "not entitled to the name christian; because they fail to follow Christ in faith and practice."[85] Unfortunately, his logic backed Parker into an epistemological corner. For it some of the elect had become members of non-Baptist churches, this invalidated the concept of the pre-Creation union of Christ and the true Church.

Instead of shoring up Parker's discredited reputation, the *Views on the Two Seeds* sparked further division among his associates and friends. Although Thomas Kennedy and Daniel Parker had shared leadership roles in the La Motte congregation, Kennedy still served as the official pastor.[86] As shepherd, Kennedy felt bound to protect his flock from heresy. Kennedy feared that the Two-Seed doctrine embraced a coeternal and cocreative Satan. If the elect had origins in the divine seed, the nonelect remained the offspring of Satan. If Satan could spawn descendants, then the Adversary rivaled the creative power of God. Furthermore, Kennedy questioned the orthodoxy regarding the eternal union between Christ and the Church. Kennedy contended that the union between Christ and individual members of the Church only took place at the conversion of a believer.[87]

After several conversations with Kennedy, Parker sought to clarify the doctrine. Parker added "A Supplement or Explanation of My Views on the Two Seeds" to his *Two Seeds* pamphlet. In this addition, Parker denied the existence of a cocreative Satan. Rather, he maintained that "the power of creation belonged to God alone. . . ."[88] In order to evade an ontological obstacle, Parker focused on the transgression of Eve. Parker maintained that the weakness of Eve had caused her to become tainted with the sins of pride and unbelief. Parker fortified his interpretation with an elaborate allegorical framework of biblical characters and events. The descendants of Eve, the nonelect, merely had inherited the propensity to sin. This weakness therefore did not mark them as the spawn of a cocreative cosmic being.[89]

The attempt of Parker to dispel questions of heterodoxy only stirred more discord. His apologetic contained numerous inconsistencies. For example, Parker attempted to quell the critics of limited atonement by structuring a logical alternative to an arbitrary God. Once again, his theological house of cards teetered. Instead of fortifying Two Seedism, the argument of Parker diminished its importance in conversion.

> Now remember my dear reader, that if you die in your sin and unbelief, that just as shure [sic] as there is a God, that shure [sic] you may be of sinking into an awful hell, and your eternal condemnation will not be because that you were of the serpent's seed, or non-elect, but because of your sin against God in his divine law, and unbelief in Christ, ...[90]

In their initial acquaintance, Daniel Parker and Thomas

Kennedy had developed a close relationship. By 1826 they had been ministerial associates for eight years. Parker credited Kennedy for being "my greatest friend and nearest companion in the work of the ministry. . . ."[91] Although eclipsed by the pulpit abilities of Parker, Kennedy supported Parker's ministry. Apparently their friendship had endured even though in an official capacity Kennedy had conflicted with the interests of the Parkers. In 1821 Kennedy, as agent for Crawford County, had entered a $500 suit against Benjamin Parker.[92] Benjamin, a brother of Daniel, served as a deacon in the La Motte Church. The legal proceedings endured from 1819 through 1824. Although these years coincided with the most rancorous developments in the missions controversy, Kennedy stood firmly with Parker. An even closer tie occurred in early 1825. On February 10, 1825, Joseph, the eldest son of Thomas Kennedy, married Abigail, a daughter of Daniel Parker.

But later that year, the good will between Daniel Parker and Thomas Kennedy exibited signs of deterioration. In November 1825 the circuit court subpoenaed Kennedy to present the minutes of the La Motte Church in the *Daniel Parker v. Wickliff Kitchell* case. On two days Kennedy appeared in court as a witness for Wickliff Kitchell.[93] After the publication of *Views on the Two Seeds*, Parker and Kennedy had several discussions concerning the innovative theology. On February 11, 1826, in the presence of the La Motte congregation, their first public clash over the Two-Seed doctrine occurred.[94] In March 1826 other members of the La Motte Church voiced opposition to Parker and Two Seedism. Elder Brice Fields, a newly arrived Baptist preacher from Kentucky, had privately counseled Kennedy and members of the La Motte Church.[95] On March 4, at the Glady Fork Baptist Church in Lawrence County, Illinois, Joel Cheek, a member of the La Motte Church, attempted to preach for the first time. Cheek had known Parker for several years. After serving as tax collector for La Motte Township in 1816, Cheek had stood as a candidate for Crawford County commissioner in 1822.[96] Newport, a Parker backer, pastored Glady Fork. The novice preacher did not mince words in the presence of Newport. Cheek took his text from Jonah 1:6. From the pulpit he echoed the accusations of Wickliff Kitchell. Cheek proclaimed that as Jonah had taken a journey, so had Daniel Parker gone "in search of wealth and popularity."[97]

On Saturday, September 9, 1826, the La Motte Church met for

monthly conference. At least thirty-nine adults crowded into the small log meeting house.[98] The followers of Parker anticipated a dispute and sought to shore up support. Parker had lost a majority in La Motte but maintained strong backing in the Little Village Church. Two weeks prior to the conference, the Little Village congregation had replaced Kennedy with Parker as moderator.[99] At least twelve visitors from Little Village, the majority of the membership, gathered at La Motte to hold up the hands of Parker. Because the conference officially concerned the affairs of the La Motte Church, only the membership of La Motte had voting privileges. As the conference progressed, Kennedy accused Parker of preaching heterodoxy. If upheld, the charges likely would have resulted in the exclusion of Parker from La Motte and censure of his ministerial credentials. When the moderator called for a vote, the members of La Motte sustained the charge by a vote of ten to zero. Yet sixteen of the church members remaining did not vote.

Parker immediately raised an objection. He contended that the decision had been one-sided. Accordingly, the moderator had elicited the opinion of opponents, but the voices of adherents had not been heard. Parker argued that the vocal absence of fifteen to sixteen votes equated a victory for him. With this argument, he insisted that the congregation supported his Two-Seeds preachments by a silent majority of five. Feeling exonerated, Parker demanded possession of the building and official records of the church. The Kennedy faction denied the request. Whereupon, Parker, supporting visitors, and approximately fifteen members of La Motte promptly left the building and the eleven pro-Kennedy members and withdrew to the "shady forest."[100] Ignoring the official vote of the church, the Parker element proclaimed themselves to be the true La Motte Church. They elected a moderator and clerk and formulated charges against the Kennedy faction. On September 26, four days before the opening session of the 1826 Wabash District Association, the Parker faction excommunicated the rival La Motte congregation.

Delegates from both groups appeared the following Saturday at the Wabash District Association. Each delegation claimed authority as the representatives of the legitimate La Motte Baptist Church. Elected to the moderatorship the previous year, Parker presided until the election of a new moderator. But as associational clerk, Kennedy also held parliamentary power. Kennedy had been elected clerk in 1825. Like Parker, he too held the right of office until replaced by the associational messengers at the 1826 meeting. The selection of new officers traditionally took place following the annual sermon and the enrollment of messengers. Parker immediately saw a possible difficulty with the routine procedure. Before a new clerk entered office, Parker feared that Kennedy would seat only the messengers from the pro-Kennedy La Motte Church. Elder Newport delivered the introductory sermon. Immediately after Newport ceased, Parker countered the anticipated move by Kennedy. Without the formal consent of the messengers, Parker announced that "in his opinion the former Clerk was disqualified."[101] As presiding moderator, Parker thereupon appointed Asa Norton, a Parker ally and member of the Little Village Church, as temporary clerk. Following these maneuvers, the association recognized the representatives from the Parker congregation. The officially seated associational body then refused to acknowledge the Kennedy faction. After reviewing the La Motte schism, the association voted to refer the controversy to member churches for their individual deliberation. Accordingly, the messengers voted to receive the voice of the churches at the 1827 conference.

Parker and his rival congregation gained associational approbation, but Parker lost a valuable comrade. In 1827 the association recognized the Parker faction as the true La Motte congregation. This action accomplished little in terms of justifying Parker. By that time, the Kennedy group had joined the Union Association. Kennedy and Parker never reconciled. Kennedy shifted support to the missions cause. By 1827 Parker had lost an important lawsuit and a senatorial election. In denominational affairs he had been instrumental in the division of the Wabash District Association and the La Motte Church. Finally, he had alienated Kennedy. As a county probate judge and respected minister, Kennedy had remained the most influential stay of Parker. This unfortunately did not prevent Kennedy from becoming a rival in the eyes of Parker. Even the connubial link between his daughter and the son of Kennedy did not preclude Parker from breaking with his longtime ally.

With his circle of supporters growing smaller, Parker again turned to the press in his struggle against perceived encroachments on the Baptist Church. In October 1829 he began publication of the *Church Advocate*. Published monthly, this organ attacked missions and the Reformation movement of Alexander Campbell. Like Parker, Campbell condemned camp meetings and mission boards as unscriptural addenda. But he exceeded the penchant of Parker for purity by also shelving associations and articles of faith. By the mid-1820s Campbell had used his paper, *The Christian Baptist,* to siphon off Baptists in the Ohio Valley into a new denomination. In the 1830s the followers of Campbell came to be known as the Disciples of Christ. Through the pages of the *Church Advocate,* Parker condemned Campbell's espousal of baptismal regeneration and attacks on Two Seedism. Parker also targeted John Mason Peck and the missions system. In 1830 Peck countered the *Church Advocate* with a promissions paper, *The Western Baptist.* In retaliation, Parker spared no ink in his denunciation of Peck. Finally, Parker used the *Church Advocate* to mount a rearguard defense of Two Seedism.

The *Church Advocate* continued publication for two years with a wide circulation. Most of its readers resided in Illinois and Indiana, but some subscribers lived as far away as New York, Virginia, and Louisiana. In spite of a wide audience, the publication encountered insurmountable obstacles. The endeavor taxed the time and personal finances of Parker. Each issue contained twenty-four pages. In addition to lengthy articles by Parker, the *Advocate* contained numerous letters from readers. Parker no doubt devoted many tedium-filled hours to penning manuscripts and organizing articles. Furthermore, the fifty-mile round trip from Palestine to the printer in Vincennes likely occupied two days per month. These trips took Parker away from his farm and livelihood. Other difficulties beyond the control of Parker interfered with production. Poor paper stock yielded unsatisfactory copies. Almost from the beginning, financial woes hampered publication. Parker made intermittent pleas for payment of postage and overdue subscriptions. After the first year, Parker considered the termination of publication. But he continued another year with the hope that a printing press might be moved to Palestine. Such a convenience either failed to occur or could not offset other printing costs. Finally, Parker ceased publication near the end of 1831.[102]

Although the Wabash District Association had experienced schism, Parker diligently worked to expand its influence. He remained busy in the organization of new churches and associations and the strengthening of antimissions sentiment in existing associations. For example, in 1829 he attended three associations in Indiana within a five-week period.[103] The efforts of Parker bore fruit. Between 1826 and 1830 the churches of the Wabash District Association increased in number from seven to seventeen. In congregational membership the association climbed from 205 to 483.[104]

The last ecclesiastical issue in which Parker participated while in Illinois concerned the organization of an Illinois Baptist convention. By 1830 Baptist conventions had been formed in South Carolina, Georgia, New York, Connecticut, Virginia, Maine, Vermont, Alabama, New Hampshire, Pennsylvania, New Jersey, and North Carolina.[105] These state organizations united individual Baptist associations with local Baptist charities and missionary societies. The primary focus of conventions concerned the presentation of a unified Baptist front. In 1831 Parker warned against the motives of the Edwardsville (Illinois) Baptist Association and its plan to form a "Baptist Union" in Illinois.[106] Parker feared that this initiative remained an insidious ploy by his old nemesis Peck. Parker anticipated that the proposed convention threatened to overthrow of "the predestinarian doctrine" and "the rights and true order of the gospel church."[107]

In the face of this challenge, Parker countered with his own plan of union. He had initially proposed this goal in 1824 after disagreement had arisen over the definition of a Baptist union.[108] The design of Parker would have established an informal worldwide Baptist network.

> The plan is. For some three, four, or five associations, . . . to meet together yearly by their messengers. One or two messengers with their letter from each association, will be sufficient to correspond with the whole number of associations thus united. . . . These corresponding meetings to have no power, nor do any thing except preach; but to receive the information from the several churches . . . and transmit the same back. . . . In this way, a few corresponding letters by way of those corresponding meetings, will cultivate an acquaintance with all of the same faith throughout America, or even Europe; and the council of the whole Union may be obtained, on any particular subject in a short time.[109]

Through his proposal, Parker confirmed the need for wider communication among Baptists. The blueprint for a closer union tacitly implied that the advances of promissionary forces necessitated expanded organizational opposition by the antimissions party. In the closing sentences of the last issue of the *Church Advocate,* Parker announced a special meeting. He urged that messengers from associations composed of predestinarian Baptists assemble at Mount Zion meeting house near Palestine on Thursday, October 11, 1832. Three days following the annual adjournment of the Wabash District Association, these representatives then would establish plans for federated associational meetings.

Talk of the meeting circulated as late as July 1832.[110] Yet the assembly may not have materialized. If representatives did gather, associations apparently did not manifest sufficient interest to implement the option. Surviving associational minutes omit any reference to such a conference. Thus, attempts to form a Baptist "union" seem to have disintegrated. Furthermore, by the autumn of 1833 Parker and his family had departed for Texas. If the organization had been successful, Parker probably would not have abandoned it so soon. If organized, the implementation of the plan would have encountered impossible obstacles. By the 1830s churches in Indiana and Illinois, which previously had remained sympathetic to Parker, had begun to raise serious reservations concerning the Two-Seed doctrine. Instead of unity, the presence of Parker among Illinois Baptists probably would have engendered continued strife.

The 1820s marked both the peak and the decline of Daniel Parker. During this decade Parker also entered midlife. With the years slipping away, he became absorbed in efforts to gain acclaim in the realms of politics and religion. An analysis of Parker and his efforts to thwart the missions system in Illinois offers several possible personal motivations.

It has been suggested that racial antagonism for Indians may have turned Parker against the ministry of Isaac McCoy.[111] Parker had cause for such views. Around 1812 his brother, John, had been killed by Delaware Indians near Cape Girardeau, Missouri.[112] In 1818 Indian conflicts in the Wabash Valley during the War of 1812 remained fresh on the minds of Illinois frontiersmen. Moreover, in March 1819 William Kilbuck, a Delaware Indian, had stabbed Crawford County resident Thomas McCall to death. The incident took place in the locality of the Little Village congregation. Kilbuck blamed his actions on a liberal consumption of alcohol. While Kilbuck remained incarcerated, McCoy had ministered to him and two other Indians charged as accomplices. In several visits, McCoy brought the three Indians bread and cloth for calico shirts.

Whether Parker knew of the ministry of McCoy to the imprisoned Indians remains unanswered. Certainly Parker knew about the murder and trial. Newspapers in Indiana and Tennessee had reported the crime.[113] Also, Parker personally knew several members of the impanelled jury. On July 10, 1819, the court sentenced Kilbuck to a speedy trip to the gallows four days later. Fortunately for Kilbuck, he broke out of the Vincennes jail and escaped the hangman. Because of insufficient evidence, the court allowed the other two Indians to go free.[114]

Yet the writings of Parker do not reveal noted animosity toward Indians. Rather, his opposition to benevolence for Indians centered around sponsorship. Parker viewed the missionary activities of the Baptist Board and the Maria Creek Church as an encroachment upon the evangelistic authority of local congregations. He also considered the employment by mission authorities of three auxiliary workers, a cobbler, blacksmith, and farmer, to be a mixture of the secular and sacred. According to Parker, the Baptist Board had exceeded its authority by requesting these personnel. Moreover, the United States government had erred in permitting McCoy to open a mission on a government reservation. Parker regarded this development as an unholy alliance between church and state.[115]

Rather than racial animosity, Parker's resistance to missionary societies may have been prompted partially by class and sectional resentment, the frontier economy, and personal rivalries. The antimissions movement definitely involved class and sectional issues.[116] In 1823 Corbly Martin had traveled to Kentucky for the purpose of collecting donations for the McCoy mission. While there, Martin became alarmed at the unsavory remarks hurled at him and the missions system.

> It may be satisfactory to you to hear that I am often received kindly by the Kentucky brethren. But I have been persecuted by many worldlings *(not to say brethren)* as though I were an evil genus immediately from the nether regions. I have been frequently called Tory, Yankee, Begger *[sic]*, impostor, D[amne]d fool, and by many such ignominious epithets. Some have said to

my face and that in a vociferated dogmatical tone. These cattle, every one of them, are going to the Pickaway [Ohio] plains to be intended for the eastern market.[117]

Apparently, the treatment of Martin did not improve. He continued to encounter verbal abuse and intimidation for the remainder of his visit. Some Kentuckians regarded contributory solicitor Luther Rice as "a most notorious scoundrel."[118] Others threatened to "set their Negroes" and "some their dogs" after Martin.[119]

Parker held little sympathy for eastern wealth, polish, and snobbery. Letters and articles in the *Church Advocate* by contributing writers scorned eastern pomp. In the last edition Joshua Lawrence of North Carolina excoriated salaried preacher dandies.

> . . . these proud hirelings, these men that can't preach without pay, these stiff, glove-handed, school polished gentlemen, that are now strutting through our country seeking a place of profit almost in every town and village, to live in idleness on the honest labors of the farmer and mechanic. I have heard many of them preach, and so far as my knowledge extends about preaching, I would not give an old jack knife for a cowpen [sic] full of such grammer [sic], Latin, Greek, gospel spoiling fellows, to preach to me.[120]

Ironically, the high-handed opposition of Parker, not easterners, drove many of his would-be western allies into the fold of the Baptist Board. Parker contended for the autonomy of local churches. At the same time, he felt compelled to withstand nonbiblical missionary societies. In 1819 the Wabash District Association had formally ceased correspondence with the Baptist Board. On the other hand, the Maria Creek congregation and several other of its like-minded neighboring Baptist churches continued support. As autonomous congregations, these churches could have remained correspondents and not have breached the official sanction of the association. But Parker did not tolerate this prerogative. His efforts to censure Maria Creek violated this premise. Neither did he suffer other associations to follow their wills.

Parker justified the imposed strictures as necessary for the defense of the faith. Possessed of an all-consuming desire to protect and advance orthodoxy, Parker deemed his crusade as a faithful service to God. Peck examined the opposition of Parker in a different light. The New England missionary criticized the increasingly proscriptive power of associations over some local congregations. Peck warned that associations, intended as advisory councils, in some cases assumed the character and force of ecclesiastical law.[121] Moreover, Peck observed that there had been many antimissionary Baptists in the West who felt unduly restricted by other antimissions brethren. As a result, some from the disgruntled antimissions faction refused to ally with Parker. Their lack of support for Parker and his associates did not necessarily indicate approbation of the missions system. Instead, their anti-Parker stance reflected concern over a Parkerian hegemony.[122]

Another possible explanation for the antipathy of Parker concerns the frontier economy. In his writings a prevailing theme concerns the evil accumulation of wealth and power. The economic plight of the West affected attitudes toward religion as well as government and banking. Other Wabash Valley settlers besides Parker had linked the accumulation of wealth with the missions system. On June 24, 1820, about the same date that *A Public Address* appeared, the *Indiana Centinel* printed an anonymous letter. The article commented on the economic distress of the frontier and posited some reasons for the money shortage. Among the many "wise people" who "have sagaciously given their opinions respecting the cause," some attributed the specie scarcity "to the Mission Societies, who send out all the silver they can get, to convert the Chinese to Christianity. . . ."[123] In *A Public Address* Parker also warned of economic consequence. He forecast a dominance of wealth and power by the missions system. In his view, the Baptist Board intended on planting missionary families in order to establish schools and raise "stocks, flocks and herds, of various kinds, all belonging to the mission system."[124]

Parker had striven to achieve prosperity. His move to the Wabash Valley had generated more wealth than he had previously enjoyed. By 1817 he had entered 516 acres in Crawford and Clark counties. In 1824 he sold a mill in Clark County for $1,000.[125] Yet the unstable Illinois economy did little to boost his hopes for prosperity. Also, the struggle against missions had diminished the personal wealth of Parker. Part of his proceeds from land sales had gone to pay for the printing of *A Public Address, Plain Truth,* and

The Author's Defence. These works had been published within a four-year span. Because printing came high in the backcountry, publication had taxed his financial resources. In 1827 Parker confessed that he had incurred great financial loss in defense of the truth. He estimated that at least three-fourths of his outlay remained beyond recoupment.[126]

Parker jealously guarded the Wabash Valley against trespass by eastern missionary societies. Yet almost all of the supporters of the missions' cause along the Wabash had come from the same stock and mould as Parker. With the exception of Peck, very few Baptist preachers along the Wabash had eastern roots. Unlike the scurrilous depiction by Joshua Lawrence, most western Baptists lacked wealth and refinement. Similar to Parker, they had immigrated from frontier Kentucky or Tennessee. Parker therefore had little reason to fear direct eastern domination through the efforts of kindred backwoodsmen.

As in Tennessee, the missions controversy became entwined with personal rivalries. After Isaac McCoy exited the Maria Creek Church, Parker vied with William Polke, John Mason Peck, and Thomas Kennedy. All but Peck had been members of the Maria Creek Church. From its organization, William Polke and his kindred had provided congregational leadership. Eight of the thirteen charter members belonged to the Polke family.[127] Several of the later additions to the Maria Creek Church married into the Polke clan. The Polke family remained a closely knit network of church and social acquaintances. Against this setting the politically prominent William exerted influence in western Indiana.

Compared to the Polkes, Daniel Parker had arrived late on the Wabash. Yet members of the Parker family held positions of leadership in two pro-Parker churches of the Wabash District Association. Four of the Parker brothers, one brother-in-law of Daniel, and father John served as messengers to the association in the early to mid-1820s.[128] These years coincided with the peak political years of Parker and his efforts to oust the Maria Creek Church. Through family members, associates, and allied preacher brethren, Parker vied for power with William Polke.

The characteristic distaste which Parker exhibited toward prominent rivals resurfaced in his efforts to discredit Polke. In 1824 the La Motte Church had presented a query to the Wabash District

Association. La Motte asked the association to rule on the moral qualifications of slaveholders who belonged to churches of the association.[129] Parker no doubt aimed this dart at promissions slaveholders William Polke and Martin Rose. Polke held membership in Maria Creek while Rose belonged to the Wabash Baptist Church.[130] Rose had owned slaves since 1807.[131] In 1820 his slave inventory numbered seven. In 1820 William Polke owned a female slave no older than fourteen years of age. This bond harbored potential scandal. By June 1823 the girl had given birth to an illegitimate mulatto baby. Although Polke may not have fathered the infant, he made sure to absolve himself from any responsibility. Polke proffered that the pregnancy had been the result of Priscilla having been hired out to a household in Vincennes.[132]

Slavery had been frowned upon for some time by the majority of Baptists along the Wabash. In 1815 the Maria Creek Church had issued a lukewarm condemnation of slavery. Although the church considered slavery unjust, it failed to chastise slaveholders. The church members felt that the statutes of Indiana had effectively curbed slavery.[133]

Parker waited until October 1824 to raise the issue of slavery. This delay indicated that the condemnation of slavery was not the primary motivation of Parker. Two months before the associational meeting, Illinoisans had defeated the legalization of slavery. To have been politically effectual, proscriptions against slavery should have been voiced at the 1823 association. The real reason for illuminating the issue in 1824 seems to have revolved around the efforts of Parker to turn Baptists against Polke, Rose, and the Union Association. Although some associations in Illinois and Indiana had not firmly chosen a side in the missions controversy, human bondage remained a creditable example of moral turpitude. If the exclusionary move against slaveholders had succeeded, the Wabash District Association could have fortified its grievance with the Union Association on grounds other than the missions question. The slavery issue would have facilitated efforts of the Wabash District Association to rally opposition against the Union Association. In 1825 the Wabash District Association ruled that the failure of slave-owning Baptists to seek gradual emancipation of slaves provided cause for the cessation of correspondence.

Yet efforts to mount an attack based on slavery proved futile.

By October 1825, Parker as the chief spokesman of the Wabash District Association, had lost support among several Baptist associations in Indiana. The White River Association in Indiana had sided with Peck. These associations did not censure the Union Association for harboring slaveholders in member churches. Instead of fomenting opposition to the Union Association among several Indiana associations, the actions of Parker had resulted in the rupture of fellowship between the Wabash District Association and many Indiana Baptists. The issue of slavery therefore failed to stir opposition against Polke, Rose, and the Union Association.

In terms of personal rivalries, Parker held more contempt for Peck than any other opponent. In return, Peck dismissed the hostility of Parker as intense jealousy.[134] But Peck underestimated the deep-seated animosity of Parker. Believing that Peck felt threatened financially by antimissionism, Parker saw Peck as a sinister foe. Moreover, he deemed the opposition of Peck as nothing short of personal hatred. He felt that Peck remained bent on his destruction. Parker shielded himself against this perceived onslaught through the pages of the *Church Advocate*. In order to accomplish this, Parker asserted that Peck had received "a flood of wisdom and wealth from the old [eastern] states."[135]

Unlike the contention of Parker with Polke and Peck, the missions system did not initiate the break with Kennedy. Kennedy held the pastoral leadership of the La Motte congregation when Parker had arrived in Crawford County. Instead, Parker attributed the opposition of Kennedy to ministerial jealousy. Parker insisted that Kennedy felt threatened and sought his overthrow.[136] Moreover, Parker charged that the objections of Kennedy to the Two-Seed doctrine remained a smoke screen to obscure the personal animosity of Kennedy toward Parker. Waving the frayed banner of persecution, Parker asserted that Kennedy "possessed a prepossessed prejudice or hurt" against him.[137] But Parker became convinced that the supposed malevolence of Kennedy exceeded mere jealousy. He fully believed that Kennedy intended to kill him.[138] Unfortunately, Parker failed to distinguish contrary theological stances from personal antipathies. Kennedy objected to the Two-Seed hermeneutic on doctrinal grounds. But Parker viewed the opposition of Kennedy as tantamount to the enmity of Satan.[139] Realizing that he had been ousted by the majority of La Motte Church, Parker felt undermined by the Kennedy faction. In turn, Parker retaliated. In 1826 he brought about the swift excommunication of Kennedy and the Kennedy partisans from the Wabash District Association.

The Illinois ministry of Parker resulted in irony and inconsistency. He continued to guard Baptist ranks against missionary and benevolent societies. On one plane his antimissionism may evidence a local response to social and religious challenges posed by increased centralization. In the second and third decades of the nineteenth century, industrialization and commercialization made Americans aware of national political and economic forces.[140] In this vein Parker simply strove to maintain the authority of local pastors and the autonomy of congregations against a centralized denominational body. Yet the anxiety over an increasingly complex political and economic environment places Parker in a broader context.[141]

The egalitarianism of Jeffersonian republicanism had influenced American Protestantism. The Revolution had helped to crack the class distinctions which previously had barred the common man from leadership in political and ecclesiastical leadership. In post-Revolutionary America the backwoods preacher, insisting on the right to interpret scripture for himself, often upstaged the professional theologian. Although Thomas Jefferson felt that the educated elite should fill the higher offices, he encouraged voting and political discussion among yeomen. As Jeffersonianism had popularized a certain degree of egalitarianism in government, it also promoted a commitment to pure republicanism by the yeomen electorate.[142]

Accompanying the idealization of pure republicanism, some churches and religious movements manifested a desire to restore primitive Christianity.[143] The purpose of Revolutionary America had aimed at the political redemption. The penchant for spiritual purity had paralleled this goal. In the 1820s Alexander Campbell discarded creeds, organizational patterns, and practices not explicitly exampled by the New Testament. Endeavoring to recapture the communal nature of ancient Christianity, some groups experimented with radical social and familial innovations. The Shakers, a communal denomination, banned sexual activity even among married partners. In western New York, an area which had experienced intense revivalistic fervor in the 1820s, John Humphrey Noyes established the Oneida Community. Members of this community practiced communal marriage. In an effort to promote perfect unity and understanding among the membership, Noyes required, except for procreative purposes, male continence. At the same time he paradoxically discouraged possessive husband-wife marriages. Each adult became a possible spouse to every other adult in the community. In the late 1820s Joseph Smith, another resident of western New York, laid the foundation for the Mormon Church. Smith propagated that Christ had accomplished a pre-New Testament revelation among Native Americans. Smith later sought to induce a sense of primitive society by introducing polygamy to his followers.

Parker did not condone such radical social experiments, even though there is no doubt he would have repudiated the Shakers, Oneida Community, and Mormons as heretical departures from true Christianity. Yet the ministry of Parker manifested characteristics of primitivism. Parker jealously resisted the corrupting influences of modern society. Institutions for missions, benevolence, and education did not example the pristine nature of ancient Christianity. Like Campbell he endeavored to rid Baptist ranks of the dross of ecclesiastical innovations. Unlike Campbell and others he did not attempt completely to restore primitive Christianity. Rather, Parker sought more readily to maintain the ancient Church as he perceived it to exist among Baptist churches.

In his role as a religious leader Parker evidenced strains of Jeffersonian and Jacksonian thought. Echoing Jeffersonianism, Parker struggled to protect and preserve purity. In this case, freedom from taint involved what he considered to be the true Church as well as republican government. Like Parker many early nineteenth-century Americans viewed politics as a struggle between the forces of good and evil.[144] In this conflict the virtuous champions of republicanism battled tyranny, monarchy, and corruption. Yet Jacksonian characteristics also surfaced. The Jacksonian emphasis on the common man boosted religious innovation. Self-made theologians such as Smith and Noyes felt freer to expound their own interpretations of scripture. In keeping with this trend, Parker likewise made theological pronouncements. His Two-Seed doctrine attempted to explain the agelong warfare between the followers of the Lamb and the powers of darkness. Through its complexities, Parker not only bolstered election but also returned the true Church to Edenic bliss.

In religion as well as politics Parker manifested faction and rancor. Perhaps more than any other characteristics, these aspects indicate Jacksonian tendencies. As Jackson fought against the national bank and eastern money lords, so did Parker struggle against the national mission board and eastern-rooted missionary John Mason Peck. Parker felt that ecclesiastical innovations tainted religious and political organs. Linking religion to politics, Parker warned that an alliance between the missions system and the government threatened "our national liberties."[145] Furthermore, Jackson sought to destroy his political enemies. In a similar vein, Parker lashed out against Kennedy, McCoy, and Polke, fellow Wabash Baptists who disagreed with him. In the process, he experienced personal and financial loss, but hope remained for a new opportunity. The prairies and forests of Texas beckoned.

Chapter 4

The Texas Years: Pioneer and Political Leader

ON TUESDAY EVENING, November 12, 1833, a caravan of approximately forty to fifty Texas-bound families had encamped for the night. One or two wagons, drawn by horses or oxen, conveyed the possessions of each family. Shortly after midnight, a celestial phenomenon occurred. A shower of meteorites illuminated the heavens. Across North America onlookers gazed at thousands of shooting stars. In Coles County, Illinois, a minister thought the "falling drops of fire" portended the end of the world.[1]

Among the immigrants at least fifty adults and children belonged to the Daniel Parker party.[2] The group included fifty-two-year-old Daniel Parker, his wife, ten children, other relatives, and church acquaintances from Illinois and Indiana. Parker did not record his sentiments concerning the heavenly spectacle. Perhaps his thoughts returned to a phenomenon experienced twenty-two years earlier. The New Madrid earthquake of 1811 had coincided with his rise to prominence in Tennessee. Whether Parker augured the astral display as a curse, favorable omen, or benign coincidence, he did not turn his team and retreat to Illinois. Rather, Parker never visited Illinois again. He spent the remaining eleven years of his life on the Texas frontier.

The move to Texas marked a new beginning for Parker. Within two years of the nocturnal episode, Texas would erupt in revolution. In the turbulent days of the Texas Revolution, his prior legislative experience enabled Parker to provide valuable leadership to the Anglo government. After independence had been won, he amassed more land than he could have hoped to acquire in Illinois or Tennessee. He also experienced a successful ministry. The expanse of the Texas frontier partially insulated him from interference by advocates of missionary societies and opponents of Two Seedism. In Texas he enjoyed more liberty to indoctrinate congregations according to his convictions.

Yet the journey to Texas did not remove Parker from sorrow, disappointment, and frustration. Indian raids claimed the lives of friends, two brothers, and his father. Two adult children, Rachel and Dickerson, suffered premature deaths as a result of hardships encountered in Texas. The phantoms of economic and political controversy reappeared under the Lone Star. Texans encountered ambitious politicians and dishonest land speculators—while not all land dealers proved fraudulent. In the face of these threats Parker remained vigilant to incursions by the wealthy and privileged in government and finance. Faced with a different political and economic scenario, conditions in Texas resulted in an amelioration of the antislavery struggle which had underscored the political career of Parker in Illinois. The acquisition of large tracts of land and the hopes for economic development muzzled his protest against slavery. Parker not only failed to vocalize opposition to slavery but abetted the construction of constitutional supports for bondage.

In the second decade of the nineteenth century, reports from Spanish Texas had filtered back to the United States through travelers and newspapers in Natchitoches and New Orleans, Louisiana. As early as 1820 a Vincennes, Indiana, newspaper relayed reports from Texas. The article extolled Texas for its virtually limitless supply of silver, fertile soil, and sparse population of Indians.[3] In January 1821 Missouri resident Moses Austin negotiated a contract with Spanish officials for a land grant in Texas. Austin received permission to settle 300 Catholic families in Texas along the Brazos River. Unfortunately, death claimed Moses before he realized his dream. Coincident with the death of Moses in 1821, Mexico achieved independence from Spain. In 1823 Stephen F. Austin, a son of Moses, renegotiated the colonization contract of his father with the infant Mexican government. Yet political instability and fear of foreign encroachments made the Mexican government hesitant to honor the contract with Stephen F. Austin. For three years the future of the Austin colony remained in doubt.

Fortunately for Austin, Mexican lawmakers permitted the door to American immigration to slowly open. The National Colonization Law of August 18, 1824, allowed the states of Mexico discretionary control over immigration within their borders. The State Colonization Law of March 24, 1825, expanded immigration opportunities for Americans. Under its administration Stephen F. Austin, Green C. DeWitt, and several others became official *empresarios*. Each *empresario* received 23,027 acres for every 100 families which had been settled. These contracts stipulated that the apportioned grants should be occupied and under cultivation within twelve years.[4] The distribution of thousands of acres therefore depended on the rapid introduction of immigrants. *Empresarios* hastened to recruit potential colonists. Letters by Austin, appearing in the *Illinois Intelligencer*, lauded the climate, crops, and healthy conditions in Texas and encouraged American immigration.[5]

James W. Parker first peaked the interest of his brothers in Texas. James, who resided in Clark County, Illinois, about thirty miles west of Paris, began to focus attention on Texas in the mid-1820s.[6] In 1824 the Solomon Duty family, acquaintances of James and relatives of his wife, had left the Wabash and moved to Texas with the first colonists recruited by Austin.[7] By the mid-1820s James had fallen on hard times. The winter of 1825 had been unusually severe.[8] The weather and climate brought ill health to his family. His wife remained sickly and three of his children died.[9] Economic reversals also had overtaken him. In May 1826 an Illinois bank attempted to repossess some belongings of James' for nonpayment of a loan. Evidently, James had either absconded with or lost possession of the property, for a county official doubted the retrievability of the goods.[10] In the late summer or early fall of 1830, James and his brother, Joseph A., moved to Conway County, Arkansas Territory.[11] By this time James seriously had considered a move to Texas. In July 1830 he had applied as a potential colonist.[12] In the winter of 1830–1831 James left his family in Arkansas for an excursion to Texas. He arrived in February 1831 and spent the next eight months along the Angelina, Colorado, and Brazos rivers. James hunted and surveyed the game, terrain, and Indians. By December 1831 he had returned to Conway County and sold his Arkansas land to Joseph.[13]

Meanwhile, the Mexican government had resumed restrictions on immigration from the United States. Alarmed at increasing numbers of Anglo-Americans and the lack of assimilation, the Mexican government passed the Law of April 6, 1830. This act rescinded unfulfilled *empresario* contracts but honored the agreements with Stephen F. Austin and DeWitt. These *empresarios* already had introduced 100 families. Two years later, the provincial congress of Coahuila and Texas passed Decree 190. This ordinance confirmed the repeal of the Colonization Law of March 24, 1825. It encouraged the settlement of northern Mexico and Texas solely by Mexicans. Passed on April 28, 1832, Decree 190 confirmed previously fulfilled contracts but specified an eighteen-month limit on the completion of new agreements.[14]

Decree 190 aimed at firmly blocking Anglo-American immigration. Ironically, the wording of the legislation actually encouraged the immigration of non-Catholic citizens of the United States. A cursory reading of Decree 190 implied less stringent religious conformity. Previous statutes had mandated the Roman Catholic faith as the only legally tolerated religion in Mexico and Texas.[15] While Decree 190 did not excuse immigrants from the required allegiance to Roman Catholicism, it did not specifically exclude Protestants. Providing a possible loophole for Protestants, it only mentioned that foreigners had to furnish adequate proof "of their christianity and good moral character . . ."[16]

In June 1832 James Parker corresponded with Austin. James apparently realized that the door to immigration might soon slam shut. The eighteen-month period of grace required quick action on the part of Texas-minded immigrants. With Decree 190 becoming effectual at the end of 1833, it became urgent that prospective settlers relay their intentions to legally immigrate to Austin or DeWitt. James presented himself to Austin as the representative of fifteen to twenty families that depended on James for his "judgment of the country."[17] James disclosed that several among the prospective immigrants professed the Baptist faith and wanted the guarantee of religious freedom. Having described his candidates, James requested permission to settle twenty-five to thirty families in "Eighteen Months or less time" along the Brazos River.[18]

According to Parker family tradition, James interested Daniel in exploring Texas.[19] Not all accounts from Texas had been positive.

An Illinois newspaper had published negative reports. In 1822 a correspondent had cautioned citizens of the United States against immigrating to Texas. The reporter warned that the Texas population "is composed of the most abandoned of the human race."[20] Three years later a writer from Little Rock, Arkansas Territory, reported flooding, crop failures, and famine in Texas.[21] In spite of disparaging accounts, Daniel Parker had heard sufficient testimony to prick his interest. After another defeat for the Illinois Assembly in 1832, Daniel seriously considered new opportunities in Texas. He nevertheless felt it advisable to make an exploratory tour of Texas.

Daniel Parker first journeyed to Texas late in 1832. Before departing, he continued to fulfill ministerial obligations in Illinois and southwestern Indiana. Parker attended an associational meeting in Harrison County, Indiana, on September 8, 1832. Two weeks later he visited the annual assembly of the Salem Association in Gibson County, Indiana. On September 23 Parker graced the pulpit of the Providence Meeting House in Gibson County.[22] Presumably, Daniel departed for Texas some time following the scheduled functions of the Wabash District Association in early October 1832.[23] If so, he left Palestine, Illinois, in the late fall or early winter of 1832.[24] Daniel likely rode to Arkansas Territory, where brother Joseph joined him. In company with Joseph, Daniel reached the Austin Colony by March 1833. **Figure 2** illustrates the main roads on which immigrants such as Parker traversed in 1833. On March 16 Daniel took the oath of allegiance to the Mexican government. After completing this obligation, he announced plans to return with his family by January 1, 1834.[25]

Preparations for immigration and travel occupied most of the next nine months. Daniel lost little time in getting back to Illinois. On May 25, 1833, he preached at the Little Village Church. The following month he finalized plans to organize prospective Baptist immigrants into a church. On July 26, 1833, these immigrants formed the Pilgrim Predestinarian Regular Baptist Church.[26] The Texas-bound caravan departed sometime after August 11. By October 20 the Parker party had reached Claiborne Parish in northwestern Louisiana. Traversing the Red River at Natchitoches, they crossed the Sabine River into Texas at Gaines Ferry. In January 1834 they stopped in the Austin Colony east of present Navasota, Texas. There, the family of Daniel Parker set up temporary shelter beside the San Antonio Road.[27]

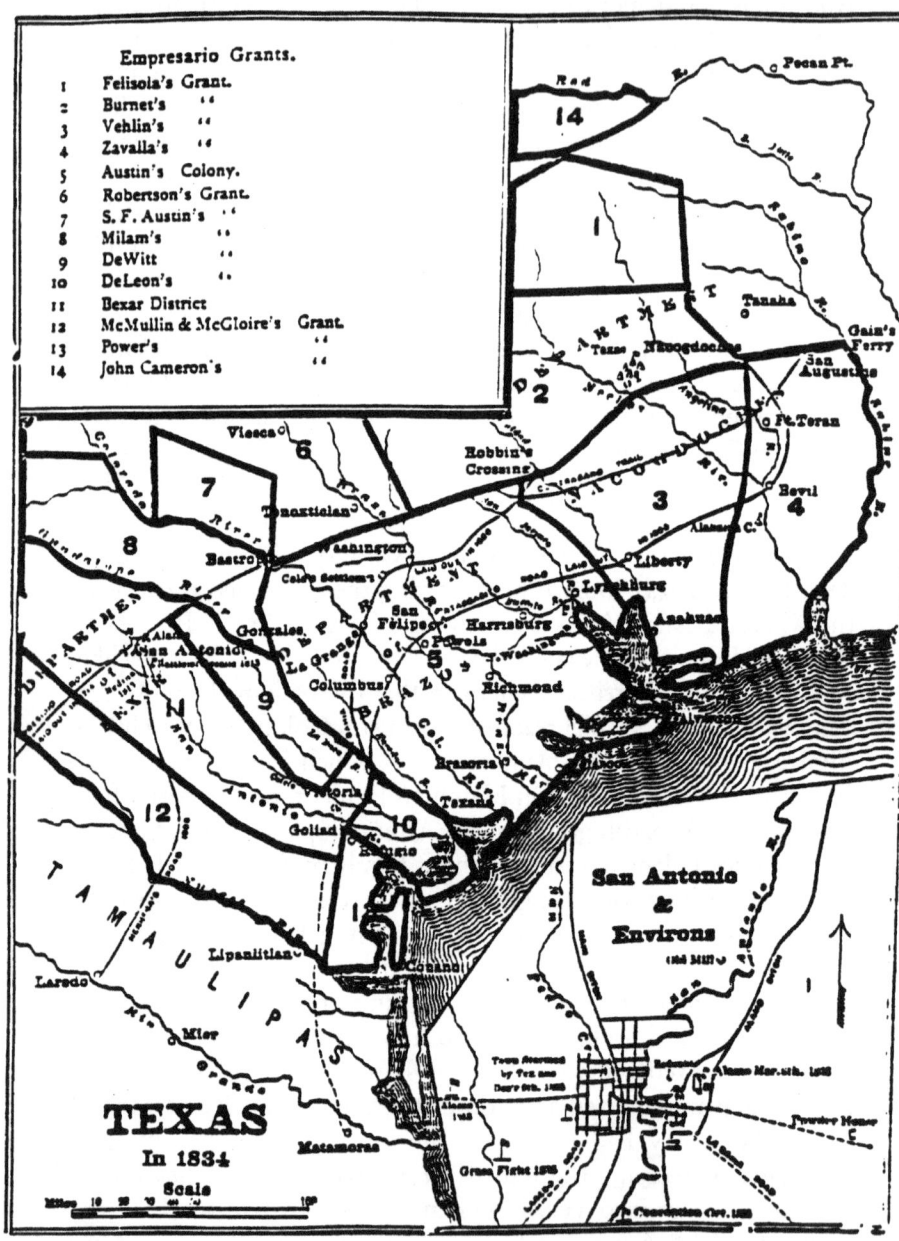

Figure 2. Texas in 1834. From Texas in 1837 *by Andrew Forest Muir. Originally in* A Pictorial History of Texas *(1879) by Homer S. Thrall.*

If all of the Parker clan anticipated settling in the same locality, their plans did not materialize. The family soon began to disperse. In the late fall of 1833 James and Silas Mercer Parker, another brother of Daniel, already had settled on the headwaters on the Navasota River near present Groesbeck. Along with Elisha Anglin, James and Silas set about building a stockaded log blockhouse known as Fort Parker.[28] Joseph Parker claimed land near the modern city of Houston. In 1834 Isaac arrived in Nacogdoches where he clerked in a store. In late 1834 Daniel relocated approximately 100 miles to the northeast in the Burnet Grant. He settled on San Pedro Creek, about sixty-five miles northeast of Fort Parker.[29] In August 1834 Benjamin Parker, another brother of Daniel, lost an election bid for the Ninth Illinois General Assembly. Between the fall of 1834 and 1835 Benjamin and John, the seventy-seven-year-old Parker patriarch, joined James and Silas at Fort Parker.[30]

Daniel Parker experienced difficulty in 1834. After an arduous journey from Illinois, Texas posed numerous hardships. In June the Texas frontier claimed the life of Patsy Brown, his three-year-old granddaughter. The move from the Austin Colony to the Burnet Grant occurred during the winter. The felling of trees for shelter and the clearing of land challenged endurance. These exigencies of frontier life disrupted the social and religious activities of family and friends. Pilgrim Church did not assemble from October 1834 until July 1835.

But others besides Anglo settlers experienced anxiety. Developments in Texas also distressed the Mexican government. By the summer of 1835 Texas rumbled with impending revolution. A continued influx of Anglo-Americans signaled their growing dominance in Texas. The antiimmigration provisions of the Law of April 6, 1830, had failed to halt American immigrants. By 1834 an estimated 20,700 Americans with their slaves had found homes in Texas. In an effort to relieve tensions, the Mexican Senate rescinded the antiimmigration clause of the Law of April 6, 1830. The annulment initially raised hopes for American settlers. But events soon turned sour.

In May 1834, coincident with the repeal of immigration limitations, General Santa Anna seized power. The state-supported Roman Catholic Church, the military, and centralist politicians backed Santa Anna. The Mexican general reciprocated by abolishing the federalist Constitution of 1824 and dissolving state legislatures. Mexican liberals protested the usurpation of power, and rebellions surfaced in several Mexican states. In this time of instability, Mexican military leaders near Texas remained wary of Texan insurgents. General Martin Perfecto de Cos, commander of northeastern Mexico, requested military reinforcements from Santa Anna. The action of Cos only provoked Anglo-Texan radicals. From June to October 1835 skirmishes flared between Texans and Mexican troops at Anahuac, Gonzales, and Goliad. Encouraged by success, Texas radicals advanced on San Antonio.[31]

Some Texans worried that Santa Anna would not ignore infractions of Mexican sovereignty. Residents along the coastline of Texas felt particularly exposed to reprisals by the Mexican military. With the threat of retaliatory Mexican action, a fifteen-man "committee of safety" met at Columbia on August 15, 1835.[32] The committee called for a consultation of elected representatives from the districts of Texas, known as municipalities, to assemble the following October 15. The committee aimed at uniting Anglo-Texans on a policy toward the central government. Texans remained divided over the best course of action. The radical war party favored immediate military advances. Moderates preferred caution to armed conflict. They hoped that Texan resolve would encourage Mexican liberals to rally against the centralists. The formation of a national liberal front might therefore topple the centralists and restore the federalist regime. The third group, the loyalists, opposed war at any cost. They regarded resistance as foolhardy provocation.[33]

While municipalities selected their delegates, the crisis continued to brew. Austin wrote from San Felipe to former Tennessee governor Sam Houston in Nacogdoches. Austin warned Houston and other key citizens of Nacogdoches of the inevitability of war. On October 5 Houston dispatched Isaac Parker to Louisiana with an appeal for arms and volunteers. The appointed courier rode the approximate hundred miles without delay. Two days later the *Red River Herald,* a Natchitoches paper, published the plea. Within a month papers in Arkansas, Tennessee, and Kentucky had printed the message of Houston.[34]

By the first week in October the Nacogdoches municipality had selected Daniel Parker as one of three delegates to the Consultation. On October 3 Parker presided over a meeting of Pilgrim

Church. The church agreed that Parker faced the possibility of an extended absence from the congregation. In the place of Parker, members selected Elder Garrison Greenwood to serve as moderator.[35]

As the date for the assembly neared, fifty-five representatives from thirteen jurisdictions began to converge at San Felipe. Daniel Parker, along with Sam Houston and James W. Robinson, composed the Nacogdoches delegation. Parker arrived in time for the anticipated opening session on October 15. Unfortunately, a quorum failed to arrive. On October 17 Parker moved for a postponement of the Consultation until November 1. Delegates hoped that the delay would facilitate the arrival of a sufficient number of delegates. A quorum having finally convened, the opening session of the Consultation assembled at 9:00 A.M. on November 3.[36] For the next fifty-nine days Parker participated in governmental organization and the formulation of policy.

On November 3 the Consultation learned that Texas troops had defeated General Cos at Concepcion mission near San Antonio.[37] Aware of the necessity for immediate defense, the Consultation named Parker and Sam Houston to a five-man committee to assess American support for Texas in New Orleans.[38] Parker did not urge rash action. At the same time, the protection of his kindred weighed heavily on his mind. On November 6 a report rumored the imminent approach of the enemy.[39] The following day, Parker and four others served as an official committee to study the organization of ranger units. On November 9 Parker, as committee chairman, recommended the formation of a twenty-man ranger company and the extension of ranger patrols from the Colorado River to the Cibollo Creek. Moreover, he urged the official recognition and enlargement of a second company of rangers recently raised by Silas Parker.[40]

Meanwhile, the Consultation became more vocal in its criticism of the Mexican government. On November 7 the Consultation approved a declaration which decried the encroachments of the centralists. The delegates pointed to the violation of the Constitution of 1824 as justification for continued resistance to Mexican authorities. The declaration announced that "Texas is no longer morally or civilly bound by the compact of union."[41] Although the proclamation failed to endorse independence, its adoption moved

Texas a step closer to self-government. On November 12 delegates organized a temporary government. They elected Parker and twelve other representatives, one from each municipality, to be members of the General Council in the Provisional Government.

The Provisional Government consisted of a governor, lieutenant governor, and a thirteen-man council. The Council of the Provisional Government assembled for deliberation on November 14.[42] The ad hoc government transacted the organizational, financial, and military affairs of the embryonic republic. On November 16 Provisional Governor Henry Smith appointed Parker to the Affairs of State committee. The duties of committeeman Parker ranged from the important to the trivial. Mundane assignments included the location of rooms in San Felipe for committee meetings and the procurement of mounts for couriers. More weighty responsibilities involved the nomination of judicial and military officers. Along with other members of the Council, Parker recognized the need for an expanded military capacity. On November 18 he offered a motion for an election of militia officers and the organization of local defense units. He also urged the enlargement of the army by 5,000 volunteers. His most significant legislative action initiated developments which resulted in a declaration of independence. On December 3 he moved for the election of members to a constitutional convention which would convene March 1, 1836.[43]

In the midst of affairs of state Parker also remained aware of developments which affected his economic interests. Conflicting land claims had plagued settlers in the Nacogdoches district. Violence flared in 1826 when *empresario* Haden Edwards, with official land titles in hand, had attempted to dislodge Mexican settlers who did not possess clearly recorded land claims. After an abortive coup by Edwards, the Mexican government cancelled his grant. Three succeeding *empresarios* sold their grants to a consortium of land speculators. This firm, the New York-chartered Galveston Bay and Texas Land Company, practiced questionable business transactions. As as result, new settlers in Nacogdoches encountered difficulty in securing legitimate titles.[44]

While in San Felipe, Parker attached particular concern to resolutions which dealt with land titles. In Nacogdoches several local Anglo officials, headed by Henry Rueg, coveted the land of Mexican settlers. Some members of the Consultation looked askance at the perceived motives of Rueg. They believed that the Nacogdoches officials wanted to thwart allegiance to the Consultation. It seemed that Rueg and company intended to secure land claims for themselves and establish control over the government in Nacogdoches.[45] On December 6 Parker moved to refer several communications from Nacogdoches concerning land officials to the Committee on State Affairs and Judiciary.[46] The membership of Parker in this committee thus provided him with an opportunity to safeguard personal land holdings.

Ironically, the last official responsibility of Councilman Parker addressed slavery. This issue, so hard-fought in Illinois eleven years before, affected the economic and political development of Texas. While slavery had waned along the Wabash, it had expanded among Anglo settlements along the Sabine and Brazos. Yet the status of slavery in Spanish areas had remained limited. Under Spanish rule slavery only occupied a position of importance around Veracruz. Because few slaveholding Spaniards chose to settle in the hinterlands, the slave population of Spanish Texas remained small. Slavery also failed to find widespread approval under the Mexican flag. During the Mexican Revolution of 1810-1823, leading Mexican revolutionaries condemned slavery. After Mexico gained independence, the legality of slavery teetered in the balance. Although Mexican leaders generally opposed human bondage, they found it difficult to eradicate slavery. To encourage foreign settlement and protect property rights Mexican lawmakers compromised. The Imperial Colonization Law of 1823 prohibited the slave trade but remained unclear concerning the introduction of slaves by their immigrant masters. Hence, legal ambiguity permitted Anglo slaveholders to import their bondsmen. Between 1822 and 1825 some of Austin's colonists took advantage of the policy and transported their slaves into Texas.[47]

By 1825 human bondage had gained a tenuous footing in Texas. Anglo settlers set about to implement the institution much as it had been observed in the southern United States. In 1827 the Constitution of the State of Coahuila and Texas emancipated all children thereafter born to resident slaves and prohibited the importation of slaves. If enforced, this statute promised to eradicate slavery. Yet slaveholders bypassed the law by either ignoring these decrees or evading them under the subterfuge of indentures. In 1834

Mexican official Juan N. Almonte estimated that African-Americans, the majority of whom remained in bondage, composed 2,000 of the 21,000 non-Indian inhabitants of Texas.[48]

Stephen F. Austin had treated the subject of slavery delicately. Austin recognized that the prohibition of slavery threatened to impede southern immigration. Cotton producers argued that economic necessity demanded slavery. The challenge of labor shortages coupled with the availability of large tracts of arable land seemed to impel the preservation of involuntary servitude. Yet Austin had to placate the antislavery sentiment of the Mexican government. In an effort to clamp down on violators of the slave code, the Law of April 6, 1830, called for the strict enforcement of antislavery statutes. Austin chose to acquiesce to the Mexican government. But the law did not end the importation of slaves. Slaveholding immigrants continued to register their human property as indentured servants.[49]

Besides Mexican reluctance toward slavery, Texas slaveholders raised concern about another development. The desire of abolitionists to colonize Texas with African-Americans already had disturbed slaveholders. In August 1834 Benjamin Lundy, a Maryland abolitionist, had visited San Felipe. Many southerners, especially Texans, had not been charmed by Lundy. In 1832-1833 he had published a colonization plan for African-Americans. Lundy designed to make Texas a haven for former slaves and free blacks. The visit of Lundy stirred suspicion and ill will among the Anglo residents of San Felipe. While he lingered at San Felipe, Lundy became a close acquaintance of Mexican Colonel Juan N. Almonte. With anti-Mexican sentiment brewing, San Felipians looked askance at the friendship between a noted abolitionist and a Mexican official. Word spread that townsmen intended to tar and feather Lundy. Only the influence of Almonte saved the Maryland abolitionist from possible violence.[50]

Furthermore, slaveholders deemed that free blacks remained catalysts for insurrection. The presence of free African-Americans thus seemed a danger to the authority of masters over bondsmen. With the anticipated 1835 advance of the Mexican Army, slaveholders feared Mexican-inspired slave insurrections.[51] These apprehensions unnerved jittery masters. In response, the Beaumont Committee of Public Safety implored the Provisional Government to prohibit the immigration of free blacks.

On 23 December the Council referred the request from the citizens of Beaumont to the Committee on State Affairs and Judiciary. Don Carlos Barrett and William Menifee served with Parker on the three-man committee. The abolition of slavery troubled Barrett, Menifee, and most of the Council. The majority of the Council either owned bondsmen or supported slavery.[52] Fear of insurrections and abolitionist-sponsored colonization projects provided a backdrop for the actions of the Committee on State Affairs and Judiciary. On January 1 the committee, chaired by Barrett, recommended harsh measures concerning the future immigration of African-Americans. The report proposed the immediate cessation of free-black immigration and authorized the legal reenslavement of violators.[53] On January 5, 1836, the Council adopted the resolution.

The sentiments that Parker expressed to the committee remain unknown. His antislavery stance in Illinois likely had not gone unnoticed during the numerous closed committee meetings. In the midst of this portentous issue, the Provisional Government assigned Parker a menial task. The Council requested that Parker dispose of two horses which belonged to the government. The animals had been left at the home of William Perry. Perry resided between Washington-on-the-Brazos, some fifty miles distant, and San Felipe. The attention given to this matter indicates the desperate financial straits of the government. The assignment also may have been a ploy to get the antislavery Parker out of San Felipe. In his absence the body might avoid lengthy debate.

Yet the records of the Council do not indicate a breach between Parker and the Council concerning the harsh measures proposed toward free black immigrants. Furthermore, with a proslavery majority in the Council, Parker had no means of effectively blocking proslavery measures. Outvoted in committee and Council, perhaps Parker realized that the threats of invasion and insurrection temporarily overshadowed antislavery ideals. His political future also teetered in the balance. In Illinois few slaves had resided in the senatorial district of Parker. Most of his Prairie State constituents had opposed slavery. Conditions differed in Texas. The Nacogdoches jurisdiction of Parker accounted for 1,000 of the estimated 2,000 slaves in Texas.[54] The fear of insurrection remained quite real to the residents of the Nacogdoches jurisdiction. Serious conflict between Parker and the Council over slavery apparently did not arise, for the issue did not rupture their amiable relationship. On January 8, 1836, Parker penned a letter to Barrett, whom Parker addressed as "My dear colleague in labor and hard trials."[55] Furthermore, Parker announced intentions to return to the Council and sent greetings to the rest of his "dear friends" at San Felipe.[56]

As December closed Parker had been away from his family for almost three months. His duties in the Council had been weighty and the days long. Delegates sat in Council or committee meetings seven days a week. Debate and legislative assignments often occupied twelve hours a day. Parker had grown weary. His report regarding the two horses revealed a note of frustration. On December 27 Parker notified the Council that he had "met no opportunity of disposing of said animals, and requests to be relieved from any further consideration on that subject."[57] The following Friday, January 1, 1836, he tendered his resignation. The Council accepted the formal notification and officially thanked Parker "for his constant attention and devotion to the interests of his country as a member of this Council."[58]

Several reasons may have influenced the resignation of Parker. Discord had developed between Governor Smith and the Council. Decidedly anti-Mexican, the governor resented moderates and opposed cooperation with Mexican liberals. Barrett and Wyatt Hanks, influential moderates, had quickly entrenched themselves in several important committees. Barrett chaired the Committee on State Affairs and Judiciary. He not only favored cooperation with Mexican liberals but remained reluctant concerning independence from Mexico. Hanks, who sat on the Military Affairs Committee, and other members of the Council advocated joint military operations with Mexican liberals against Matamoros. Smith inclined toward a different course. A resolute proponent of independence, Smith nettled the councilmen.

The actions of Hanks and Barrett also rankled General Sam Houston. As commander-in-chief of the Texas army, Houston jealousy guarded his military authority. Houston felt that Barrett and Hanks had interfered with military affairs. Instead of placing all units under the command of Houston, the Council had commissioned independent ranger, militia, and cavalry units. Because the Council held the reins of these auxiliary forces, Houston deemed that his right to command stood in jeopardy. Houston also felt shackled by self-serving politicians. He particularly resented Hanks. Conscious of a potentially lucrative opportunity, Hanks desired appointment as army sutler. By serving as official supplier to the army and on the Military Affairs Committee, Hanks postured himself for a potentially handsome profit.

Dissension between Smith, Houston, and the Council peaked in December 1835. On December 6 the Military Affairs Committee urged that Houston headquarter the army at Gonzales, "or some other suitable place on the frontier."[59] Houston later charged that this action purposely aimed at removing him from the scene. Houston felt that his absence facilitated the designs of Barrett and Hanks.[60] The motion placed Parker in an awkward position. He had to choose between the Council and his friendship for Houston. Parker countered with a recommendation that Houston fix his headquarters "at such a place as he (Houston) may think best."[61] On December 11 the Council struck the recommendation of Parker and ordered Houston to move his command fifty miles distant to Washington-on-the-Brazos.

The ultimate downfall of Smith resulted from the election of Barrett as Judge Advocate General. Hanks had nominated Barrett for the post. Parker and his fellow council members unanimously elected Barrett. This position not only gave Barrett leverage in the army but also stirred the ire of Smith. Barrett had become the chief nemesis of Smith in the Council. The governor responded by refusing to confirm the election of Barrett. In a communique to the Council, Smith accused Barrett of forgery, dishonesty, and counterfeiting.[62] Smith felt that the election of Barrett represented an attempt by the Council to curb his executive authority. On December 25, in a resolution by William Menifee, the Council censored Smith for prohibiting the appointment of Barrett. It candidly refused to recognize any veto power of the Executive and ordered Smith to commission Barrett. The friction ultimately led to the deposal of Smith by the Council on January 11, 1836.[63]

Intergovernmental dissension may have influenced Parker but likely did not seal his decision to resign. A retreat from conflict did not characterize him. By 1835 he had experienced almost thirty years of ecclesiastical and political wrangles. Other obligations, primarily familial, beckoned. On December 24 Joseph A. Parker had arrived in San Felipe to obtain much-needed supplies for the rangers under the command of Silas Parker. Only six days before, Joseph had spoken with Silas at Fort Parker. Joseph spent three days in San Felipe. While there, he surely informed brother Daniel about the state of military preparedness on the frontier.[64]

The nature of military affairs in Texas remained uncertain. Few barriers protected Texas from invasion. San Antonio had fallen to Texas volunteers on December 10. For the moment no Mexican troops remained in Texas. It seemed that the respite had lulled Texans into a false sense of security. Unfortunately, Texas troops, many of whom had volunteered for three months, began returning to their homes. Settlers near San Pedro Creek remained exposed to attack. Separated from his family by 150 miles, Daniel wanted to insure their security before weather, personal illness, or military operations intervened. Besides, spring planting neared. Before going to San Felipe, Parker had spent only eight months improving his new farm. Much preparation remained in advance of corn planting around the first of March.

The opportunity for future political life may have influenced Parker to step down temporarily. His departure from the Council in January 1836 did not indicate a renunciation of political activity. Instead, Parker anticipated possible election to the forthcoming constitutional convention. With trouble brewing between the Council and Smith, a short absence would have distanced Parker from any negative political repercussions in a showdown with Smith. On January 8, 1836, only seven days out of office, Parker wrote to Don Carlos Barrett. Parker promised that if "it is necessary that I should return to my seat, I will try to do so in a short time."[65] Although he failed to win election, Parker stood as a candidate to the Constitutional Convention in February 1836.[66]

Events proved momentous and tragic for Daniel Parker in 1836. By February 6 Parker had returned to his family and congregation in the Nacogdoches jurisdiction. Soon, sons Dickerson and Daniel, Jr. went to serve with the Texas Army. With the fall of the Alamo on March 6 and the eastward advance of the Mexican Army, panic spread throughout Anglo settlements. In what became known as the Runaway Scrape, thousands of settlers slogged along rain-drenched roads toward the Louisiana border. The minutes of Pilgrim Church for April 2 record the "appearant [sic] danger and unsettled state of the country. . . ."[67] Shortly thereafter, the imperiled church members joined the throng of refugees. Settlers from recently established Forts Parker and Houston also fled. Fort Houston, two miles west of present-day Palestine, defended the area in which Daniel Parker recently had settled. Elder Greenwood, acting militia commandant of Fort Houston, escorted settlers across the Angelina River and toward Louisiana. Presumably, Parker either remained to help defend Fort Houston or accompanied the refugees.[68] Fortunately, the flight soon halted. On April 21 General Houston routed the Mexican Army at San Jacinto. The stunning Texas victory and subsequent capture of Santa Anna allayed the fears of the refugees. Displaced Texans breathed sighs of relief and began to trickle back to their homes.[69]

At Fort Parker the ranger company under the command of Silas Parker disbanded and resumed cultivation. Their relaxed vigilance proved tragic. During the first part of May, word reached Fort Houston that Fort Parker stood in danger. An Indian had informed a son of Daniel Parker that 500 hostile warriors had started toward Fort Parker.[70] Unfortunately, the defenders of Fort Houston failed to aid Fort Parker. The decision had fatal consequences.

Anglo-Indian hostilities had been brewing along the Colorado and Brazos river valleys for three to four years. In May 1835 Henry Rueg, a governmental official in Nacogodoches, received word that Anglos along the Red River, with a large cache of ammunition, had incited the Comanches on the Colorado to attack Mexican settlements. The raiders also seized the opportunity to swoop down on Anglo settlements. In the summer and early fall of 1835 several Anglos met death at the hands of Indians near present Bastrop and Gonzales, Texas. In retaliation Anglos had murdered two friendly Caddoes near present Marlin, Texas. Incensed, the Caddoes joined the hostile Comanches in the area. Settlers further antagonized the local tribes by organizing four mounted companies. One of these ranged as far north as the subsequent site of Dallas in search of Indians. In August 1835 the four commands, in total numbering between 80 and 100 men, rendezvoused at Fort Parker. Shortly thereafter, the command launched an attack on a friendly Indian village. Fortunately, the Native American inhabitants had fled. Yet Fort Parker, with its own shortly-to-be-organized company of rangers, became a retaliatory target by Comanches and Caddoes.

Around midmorning on May 19 a large party of Indians, primarily Comanches along with some Caddoes, approached Fort Parker. The main body of warriors halted at a distance from the fort. Two warriors approached the fort under a white flag, requested a beef and asked directions to a spring and suitable campground. Fortunately, most of the thirty-four settlers had left the stockade to work in the fields. Benjamin Parker parlayed with the two outside the fort. During the course of conversation, other warriors, seeming friendly, entered the fort. Benjamin returned to the stockade and warned the occupants of impending danger. Apparently, both sides felt uneasy. In a last effort to avoid conflict or stall attack, Benjamin again approached the Indians. His efforts proved futile. A body of Indians promptly surrounded and speared him. Whereupon, Silas began firing from the fort. The remainder of the attackers rushed the stockade. Witnessing or hearing the attack from a distance, the inhabitants of the fort, most of whom belonged to the Parker family, scattered in horror. Brothers Benjamin and Silas Parker, father John Parker, along with Robert and Samuel M. Frost, met death at the hands of the attackers. One of the women from the fort escaped before hostilities erupted and warned the settlers at work in nearby fields. Some of the men returned but watched helplessly as the war party made off with white captives. The marauders captured five children and two women. The women captives included a married daughter and a sister-in-law of James Parker.[71] Fearing another assault, the terrified settlers fled. The uncaptured but traumatized survivors trekked back toward Fort Houston under cover of darkness. After an exhaustive journey, they reached safety on May 25.[72]

The attack on Fort Parker underscored the need for military preparation. The following year Daniel Parker became instrumental in the defense of settlements around Fort Houston. Settlers continued to live in fear of Indian depredations or Mexican invasion. The Comanches made sporadic raids along the Trinity, and Caddoes lived and hunted near white settlements. After the raid on Fort Parker, Daniel Parker suspected that the neighboring Caddoes might prove hostile. On June 18, 1836, while a fourteen-man burial party returned to Fort Parker, Daniel Parker wrote a vivid description of the raid.[73] He evidently wished to impress readers that Caddoes, possibly those from neighboring villages, shared some of the blame. It seems that these developments prompted General Houston to assess the need for frontier defense. On September 8,

1836, three days after his election as president of the Republic, Houston commanded Daniel Parker to build a blockhouse and ferry on the Trinity River above Comanche Crossing and near Fort Houston.[74] Houston instructed Parker to detail twenty garrisoned soldiers for the task.

Parker tried but failed to complete the assignment. In January 1837 Parker informed Houston that the two commanders near Fort Houston had refused the order. Although Parker recently had supplied provisions to the troops, the commanders remained uncooperative.[75] Instead, some members of the command had been detached to refine salt for private purposes.[76] Parker apologized for the failure and asked to be excused for not drawing on his private resources of labor and material. He had moved back to San Pedro Creek but suffered hardships. Efforts to improve his farm twelve miles south of Fort Houston and poor health had taxed his physical and financial reserves. Parker also reminded Houston that settlers in the area relied on home guards for defense. If the male defenders received orders to leave their homes for duty elsewhere, the settlers around Fort Houston would stand vulnerable to attack. After complaining of Indian raids, Parker implored Houston that the powder and lead of the defenders "is much needed amongst us."[77] Houston responded with a scorching denunciation of the soldiers who had disobeyed orders. At the same time, he promised to honor the request of Parker and not leave Fort Houston defenseless.[78]

Indian raids nevertheless continued. Three days after Parker wrote to Houston in early 1837, a party of Indians killed three Fort Houston residents.[79] In October 1838 Indians attacked the Eden household on San Pedro Creek. The settlers lost six members. Two women died and four suffered capture.[80] Having experienced tragedy, some settlers considered moving to less hostile areas. In March 1837 Garrison Greenwood had moved to Shelby County, near the Louisiana border. In light of the Eden massacre, most of the membership of Pilgrim Church decided to join Greenwood. By January 1839 Parker also had moved to Shelby County, where he resided until the summer of 1841.[81] **Figure 3** shows the approximate locations of the San Pedro Creek and Shelby County settlements.

The move to Shelby County had political consequence. In the fall of 1839 Parker once again made a bid for public office. The desire for political positions in Texas had influenced other members

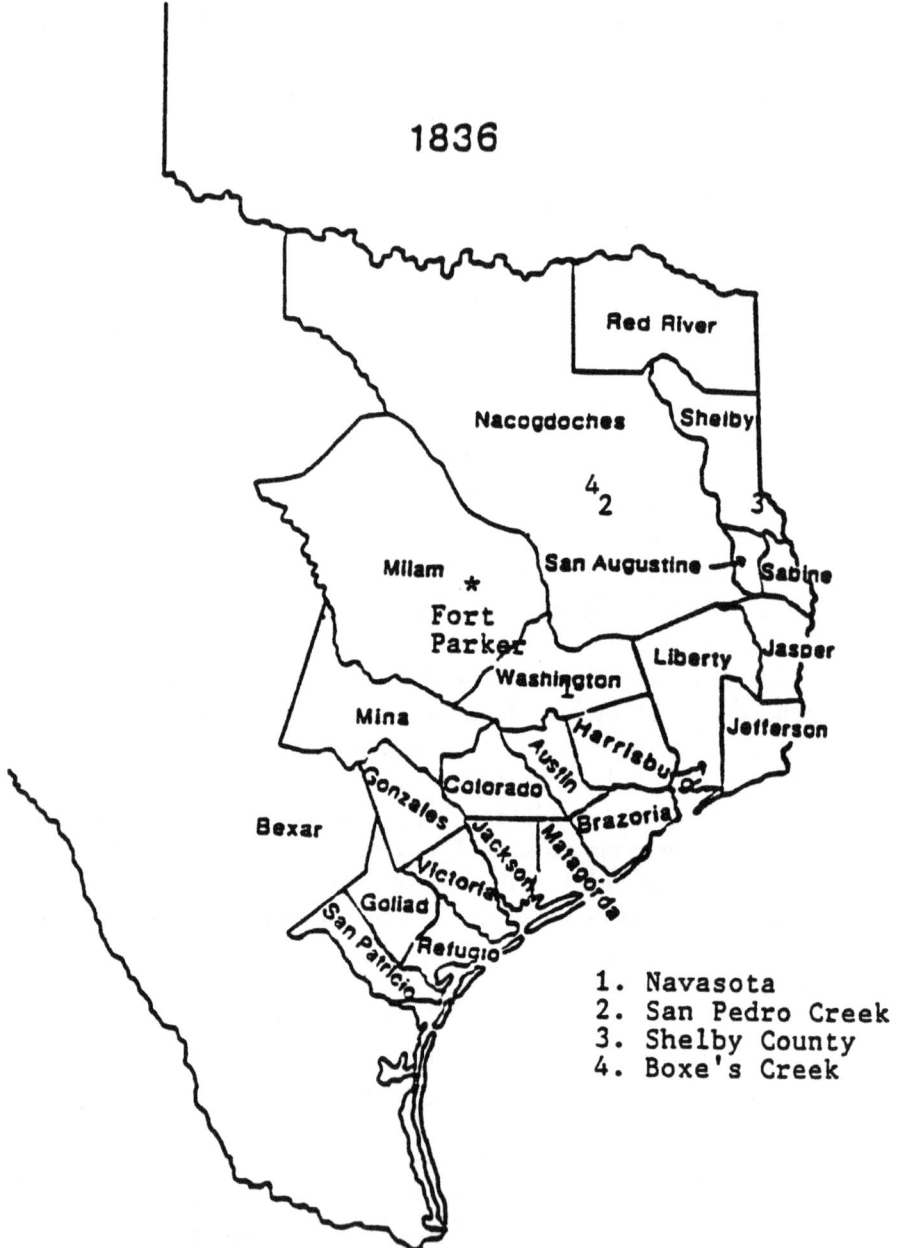

Figure 3. Locations in which Daniel Parker settled. Based on Historical Atlas of Texas by Ray A. Stephens and William Holmes.

of the Parker family. During 1838 brothers Isaac and Joseph had served in the Texas House of Representatives. In 1839 Isaac returned to legislative duties as a representative from Houston County. On September 2 the voters of Shelby County elected John H. Hansford and Daniel Parker to the Texas House of Representatives. Front-runner Hansford and Parker, the runner-up, garnered the highest totals, while John Houston finished third.[82]

By accepting the office, Parker stood in direct violation of the Constitution of the Republic of Texas. Adopted March 17, 1836, the Constitution expressly forbade any "minister of the gospel or priest of any denomination whatever" to serve the Republic as president or as a legislator.[83] Perhaps Daniel remained ignorant of this constitutional roadblock. After all, ministerial activities had not prevented his candidacy for the convention in February 1836. But if Daniel knew of the constitutional prohibition, he chose to evade or ignore the regulation. Because he was not a salaried minister, he may have reasoned that this status implied exemption.

Daniel Parker took his seat in the House on November 11, 1839. The capital recently had been relocated from Houston to Austin, which lay 325 miles from Shelby County. The ten-day ride likely fatigued the fifty-eight-year-old Parker. The House quickly organized and appointed Parker to a committee. His congressional tenure proved brief. On November 12 John Houston appeared before the House.[84] Houston protested that Parker had taken his seat in "defiance of the constitution."[85] Houston bolstered his claim with documents from officials in Shelby County. A statement signed by the Shelby County Clerk of Court on November 1, certified that Parker had performed a wedding in Shelby County on June 20, 1839. The marriage certificate revealed that Parker had referred to himself as "a regular ordained minister of the gospel."[86] John Houston contended that the paper documented the ineligibility of Parker.

The House referred the matter to the Committee of Privileges and Elections. On November 14 the committee vacated the seat of Parker. It ruled "by the confession of said Parker that he is a minister of the gospel, and as such is not entitled to a seat in this house."[87] The next day John Houston, not Parker, answered roll call as an official representative. Although the House dismissed Parker, it did not negate his brief term as fraudulent. Evidently, representatives gave some credence to his claims. On November 22 the House auditor allowed him $150 for four days service and travel expenses.[88]

By 1841 the threat of conflict with Indians had diminished in Houston County. The Cherokees had been driven out of Texas. The Comanches, who offered greater resistance, had retreated into the Texas hinterland. Beyond the line of Anglo habitation, the Comanches temporarily ceased to raid settlements. With the pacification of the Trinity River Valley, Parker returned to Houston County and devoted himself to farming, blacksmithing, milling, church affairs, and land speculation.[89]

Like many other Texas landholders, large and small, Parker hoped to profit from the land sales that anticipated immigration might bring. Large-scale Anglo speculators had taken an active interest in Texas before the Revolution. *Empresarios* had been lured to Texas by the potential profits from land sales. In eastern Texas the Galveston Bay and Texas Land Company laid claim to huge tracts. Yet individuals such as Parker also engaged in speculation. In many respects only the amount of land exchanged and the number of transactions separated large and small land speculators. Both yeomen farmers and large consortiums remained interested in land prices and clear titles. Even pioneers, those who farmed small plots, hoped to improve their holdings and profit from land sales before moving farther West.[90]

Anxious to capitalize on the expected appreciation of choice properties, developers plotted scores of townsites. Proprietors laid off lots and gave impressive names to their enterprises. Sites such as Carolina, Rome, Pompeii, Cincinnati, and Geneva dotted the bluffs of Texas rivers.[91] Unfortunately, most of these settlements never blossomed. Around 1842 Parker, likewise hoping to profit from the town boom, laid out Parkersville. He located the proposed town on the east bank of the Trinity River seven miles below Fort Houston.[92] Planted between Fort Houston and Crockett and near principal transportation arteries, the enterprise held promise. In addition to Parkersville, Daniel Parker owned substantial tracts of land. In 1843 he held title to seventeen town lots in Fort Houston and Parkersville and 15,482 acres in five counties. His total real estate holdings approximated $10,956.50 in assessed valuation.[93] Parker anticipated growth, development, and prosperity for Texas. Yet economic distress and political turmoil yielded disappointment.

From October 22, 1836, to December 10, 1838, Sam Houston served as the first popularly elected president of Texas. As helmsman war debts and the launching of a new nation challenged Houston. The new president faced an inherited state debt of $1,250,000. Through thrift and wise management, Houston endeavored to balance the Texas ledger. Port fees, property and poll taxes, and a tariff replenished state coffers. Instead of a large and costly standing army, Houston opted for small militia units. A dismantled army also meant down-scaled operations. Strategy focused on local defense and restraint against Mexico and Indian nations. In an effort to promote stability, Houston discouraged the excesses of land speculation. In December 1836 the Texas Congress placed restrictions on bounty grants. This action intended to reduce fraudulent land claims and thereby fortify the Texas economy. Before obtaining full title to lands, the government required settlers to establish a three-year residency in the Republic and pay surveying fees on their claims. The implementation of austerity and wise administration enabled Houston to establish the Republic on a sound fiscal footing by the end of his first term.[94]

The efforts of Houston to promote solvency served to encourage stability and immigration. Consequently, the policy promised profits for land speculators such as Parker. Yet the administration of Mirabeau Buonaparte Lamar, the next president, dampened hopes for personal and national prosperity.

Lamar served from December 1838 to December 1841. Whereas Houston desired the annexation of Texas to the United States, Lamar harbored grandiose dreams of an independent empire. In an effort to realize his vision, Lamar launched Texas on a more expensive course. Salaries for public officials rose. Yearly compensation for the president amounted to $10,000 plus housing. District judges received $3,000 per annum.[95] Lamar sought to finance the Republic through foreign loans and trade agreements from European governments. Efforts to secure loans from France and Great Britain failed. But attempts at statecraft did not prove fruitless. Texas received diplomatic recognition from Great Britain, France, Belgium, and Holland.

In the quest for empire, Lamar initiated substantial military expenditures. With an expanded army and navy, he embarked on an aggressive course against Indians and Mexico. In 1839 Lamar encouraged an expedition against the Cherokees in northeastern Texas. In the ensuing campaign, Texas troops slew Chief Bowles and defeated the Cherokees. The victory resulted in the banishment of the tribe from Texas. Lamar undertook an equally provocative policy toward Mexico. The Texas president sought to expand the western border of Texas to include Santa Fe. If successful, the Republic would benefit from the lucrative customs which traders paid at Santa Fe. In an attempt to seize Santa Fe, Lamar supported an ill-fated expedition against the province of New Mexico. In 1841 the poorly prepared Texans fell victim to starvation and fatigue, and Mexican troops captured the Texans without resistance. The survivors spent months in Mexican prisons.

Because of increased military and administrative expenditures, the cost of government increased. To meet the fiscal challenge, the government printed more currency. The expanded appropriations thus touched off inflation. Unsecured currency made Texas notes almost worthless. In three short years the Lamar administration ushered Texas into a difficult economic situation.

Worldwide economic distress merely worsened the shaky Texas economy. Regrettably for the hapless Lamar, his administration coincided with the Panic of 1837. In the United States the depression had been partially the result of runaway land speculation in the West. The Panic immobilized the economy of the Union. Prices for land and crops fell. The purchasers of American land failed to recoup their investments which had been made in an inflationary economy. Beset by hard times, many Americans looked to Texas for a brighter economic horizon. As a result immigration to Texas increased. Yet immigrants did not escape difficulty. Inflation in Texas, coupled with the Panic, brought privation. Newcomers encountered scarce provisions and high prices. Moreover, an inflationary economy fueled by a shortage of specie squeezed established settlers.

The financial repercussions of the Panic pounded Texas soon after the economy of the United States declined. But the psychological effects did not dampen spirits in Texas until 1839. Even in the wake of depression, land speculation continued. Large and small speculators hoped that the anticipated rush of settlers would generate handsome profits. By December 1841 the value of the Republic's money had fallen to eight cents on the United States dollar. Because sound specie remained scarce, a barter system developed. Merchants and professionals accepted produce, animals, or slaves in payment. The dismal economy meant that many speculators who had invested in land found themselves with large tracts but few able buyers.[96]

The unsettled economy made it difficult for established Texas land owners to profit from the sale of property. Those without cash reserves proved especially vulnerable. Profit-minded settlers such as Parker initially had hoped to locate and sell enough land before disputed land titles resulted in a deluge of litigation. But this aspiration did not always materialize. Lamar continued the *empresario* system. Under this practice, huge tracts entered the possession of independent entrepreneurs and foreign capitalists. Outside consortiums instead of resident land owners often reaped profits.

In the late 1830s and early 1840s many Texas settlers experienced legal difficulties over land claims. One contemporary blamed bogus property certificates on land speculators, who "swarmed like locusts."[97] Actually, the background for faulty land claims had been laid before the Revolution. Large land companies, such as the Galveston Bay and Texas Land Company of New York, had acquired huge tracts. But the Mexican government had never legitimatized the titles. As a result many unsuspecting settlers invested large amounts of money for land certificates of dubious worth.[98] These titles, often fraudulent, resulted in an avalanche of litigation. Petty lawyers and swindlers crisscrossed Texas. Opponents did not always resolve their disputes in court. In the early 1840s violence erupted in Shelby County over conflicting land claims between early settlers and newcomers. This dilemma posed a serious consequence for Parker. Plummeting land values and bogus land titles threatened the sale of tracts in eastern Texas. Parker held 8,790 acres in Shelby and neighboring Harrison and Nacogdoches counties.[99] Yet the prevailing economic climate and the speculative craze soured his hopes for financial success.

As difficulties mounted, Daniel Parker once again turned to Sam Houston. Daniel had kept abreast of affairs of state through Isaac Parker, who with the exception of 1839–1840, had represented Houston County in the Texas Congress during the Lamar administration. In December 1841 Texas voters elected Sam Houston to his second term as president. Daniel recalled his past acquaintance with Houston and seized the opportunity to influence Houston through personal correspondence.

The lack of adequate defense and the financial instability of Texas troubled Daniel. The threat of Indian attacks had not subsided entirely. Parker remembered well the bloody massacres at Fort Parker and the Eden household. The possibility of hostilities also clouded hopes for economic development. Potential settlers, speculators, and entrepreneurs thought twice about purchasing acreage and town lots in areas which remained vulnerable to raids. In a June 1842 letter, Parker commended Houston for maintaining sobriety. In the same communique, Parker notified Houston of Indian trouble near Fort Houston. He reminded the president that Houston County remained open to attack. Parker again appealed that Houston allow the defenders from the Fort Houston settlements to remain at home.[100]

Parker also felt threatened by the unstable Texas economy. Scarcely a month after the June 1842 letter, Parker addressed a rather lengthy appeal to Houston. He called attention to three years of poor crops and the lack of money necessary to procure supplies. Parker laced his letter with scriptural admonitions concerning righteousness and national policy. Parker bemoaned governmental extravagancy and the growing number of high-salaried judges and professional politicians. Yet he felt that the legal system had disappointed commoners. He deplored the apparent absence of justice. Debt collection had not been easy in frontier Texas. Guilty parties often absconded. In cases of violent crimes, defense attorneys based their arguments on self-defense. Flowery oratory stroked a sympathetic chord in jurors, so that the accused often escaped punishment.[101] In addition to these challenges, Parker blamed land taxes for exacerbating the impoverishment of settlers. Along with individual hardships, Parker feared that the poor economy jeopardized the political independence of Texas.

To induce immigration the Texas Congress had considered colonization grants to *empresarios* from the United States and Europe. Legislators hoped that land grants would prime the economy and promote immigration to the United States. The anticipated surge of newcomers would create a demand for farmland and result in increased land prices. If the process came to fruition, Texas landholders stood to profit. On February 4, 1841, Acting President

David G. Burnet signed legislation which established a colony south of the Red River in present counties of Cooke, Grayson, Denton, and Collin. Known as the Peters Colony, William Smalling Peters, a United States resident but English citizen, emerged as the chief *empresario*. Peters represented twenty principal promoters, eleven of whom resided and held citizenship in England. Peters and associates proposed to settle 600 families within three years. By January 1842 the first settlers had ascended the Red River to Shreveport and embarked on a trek across northeast Texas to their new homes.[102]

Besides Englishmen, Texas attracted other Europeans. In the 1840s Alsatians, Swiss, and Germans began to settle west of San Antonio on the grant of Henri Castro.[103] The same year that Congress approved the Peters Colony it also deliberated the settlement of 8,000 Frenchmen on the western frontier. In conjunction with twenty frontier forts, congressmen hoped that the French would provide a buffer against the Plains Indians. Known as the "Franco-Texienne bill," the proposed legislation received the support of Representative Sam Houston. The bill raised considerable debate among the public. Many feared that such a colony would give France a foothold in Texas. Although passed in the House, the bill suffered defeat in the Senate and died.[104] In February 1842 Houston and Secretary of State Anson Jones proposed the establishment of other French, English, and Belgian colonies along the Rio Grande.[105] Lamar already had curried favor with Great Britain and France in an attempt to secure loans. Parker worried that credit obligations to foreign investors would result in disarming political entanglements. Through default on loans, Texas stood to lose title to public land and consequently national sovereignty.

Parker also cautioned Houston of the necessity for governmental austerity. He advised the president to reduce the entire judicial staff to four justices. In order to reduce the expenses of diplomacy, Parker recommended that foreign affairs be transacted through correspondence. He also advocated the replacement of professional public officials with virtuous citizens. He contended that Texas remained best served with selfless citizens in office. In words which echoed his bias against pompous eastern clergy and revealed the spelling limitations of his education, he decried the services of self-seeking professionals.

But permit me sir to say that right here lys the mistake and grait evil which is destroying our country. The grait talents that must be got for large salaries is the talents that dose not sute Texas at this time. Sir, they have come for the gold Egg. And they are so impatient that they will kill the *goose* if they are let alone. The sooner they back out from our service the better for the country. Talents raised up in the school of pride, vanity Extravigancy and vain show, Ignorant of the cituation and dificulties of a new country, and of the labouring class of men. . . . We wont none of the broke down merchents nor politions who have come here to make good off of the people. . . .[106]

Government through sound management and a virtuous citizenry anchored the political philosophy of Parker. On the other hand, he remained alert to opportunity. On a mild December day in 1843, six days after the death of his youngest daughter, the grieving Daniel Parker again wrote to Sam Houston.[107] As 1843 drew to a close the much-discussed annexation to the United States excited many Houston Countians. Most locals fondly anticipated becoming part of the Union. Yet the letter from Parker to Houston conspicuously omitted the possibility of statehood. Rather, the attention of Parker focused on a more illusory source of salvation for Texas. Over twenty years had passed since Daniel and Joseph Parker had shoveled for Spanish gold in Tennessee. Now, Daniel pondered another treasure hunt. He sought to convince Houston of the veracity of a huge cache of treasure reportedly located along the Santa Fe Trail. Daniel urgently pressed Houston to take action based upon the ideas of his brother James.

In November 1840 James Parker had availed himself of the Lamar administration's penchant for military expeditions. In several letters to the Texas Congress, James had proposed an exaggerated scheme of conquest. He dreamed of raising an army of 4,000 adventurers and marching on the Indians. In 1840 he had enlisted 150 volunteers and anxiously waited for congressional authorization. In a grandiose sweep of the prairies, he planned to discover mines and lay claim for Texas to the territory north of the Santa Fe Trail.[108] The scheme also held promise of a personal empire and fortune for James. Besides the treasure, thousands of acres might be claimed by the commander of the expedition. Fortunately for James, Lamar chose to finance another force. Members of the Santa

Fe expedition, rather than the would-be glory seekers of James W. Parker, languished in Mexican jails.

By 1843 James bordered on bankruptcy.[109] His attempts to recover his niece, Cynthia Ann Parker, had cost him almost $9,000. Grasping at straws, he revived his scheme of conquest and treasure. James shared the vision with Daniel. If successful, the enterprise would have brought enormous wealth to the Parkers. James intended on returning to Illinois where, he meant to interest brother Nathaniel Parker, an Illinois state assemblyman, in the expedition. In company with Nathaniel and Santa Fe traders, James hoped to unearth fabulous riches.[110]

With Lamar out of office, James attempted to sell his scheme to Houston. But James had also fallen out of favor with Houston. The efforts of James to rescue the Parker captives had been regarded by Houston as irresponsible. Houston felt that footloose James had incited hostility among the prairie Indians. In the process, James had threatened to undermine the more peaceful strategy of Houston toward Indians.

Daniel sought to use his personal leverage with Houston to intervene on behalf of the younger Parker brother. After all, the public looked favorably upon the possibility of Texas being annexed by the United States. If this materialized, United States officials might not be as open to influence as Houston. Daniel bolstered his petition with an appeal to patriotism. He declared that such a windfall promised to insure the solvency of Texas. Simultaneously, he reserved claim to one half of the treasure for brother James. Daniel optimistically declared: "And I shall be deceived if Texas is not made independently Rich if the object can be reached and the finder have one half which I believe is his Right."[111]

Houston put aside the request of Daniel. Weightier decisions, chiefly annexation and affairs of state, captured his attention. Besides, the Lamar-sponsored Santa Fe expedition had strained relations between Texas and Mexico, and Houston dared not allow n'er-do-well James Parker to spark another confrontation with Mexico.

Daniel Parker did not live to search for treasure or witness annexation. He died on December 3, 1844. By then he had spent almost eleven years in Texas. These years proved crucial for Texas, which had achieved independence and reached the brink of annexation. The decade also remained eventful for Daniel Parker. Except for his early childhood in Virginia, Parker resided in Texas for a shorter period than any other state. Yet as a pioneer and public servant his life in Texas had been momentous. Parker entered Texas under the shadow of political defeat, but former losses did not suppress his penchant for public office. In less than two years after immigration, he helped to mold an embryonic government and initiate a constitutional convention. Texas also unveiled economic opportunities. Although his business activities in Texas never delivered extensive wealth, he nevertheless engaged in several commercial ventures. He had established a lumber mill and blacksmith shop near his home. By 1844 he had availed himself of the opportunity for government lands. His land claims amounted to far more than his combined holdings in Tennessee and Illinois.

The Texas years reflected the firm allegiance of Parker to republicanism. The Declaration of the People of Texas, adopted by the Consultation on November 7, 1835, justified the patriotic resistance by Texans to the despotic Santa Anna. Parker moved that the Declaration explicitly contain the word "republican." The amended proclamation defended force in an effort to restore "republican principles."[112] The republicanism of Parker also safeguarded the rights and property of common citizens. Resonant with populist sentiment, he championed the sovereignty of the people.[113] In his eyes the government remained obligated to protect property rights and preserve opportunities for small entrepreneurial capitalists.

Texas afforded Parker an opportunity for economic advancement. But the economic improvement of a developing frontier tempered his view of human rights. Like most Texas frontiersmen, he saw little conflict between republican principles and the violation of the rights of Native and African-Americans. The Provisional Government had guaranteed land rights to the Cherokees in northeastern Texas. Facing an invasion by the Mexican Army, the delegates at San Felipe wished to ameliorate the chance of a Mexican-Cherokee alliance. The Consultation thus held the carrot of protected land rights before the Cherokees. Parker, along with the rest of the delegates, had signed the agreement. Unfortunately for the Cherokees, in March 1836 the Texas Congress refused to ratify the treaty. In the wake of independence, Texans cast greedy eyes on the pineywoods and post oak forests of the Cherokees. The defeat of the Cherokees in 1839 had opened these lands to settlers.

In 1840 Sam Houston, then a member of the Texas House of Representatives, presented a bill which would have restored to the Cherokees their land. Houston maintained warm personal sentiments toward the Cherokees. Before coming to Texas, he had lived among the Cherokees in the Arkansas Territory. Although well intentioned, the proposed legislation of Houston came too late. Land speculators and some settlers already had seized Cherokee lands. The politically unpopular bill failed to become law. Parker personally chided Houston for the Cherokee Bill. Parker accused Houston of a grave error in permitting personal "ambition" to interfere with settlement.[114] The pro-Cherokee sentiments of Houston had seemed to restrict resident Texans from northeastern Texas. According to Parker, the opposition of Houston had merely barred the area to small farmers and robbed the Texas treasury of much-needed revenue from land sales.

The violation of human rights for the possibility of profit also muted the opposition of Parker to slavery. The efforts of Parker in the hard-fought struggle against slavery in Illinois did not characterize his reaction toward slavery in Texas. On March 17, 1836, the Texas Congress adopted strong proslavery legislation. The Constitution of the Republic of Texas did not include a provision for re-enslavement. Yet it did intend to prevent Texas from becoming a haven for free blacks. The document required congressional approval for individual emancipations. By 1848 there had been fifteen requests for emancipation. Congress had denied all but two.[115] Furthermore, the constitution restricted settlement by free immigrants of African ancestry. Free African-Americans who entered Texas following the Texas declaration of independence had to obtain congressional approval before establishing permanent residency.[116]

While large slaveholders and planters never formed a majority of the Texas population, slavery remained an important part of the Texas economy. Only 2.3 percent of families held more than twenty bondsmen and could be called planters.[117] But considerable numbers of Texans held smaller inventories. Slightly over 30 percent of Texas families owned slaves in 1850. Moreover, the slave states furnished Texas with a majority of its immigrants. These newcomers either imported their slaves or hoped to gain sufficient wealth to purchase servants. Most Anglo-Texans, slaveholders or not, regarded the institution as an economic necessity. Labor remained scarce. With abundant land, few free laborers chose to sell their toil. They preferred instead to work their own lands.[118] Slaves therefore provided a solution to the labor shortage.

Few slaves and slaveholders lived in Houston County, the area in which Parker finally settled. Yet the antislavery activities of Parker in Illinois did not prohibit his kinsmen from acquiring bondsmen in Texas. In 1838 nineteen settlers owned a total of fifty-seven bondsmen.[119] Isaac Parker numbered among the Houston County slaveholders. By 1840 James Parker owned three slaves. In the mid-1850s Miles Bennett, a former son-in-law of Daniel Parker, and John, a son of Daniel, purchased slaves.[120]

Not only did family members own slaves, but Texas preacher Daniel Parker failed to resist slavery from the pulpit. In Illinois Parker had spoken against slavery through the auspices of the La Motte Baptist Church and the Wabash District Association. In Texas counterparts existed in the Pilgrim Baptist Church, his principal pastorate, and the Union Association of Regular Predestinarian Baptists. Unlike the platitudes against slavery by some Illinois Baptists, these Texas denominational organizations remained conspicuously silent. Before the death of Daniel, Isaac and James Parker remained some of the few, if not the only, slaveholding members of the Pilgrim Church. The congregation never mentioned slaveholding as a bar to fellowship. In 1857 the church ordained slaveholder Miles Bennett as a deacon.[121] Except for identifying some of the members as slaves, the issue of slavery never appeared in the church minutes. Perhaps the omission partially resulted from the kinship of Isaac and James to the pastor of the church. Yet familial ties usually did not excuse transgressors from church discipline.

Slavery had become a social and economic factor among southern churches. Servants had become a significant part of the social structure. Because of patronization or miscegenation, some masters considered slaves as part of the familial structure. Also, among the more prosperous congregations wealthy slaveholding members brought prestige and financial support to their places of worship. The clergy of these churches had to be careful not to alienate such members. The subsequent loss of offerings posed an economic and social threat to congregations. Parker probably did not feel jeopardized by the loss of offerings. Because of his opposition to a salaried ministry, Parker did not depend on congregational offerings for his livelihood. And, other than upkeep on crude meeting houses and congregational benevolence, his congregations had few expenses. Moreover, his members, slaveholders or not, had not come from the wealthy planter class.

A more likely reason for the muted response concerned the possible public outcry which opposition to slavery might provoke. By the 1820s and 1830s the Baptist Church had achieved a degree of societal esteem. Slaveholding, even for Baptist ministers, had become more common in the Southwest. Consequently, ministers who wished to promote the Baptist faith and their congregations in local communities remained chary of the uproar which an antislavery position might incur.[122] As in other parts of the South, Texans looked awry at antislavery enthusiasts. Those who encouraged emancipation risked being labeled as abolitionists. Such an appellation injured chances for political, economic, or social success.

Ecclesiastical rather than theological views may have mitigated the activities of Elder Parker. Parker had considered the abuse of slaves as contrary to the spirit of Christianity.[123] Yet slavery remained a practical rather than a theological issue. His Two-Seed hermeneutic defended predestination. But election determined spiritual destiny and not necessarily social rank. In Illinois there had been considerable antislavery sentiment among local Baptist churches. With such strong opposition, local congregations and associations could mount an attack on human bondage. Among Texas Baptists such a negative attitude did not exist. If Parker had wanted to resist slavery through an organized body, he would have had to ally with outside abolition societies. Yet Parker had little use for extracongregational institutions of reform. Abolition societies only presented another example of centralized benevolence. Any alliance with such groups reeked of the missions controversy.[124]

Finally, economic realities affected attitudes toward slavery. Perhaps Daniel pondered whether the economic ramifications of slavery would hasten its eventual demise. The value of slaves had remained stationary from the mid-1820s through 1835. Rapid expansion after independence had temporarily boosted the value of human chattel. But the Panic of 1837 had initiated a price dip for commodities and slaves. Between 1837 and the early 1840s the price for slaves had fallen approximately $200 per bondsman.[125] By the early 1840s human inventories proved a poor return for solely investment capital.

Yet the argument against slavery, based strictly on investment outlays, did not seriously threaten the demise of human bondage. Texas remained primarily a nation of small farmers. Upon arrival, the average yeoman farmer, typically of southern background, might not have possessed the necessary capital for the purchase of slaves. But this did not mean that small farmers would not acquire slaves once they had become sufficiently prosperous. Because yeomen hoped for economic advancement, slavery expanded rapidly during the early statehood years. Even in the years that Daniel Parker lived in Texas, the number of slaves had increased by approximately 25,000 from 1836 to 1846.[126]

Daniel Parker realized that a much stronger argument for slavery persisted in Texas than Illinois. Wabash yeomen farmers chiefly opposed slavery for economic and social reasons. In a hard-pressed economy, mechanics and laborers found it difficult to compete with slave labor. Yeomen farmers also feared that slaveholding planters possessed the capacity to out produce the small farmer. Many of the Prairie State constituents of Parker had incorporated the issue of class into the controversy over slavery. The contest pitted wealthy planters against small farmers of modest means. In the Republic of Texas the Anglo settlers still seemed more socially and politically equal in an economy structured around small farmers. Most slaveholders in Texas came from the ranks of yeomen farmers. The issue of class and economic exploitation therefore did not seem as important in Texas. Cotton-growing Texans, including yeoman slaveholders, needed slave labor to compete with the rest of the South. Furthermore, the abolition of slavery might impede southern immigration and economic development. If Texas straddled the fence over slavery, would-be slaveholders might reconsider immigration. Slowed immigration would consequently drive down the value and demand for land. Parker never held extensive property in Illinois. There, he had opposed the potential economic repercussions of slavery. In Texas he had acquired substantial acreage. Slavery therefore occupied a pivotal position in the economic future of Texas and Parker. His fiery orations in Illinois decried slavery. The economic realities of Texas had snuffed the flame.

In early 1844 many Texans anxiously awaited the annexation

of Texas to the United States. On February 28, 1844, Isaac Parker wrote to Sam Houston. Writing from Houston County, Isaac reported the enthusiastic reception of most locals to annexation.[127] Isaac mentioned that he had visited with Daniel the previous day. Preacher Parker remained in good health and sent regards to his old compatriot Houston. That may have been the last recorded communication between Houston and Daniel Parker. Before the end of the year, Daniel had died.

The experience of Parker in Texas differed in some respects from his years in Illinois. Religious controversy never reached the level as it had in Illinois. Although he possessed more property in Texas, Parker failed to gain the political prominence which he had achieved along the Wabash. Also, he ceased to speak out against slavery in Texas. On the other hand, in a broader sense the Texas years paralleled past economic and political experiences. In Texas as well as Illinois, he failed to adjust to the social and political changes which characterized a national market economy. The promise of more freedom and opportunity had lured Parker to Texas. By 1834 Texas presented the last hope of the aging Parker for a new life. Missionary societies and partisan politics had engulfed Illinois. Texas held new promise for the common man. Citizens could enjoy the egalitarian principles of untarnished republican government.

In spite of this anticipation, the murky Sabine River never equaled the solace of the Jordan. Texas held promise but was not the Promised Land. Factious politics, human bondage, and economic repercussions resurfaced. Worldwide economic trends touched Texas as well as the United States. The common frontiersman still felt the impact of developments in the urban markets of Europe and the northeastern United States. As in Illinois, the Jeffersonian dream in Texas had been squeezed by national market realities and partisan politics. As annexation dawned, an important era had passed in the history of Texas. Desiring opportunities for leadership and advancement, Parker had been one of the sturdy pioneers who had sought the Jeffersonian dream in Texas. His quest had been achieved behind the podium of public affairs as well as the pulpit.

Chapter 5

The Texas Ministry

ON MONDAY, 21 DECEMBER 1835, Elder Zacharius N. Morrell and five companions from Tennessee crossed the Sabine River at Gaines Ferry. Morrell, a self-styled "cane-break" Baptist preacher, had been familiar with the ministry of Daniel Parker. Morrell had ministered for fourteen years among churches in Obion County, Tennessee. This part of northwestern Tennessee lay near Robertson and Sumner counties, where Parker had lived before he moved to Illinois in 1817. Morrell, a distributor of the *Church Advocate* in 1830, also had knowledge of Parker's publications.[1] Morrell recently had moved from Tennessee to Yalobusha County, Mississippi, but did not feel at home there. Events in Texas captured his interest. Morrell felt that Texas would soon gain independence. An acquaintance of Morrell previously had claimed that in 1829 Sam Houston had confided plans to establish a "little two-horse republic" in Texas.[2] Believing that recent hostilities between Anglo-Texans and Mexican authorities would spark Texas independence, Morrell yearned to survey land and opportunities under the Lone Star. Once in Texas, Morrell and party rode through pine forests and red clay hills as they approached San Augustine, some twenty miles from the Sabine River. They lost little time on their journey, for they had planned a rendezvous on Christmas Day with David Crockett. The companions of Morrell had arranged to meet fellow Tennessean Crockett at the Falls of the Brazos for a bear

hunt. Crockett had suffered political misfortune in Tennessee, when he had sided with Whig champion Henry Clay against President Jackson. Having lost a reelection bid for Congress only a few weeks earlier, Crockett had decided to spread his tent in Texas.[3] Licking political wounds, Crockett already had reached Texas by December 1835.

The Morrell party passed through Nacogdoches on December 22 or 23. While there, Morrell inquired about the activities of Baptist preachers in eastern Texas. Baptist minister Isaac Reed, a Tennessee immigrant and acquaintance of Morrell, resided a few miles north of Nacogdoches. Reed had lived near the settlement for at least a year, but since moving to Texas, he had not resumed preaching. Because the Mexican law required immigrant allegiance to the Roman Catholic church, Reed feared opposition from Mexican authorities in nearby Nacogdoches. Reed therefore had remained reluctant to launch a public ministry. But the activities of another preacher circulated in Nacogdoches. Residents informed Morrell that Daniel Parker remained the only Baptist preacher "in all this wide domain."[4]

Comparable to unsettled areas in the United States, the physical and material necessities of life on the Texas frontier took precedence over religious and spiritual matters. In 1831 Texas resident William Bluford DeWees observed the indifference to religion by frontiersmen. The Kentucky immigrant and son of a Baptist minister lamented that he had not heard a sermon since passing through the Arkansas Territory in 1820. DeWees deplored the lack of religion along the Colorado River.

> The people of this country seem to have forgotten that there is such a commandment as "Remember the Sabbath day and keep it holy." This day is generally spent in visiting, driving stock, and breaking mustangs. There is no such thing as attending church, since no religion except the Roman Catholic is tolerated, and we have no priests among us.[5]

Part of the indifference had resulted from the political involvement of the Roman Catholic church in Mexico. In 1824 Pope Leo XII issued an encyclical which admonished the Mexican ecclesiastical hierarchy to support Ferdinand VII's return to power in Spain and, presumably, the monarch's plan to regain his American empire.⁶ During the 1820s, the Roman Catholic church became an important part of the conservative centralist faction in Mexico. To further their own political views, liberals sought to weaken the centralist-church link. Liberals did not oppose Catholicism but resented the powerful alliance of church and state. Because of political turmoil and the absence of diocesan leadership, the ministry of the Roman Catholic Church in Texas lagged. From 1825 to 1840 the archbishopric of Mexico remained vacant. And between 1821 and 1836 the diocese of Linares, which included Texas, lacked a bishop. By 1836, no doubt partially because of the Texas Revolution, very few priests ministered in all of Texas.⁷

In spite of the widespread apathy, all Texans did not totally ignore spiritual matters. The dearth of priests and limited access to the sacraments raised concern. Because Roman Catholicism remained the only legally sanctioned religion, Protestant ministers could not baptize, marry, nor bury colonists. In the 1820s residents of Nacogdoches made several petitions to the central government for a priest but found it almost impossible to get and retain one.⁸ "Consequently, the colonists were unbaptized; wrote out their wedding vows, . . . and were buried by laymen."⁹ Yet at times, perhaps because the lack of priestly visits had weakened the influence of Roman Catholic congregations, some Texas Protestants availed themselves of the vacuum and observed de facto freedom of worship.

Mexican law protected the Roman Catholic church against encroachments by other religions, but authorities did not strictly enforce the provision. Federal and state constitutions of Mexico and the State of Coahuila and Texas had specified Roman Catholicism as the established religion and prohibited "the exercise" of any other.¹⁰ Yet by the early 1830s Mexican policy tolerated the presence of Protestants. Official guidelines did not stipulate that incoming colonists had to be Catholics, but immigrants had to "observe" the prescribed religion.¹¹ Because of the ban on other religions, Mexican officials assumed that prospective colonists would convert to Catholicism.¹² Moreover, governmental reforms in Mexico had mitigated the stance toward non-Catholics. In 1833 the Mexican Congress curtailed clerical and church privileges such as the ecclesiastical monopoly on education and involuntary tithes.¹³ At the same time, this policy assuaged potentially rebellious Anglo-Texans. A decree dated March 26, 1834, assured Texans that

"No person shall be molested for political and religious opinions, provided, he shall not disturb the public order."[14] The following year a traveler to Texas wrote that "though the Catholic religion is required to be supported, the laws are tolerant, and there is no persecution for opinion's sake."[15] In the early 1830s the Mexican commander at Nacogdoches, Jose de las Piedras, learned that a Methodist itinerant had initiated services approximately fifty miles from Nacogdoches near the border with the United States. Satisfied that the Methodists remained innocent of horse stealing, murder, or other crimes, the commander allowed the services to continue unmolested.[16]

Parker personally availed himself of the relaxed religious directives. In May 1835, in obedience to the colonization law which required foreign colonists to provide sworn certificates of good character, Daniel vouched for the moral fortitude of one of his sons. Rather than specify a denominational allegiance, Daniel simply certified that son Dickerson held membership in the "religion cristiana."[17] Mexican officials did not regard such a confession as evasive. For the 1825 colonization law of the State of Coahuila and Texas had mandated that immigrants only had to prove "their christianity and good moral character."[18] Most authorities only recognized Catholicism as the genuine form of Christianity. Hence, the term "religion cristiana" legally implied allegiance to the Catholic Church. Yet many Anglo-Texans ignored any stipulation which encouraged conversion to Catholicism.[19]

Because most Anglo-Texans had Protestant backgrounds, Protestant religious activity initially centered around Anglo settlements on the northern and eastern borders of Texas. As early as 1818 Methodist ministers had held services along the Red River. Soon other Evangelicals penetrated the Texas hinterland. In 1824 the Reverend Henry Stephenson, a Methodist minister from Missouri, preached as far south as San Felipe. Joseph Bays, a Baptist immigrant from Missouri, had arrived in Texas around 1820. Bays preached along the Brazos River in 1826 and later at San Augustine. In 1829 Baptists established one Sabbath school at San Felipe and another at Matagorda. Following close on the heels of Baptists and Methodists, Presbyterians began services at San Felipe around 1828 and maintained their efforts along the Red River.[20]

In January 1834 Daniel Parker and the membership of Pilgrim

Predestinarian Regular Baptist Church arrived in the Austin Colony. Although organized in Illinois, the Pilgrim Church became the first formally organized Baptist Church in Texas. Family legend reports that Parker organized the church in Illinois because the Mexican government had denied him permission to form a Baptist Church in Texas. To circumvent this prohibition, his family believed that Parker sought permission from Stephen F. Austin to import a Baptist congregation. Accordingly, Austin granted approval to Daniel.[21]

There may be a germ of truth in the tradition, but its total veracity is dubious. A more plausible reason for forming the church in Illinois related to Baptist ecclesial practice. In 1832 Parker realized that Baptist churches did not exist in Texas, and very few Baptist ministers lived there. Parker firmly believed that members of organizational presbyteries had to be doctrinally sound. If not, then the credentials of the congregation and the baptisms of those immersed under its authority stood in doubt. With this in mind, Parker likely reasoned that it would be difficult to assemble an organizational presbytery of like faith and order in Texas. Furthermore, there are no documents which indicate that Parker directly sought or received permission from Austin. Perhaps Daniel appealed to his brother, James W. Parker, to intervene on behalf of Baptist immigrants. When James wrote to Austin in 1832, he mentioned that several prospective colonists professed the Baptist faith. James also volunteered that these settlers desired the freedom of worship.[22]

Daniel may have had the opportunity to approach Austin at San Felipe. While Parker visited the Austin Colony during the winter of 1832 and 1833, Austin had remained at San Felipe. Yet with Anglo settlements under close scrutiny by Mexican authorities, Austin likely did not encourage any Protestant activity by Parker or anyone else. In late December 1832 *empresario* Austin had returned to San Felipe from a tour of Mexican settlements at Goliad and San Antonio. He had attempted to solicit the political support of Mexican settlers for the creation of Texas as a separate state within the Mexican union. If Mexico conferred statehood, Austin hoped that this action might avert a move for complete independence by Anglo-Texan radicals.[23] In the spring of 1833 Austin therefore had good cause to adhere closely to the political and religious guidelines of the Mexican constitution.

The efforts of Austin to recruit settlers had presented two major obstacles. One concerned the dubious legality of slavery under Mexican ordinances. Without the reservation of property rights to slaveholders, some southerners remained reluctant to become colonists. The other impediment dealt with restrictions on religious liberty. Freedom from coercive religion had been central to republican ideals in the predominantly Protestant United States. The required allegiance to Catholicism therefore created a potential barrier to immigration from the United States. At the same time, Austin had looked askance at vociferous Protestant evangelism in Texas. In 1824 Austin had penned his views concerning Protestant activity to Methodist clergyman William Stephenson, a resident of the Arkansas Territory. At that time Stephenson ministered along the Red River in what some considered to be part of Arkansas. Austin warned "if a methodist, or any other Preacher except a Catholic, was to go through this colony, preaching, I should be compelled to imprison him."[24]

From the initial stages of their colonization endeavor, Moses Austin and son Stephen had evaded but not directly challenged the religious requirement. Moses had sworn that his 300 settlers would be industrious and submissive to Spanish authorities. He did not indicate that they would be Catholics. Stephen also sidestepped the issue. Although Stephen had a Protestant baptism, he did not favor any denomination. Influenced by the Enlightenment, Stephen opposed sectarian wrangling and denominational competition. He especially frowned upon the exuberance of Methodist circuit riders. The younger Austin felt that Protestant preachers should not antagonize Mexican officials nor flaunt the law. Left unprovoked, Mexican authorities might thus tacitly allow Protestant worship.[25]

With or without the approval of Austin, the membership of the Pilgrim Church first assembled in Texas at the home of Daniel Parker on Saturday, January 18, 1834.[26] The church continued to meet in Parker's home near present Navasota, Texas, until November 1834. Parker then relocated near the southern edge of present Anderson County, Texas. Because of the difficulties involved in moving, the congregation did not assemble again until July 4, 1835. On that date, Daniel Parker and eight members met at his home in the Burnet *empresario* grant. Over the next eight months, the congregation convened six times, developments having interrupted regular services. During this time, Anglo-Texan tension with Mexico increased. In March 1836 Texas declared independence from Mexico. The Runaway Scrape, as Texans fled advancing Mexican troops, disrupted the church. On April 2, 1836, the congregation voted to disperse and did not reconvene until February 25, 1837. On that date, the members gathered at their previous place of worship, the home of Daniel Parker. The clerk distinctly located the residence of Parker in the newly created "County of Nacogdoches and Republic of Texas."[27]

Life on the frontier proved tenuous for individuals and religious organizations as well. In March 1837 Elder Garrison Greenwood, Parker's principal ministerial assistant in the Pilgrim congregation, moved approximately ninety miles eastward to Shelby County, Texas. Other church members soon joined Greenwood. To accommodate the widely scattered membership, the congregation agreed to hold separate services, one for the members in Shelby County and another for those who remained in Nacogdoches County. This arrangement continued until December 1838. By then most of the congregational remnant in Nacogdoches County had moved to Shelby County.[28] Yet in spite of the difficulties imposed by distance, Parker maintained worship services in Shelby County and organized a second congregation in Nacogdoches County. On September 17, 1837, he assisted in the formation of the Hopewell Baptist Church, approximately fifteen miles west of Nacogdoches.[29] This congregation, composed of only eight members, may have been the second Baptist church officially organized on Texas soil.[30]

Not only did Parker plant churches, other Baptists did as well. The Republic of Texas lifted the religious stipulations which had been part of Mexican law. Protestants could enter Texas without legal reservations. Baptists numbered among the many immigrants from the United States. The increasing numbers of Baptists challenged Parker's leadership and also resulted in the rekindling of the missions controversy. Yet the conflict did not reach the level of acrimony which had been manifested in Illinois and Tennessee. Unlike the more thickly settled areas in the Mississippi Valley, greater distances separated Texas settlements. Although vast areas, sparse settlement, and smaller numbers of Baptist clergy resulted in a more restrained conflict, differences nevertheless soon surfaced.

In 1836 a group of Baptists in the Sparks' Settlement, four miles north of Nacogdoches, had initiated worship services in a school taught by Baptist minister James L. Bryant.[31] On Sunday, May 6, 1838, Elder Isaac Reed organized this fellowship into the Union Baptist Church.[32] Reed did not differ with Parker over missions. Like Parker, Reed stood against missionary societies. Yet Parker refused to recognize the Union congregation as a true Baptist Church.

Parker grounded nonfellowship with Union on alleged organizational improprieties. In May 1839 he listed three reasons for nonfellowship. First, Parker maintained that Union harbored Separate Baptist doctrines. By this he meant that the church had been tainted with nonpredestinarian tenets.[33] As early as 1814 Parker had alluded to the doctrinal defection by Separate Baptists to Arminianism. Second, the Union Church had been organized by an "unauthorized" presbytery. Finally, Elder Bryant had administered baptism and communion to the Hopewell congregation without having been restored "to the ministerial function."[34] Parker failed to detail the circumstances behind the lapsed status of Bryant. Yet Reed, the primary shepherd of Union, seems to have been a respected minister. If legitimate improprieties had existed, the ministry of Reed likely would have been censured by other Baptist ministers in the area.

After the organization of the Union Church, Parker fortified the churches in which he ministered against doctrinal corruption. The Union congregation had offered to extend fellowship to neighboring Hopewell. This initiative implied that Union desired mutual recognition and cooperation between the two churches. The invitation alarmed Parker, for it threatened to recognize Bryant instead of Parker as Hopewell's shepherd. On April 27, 1839, he notified the Pilgrim Church of the alleged disorder which existed among the Hopewell congregation.[35] Parker evidently offered to present in person a Pilgrim-approved letter of rebuke to Hopewell. In the May 1839 epistle Parker cautioned Hopewell to resist any overtures by Union. By June 8 Parker had delivered the letter to Hopewell.[36] His visit evoked different responses. Parker reported that the small congregation had initiated a correction of the disorders. But at least one prominent member of Hopewell seems to have differed with Parker. William Sparks, the only deacon in Hopewell, likely took offense to the Parker-borne rebuke. On June 1 Sparks had presented himself for membership to the Union Church.[37]

Although the Union congregation remained antimissionary, other Texas churches favored centralized benevolence. In November 1837, after a prior abortive attempt, Zacharius N. Morrell organized the first missionary Baptist church in Texas at Washington-on-the-Brazos. On November 7 the church appealed to the American Baptist Home Mission Society for missionaries.[38] The Washington church soon disbanded and did not reorganize until the 1840s. Yet promissions Baptists from nearby settlements along the Colorado and Brazos rivers formed an association. On October 8, 1840, messengers from three churches organized the Union Baptist Association. T. W. Cox, a promissions minister, shepherded all three of the member churches. This association recommended the support of temperance and tract societies, organizations to which Parker remained decidedly opposed. Moreover, it adopted *The Baptist Banner and Western Pioneer,* a promissions paper published in Louisville, Kentucky, as its official paper. From its inception, this association favored missions. Yet there remained at least two antimissionary ministers in the area. For the sake of unity, the associational organizers thought it best to address the missions question with diplomacy. The messengers therefore reserved the right to exercise "discretion in contributing to the support of missions." At the same time, they appealed to their antimissionary brethren "to unite with us," and "we will meet you with tearful eye."[39]

While promissionary Baptists organized, Parker lost little time in forming an antimissions association. On July 11, 1840, Daniel Parker, with brother Isaac serving as deacon, examined the ecclesiastical and doctrinal stance of the Mount Pleasant Baptist Church in Montgomery County. The church had been gathered two years earlier by another minister but seemed to have lacked a proper organizational presbytery. Consequently, Parker met with the church and weighed its doctrinal purity. Satisfied that this congregation proved sound, Daniel properly organized the church. He then requested that the Pilgrim congregation recognize Mount Pleasant as a legally constituted sister church. In August 1840 the Pilgrim Church approved the recommendation of Parker.[40] With the establishment of Pilgrim, Hopewell, and Mount Pleasant, Parker then moved to organize these congregations into an association. On October 17, 1840, seventeen representatives from four churches of like faith and order entered an associational compact.⁴¹ Mount Pleasant, Hopewell, and Pilgrim lay in Texas. Boggy Bayou, located approximately fifteen miles southwest of Shreveport, Louisiana, composed the fourth church. Known as the Union Association of Regular Predestinarian Baptists, this became the second Baptist association formed in Texas.⁴²

In Illinois the Two-Seed doctrine had resulted in acrimony and division, but in Texas the dualism did not create such controversy. The churches of the pro-Parker Union Association did not regard it as a serious doctrinal issue. The core membership of several of these churches had followed Parker from Illinois. They either agreed with Two Seedism or did not consider the doctrine a serious departure from orthodoxy. Moreover, survival on the frontier may have concerned them more than metaphysical asbstractions. Difficulties also challenged promissions Baptists. Their attention focused on the tenuous existence of the Baptist faith in Texas. Church planting and strengthening, rather than Two Seedism, occupied their efforts. Denominational papers, those organs which might have mustered opposition to Two Seedism, did not exist to fuel controversy in Texas. Furthermore, the center of promissionary Baptist activity lay along the Brazos and Colorado rivers. The ministry of Parker in East Texas remained separated from the main area of Baptist activity.

Ironically, much of the published criticism of Two Seedism came from antimissionary Baptists in the eastern United States. In late 1841 or early 1842 Parker sent an article to his old friend Richard N. Newport, the editor of *The Western Predestinarian Baptist*. In January or February 1842 Newport launched the publication in Paris, Illinois. *The Western Predestinarian Baptist* championed the principles of strict election and antimissionism which prevailed among many Baptists in the Mississippi Valley. Newport published the comments of Parker in the first edition of his paper. The remarks had been excerpted from the official 1841 minutes of the predestinarian Union Association. In the article Parker defended himself against an alleged reference which had appeared in the promissions *Baptist Banner and Western Pioneer* between 1840 and September 1841. The editor of the *Banner* commented on the beliefs of Daniel Parker and noted Two-Seed adherent Thomas Paxton of Greensburg, Louisiana. In 1829 Elder Paxton's Two-Seed sermons had ignited controversy among Baptists in southeastern Louisiana and Mississippi.[43] The editor remarked:

> It would be a blessing to the world if they were together and were compelled to reside in some of our large prairies in the Rocky Mountains, where they could scatter their two seeds among the Mustangs and wild Ass.[44]

In his article Parker refused to recant the Two-Seeds doctrine. Rather, he acknowledged, "We glory in this seed that should bruise the Serpent's head."[45]

While Parker fended off attacks from the *Banner*, his antimissionary brethren also criticized Two Seedism. By the early 1840s Baptists who espoused antimissionism and strict election had been labeled Old School or Primitive Baptists. Virginia minister Samuel Trott, a member of the Primitive fellowship, had serious reservations about Two Seedism. Trott had written to the *Signs of the Times*, an Old School paper published in New Vernon, New York, by Gilbert Beebe. Trott proposed to republish *Views on the Two Seeds*, an essay published by Parker in 1826. Included in his edition of Parker's work, Trott wanted to incorporate copious notes which illuminated the errors of Two Seedism. Trott focused on the perceived Parkerian explanation concerning the origin of evil.

The idea that God had been responsible for the origin of Satan and evil revolted Trott. Parker had incorporated the origin of evil into his doctrine to manifest the righteousness of God. He meant to prove that God did not create the nonelect to be the "subject of his eternal wrath."[46] Instead, Parker attributed the source of evil and the nonelect to the archfiend. Yet the explanation evoked more questions. If Satan had created the nonelect, then he remained coeternal with God. If not coeternal, then God must have created evil.[47]

Parker read the offer of Trott and penned a lengthy letter to the *Signs* on February 1, 1842. The veteran proponent of Two Seedism denied the scriptural basis for a Satan-backed cosmic coup which had caused a part of God's angelic minions to align with evil. Parker explained that Satan "existed eternally as the spirit of darkness and corruption, as the apposite [sic] to the spirit of light and Holiness."[48] This assertion reinforced a Parkerian apologetic written sixteen years earlier. In 1827 he had written that "those disembodied spirits, which are called angels" had not been created.

Rather, they remained "particles or proceeds" of the eternal spirit.[49] In the mind of Parker this abrogated God from any responsibility as the creator of evil.

The comments of Parker to Trott touched off a volley of letters to *The Western Predestinarian Baptist* by the supporters and foes of Two Seedism. As in the missions controversy, sectionalism colored the issue. In March 1842 H. T. Craig, coeditor of the paper, wrote: "It seems that our brethren in the east regard the western Baptists as having generally imbibed Elder Parker's views."[50] By October 1843 at least twenty letters on each side of the question had reached Newport. Although some readers held strong opinions, others had grown weary of the rancor. Approximately forty readers had urged *The Western Predestinarian Baptist* to curtail public debate over Two Seedism.[51] Yet the controversy failed to subside. In May 1844 the *The Western Predestinarian Baptist* reported that contention over the doctrine still seethed among Old School Baptists in eastern Illinois, the area which had witnessed the apex of Parker's ministry.[52]

Although Parker remained under siege from Baptist critics in the United States, his immediate concern rested with religious developments in Texas. Parker wished to keep Texas Baptists pure from the leaven of missionary societies. He also endeavored to insulate the newly formed Republic of Texas from a perceived alliance between church and state. On January 25, 1837, approximately three months after the inauguration of President Sam Houston, he wrote to his old friend. After informing the president of the deplorable state of defense around Fort Houston, Parker also urged Houston to fortify Texas against incursions by organized religious agencies. By his remarks Parker possibly recalled the work of missionary-society salaried personnel on governmentally supported Indian stations in Indiana. Parker feared that "impostors" might solicit governmental approval for the incorporation of church-sponsored institutions. By these Parker meant societies which advanced missionary, benevolent, and educational purposes. He already had alerted Houston to this possibility in a Parkerian publication, which dealt with "the impropriety of blending religious matters with national pollicy [sic]."[53] Perhaps the preacher had handed Houston his printed handiwork in late 1835, the year in which Parker had served in the Provisional Government. Parker buoyed his hopes of influencing the president by claiming extensive publication experience. He mentioned that he had written over 1,000 pages against the evils of church-state links.

But Parker's fear of a presumed church-state link soon materialized. Less than five years after independence, denominational schools began to emerge in Texas. Rutersville College, a Methodist-sponsored institution, opened near La Grange in 1840.[54] Wesleyan College in San Augustine, also a Methodist establishment, had been chartered by the Texas Congress during Houston's second presidency. The school commenced classes on March 4, 1844.[55] In December 1844 Anson Jones succeeded Houston as president. On February 1, 1845, almost two months after the death of Parker, President Jones signed the congressionally approved charter for Baylor College. In May 1846 the Baptist school, the forerunner of Baylor University, initiated instruction at Independence in Washington County.[56]

In spite of his efforts, Parker did not prevent the advance of Methodists, Presbyterians, camp meetings, centralized institutions of benevolence, and other Baptists. Fort Houston soon experienced some of these developments. As early as 1835 Presbyterians held a camp meeting near the settlement. In 1841 a Methodist missionary organized a church at the hamlet. Two years later, Methodists near the fort sponsored a camp meeting. Such efforts resulted in rapid increases among this denomination which Parker had targeted in Tennessee.[57] Baptist congregations which had not aligned with Parker also experienced progress. In 1841 the promissions Union Association, composed of churches along the Brazos and Colorado rivers, established the Texas Baptist Home Mission Society. The same year this society sponsored three missionaries on Texas soil.[58] In November 1843 the Union Church, north of Nacogdoches, and four other congregations in eastern Texas formed the Sabine Association.[59] While favoring missionary outreach, this association opposed missionary societies. In spite of similar views over centralized benevolence, Parker refused formal ties with the Sabine Association.

The controversy which surrounded the organization of the Sabine Association in East Texas evidenced Parker's penchant for faction. Bethel Church in Sabine County, one of the five congregations in the Sabine Association, had been organized under the ministry of Parker in 1841. Yet it had never joined the predestinarian

Union Association.⁶⁰ The support of missions did not originally become a basis for nonfellowship with the Sabine Association. For this association initially opposed missionary societies. Rather, the Sabine Association, the second association organized in East Texas, looked to Isaac Reed and others rather than Parker for leadership. Parker refused to condone this perceived challenge.

On August 17, 1844, the Pilgrim Church approved a letter of caution, no doubt composed by Parker, to its sister churches. The letter "warned the churches in our union against the disorder of the Bethel church in Sabine County."⁶¹ Parker resented that Bethel had first agreed to unite with the predestinarian Union Association but had joined another association "with whoom [sic] we have no fellowship."⁶² He therefore felt that Bethel should have surrendered its organizational constitution to the Union Association. Because Bethel had not relinquished the document, Parker felt that the congregation had "forfeited" the right to exist and "proved herself unsound in the faith."⁶³ In the mind of Parker if Bethel did not fall under the strictures of the Union Association, the church should dissolve.

Yet the successes of rival Baptists and other denominations did not silence Parker. The principles and doctrines of Old School Baptists remained dear to him. In the midst of economic adversity and familial tragedy he strove to plant and indoctrinate churches. In February 1842 Fort Houston resident Winnie Morgan, a former member of the Mount Pleasant Baptist Church near Paris, Illinois, described the efforts of Parker.

> We have a little church of Old fashioned Baptists. . . . We have the gospel preached to us in its purity by that old veteran of the cross, Elder Daniel Parker, ... He devotes himself entirely to the work of the ministry, and his labors are abundantly crowned with success.⁶⁴

In the ten years that Parker had resided in Texas he had organized seven churches over a broad area. Furthermore, he had led in the formation of the Union Association of Regular Predestinarian Baptists. By 1843 this association numbered eight churches, whose memberships totaled almost 200.⁶⁵ All of these congregations met in Texas. Boggy Bayou in Louisiana, an original member, seems to have disbanded or had left the association shortly after 1840.⁶⁶ As shown in **Figure 4,** the Texas perimeters of the Association ranged from present Palestine 100 miles eastward to Milam, south to present Woodville and west to Huntsville. Parker organized the following member churches: Hopewell, west of Nacogdoches; Fort Houston; Bethel, north of Milam; a church near San Augustine; Mustang Prairie in Houston County; Wolf Creek, approximately five to ten miles northeast of present Woodville; and San Jacinto near Huntsville.[67]

On April 6, 1844, Daniel Parker observed his sixty-fifth birthday. Six days later, Parker wrote his will.[68] His years had been full. He had been blessed with eleven children, all of whom reached adulthood. But their support had required frugality, hard labor, and wise management. Life on the frontier had been difficult. National economic downturns in 1819 and 1837 had resulted in short money and financial distress. The heavy burdens of family, churches, publications, and political involvement had taken their toll.

Yet Parker remained quite active. In June 1844 he had organized the San Jacinto Church. In August 1844 Parker set out to visit some churches which he had organized along the Neches River.[69] Possibly they included the recently organized Wolf Creek Church. While he traveled, Parker grieved the loss of son Dickerson, who had died August 1, 1844.[70] The annual session of the predestinarian Union Association had been scheduled for October 1844. As the meeting approached, Parker likely wanted to fortify far-flung member churches against the corrupting influences which recently had befallen Bethel. Another possible motivation for the journey concerned the proposed formation of a second predestinarian Baptist association in southeastern Texas. On November 8, 1844, five antimissionary Baptist churches organized the Louisiana and Texas Regular Predestinarian Baptist Association in Jasper County, Texas.[71] Parker may have wanted to assay the doctrinal purity of the association and assist in the formation. Unfortunately, he never completed the journey. Parker fell ill and had to return home.

Although in poor health, Parker continued to attend to private and church affairs. On October 12 the predestinarian Union Association convened at the Fort Houston Church, twelve miles from the home of Parker. His physical condition did not permit him to stand or preach. But he nevertheless attended the conference and

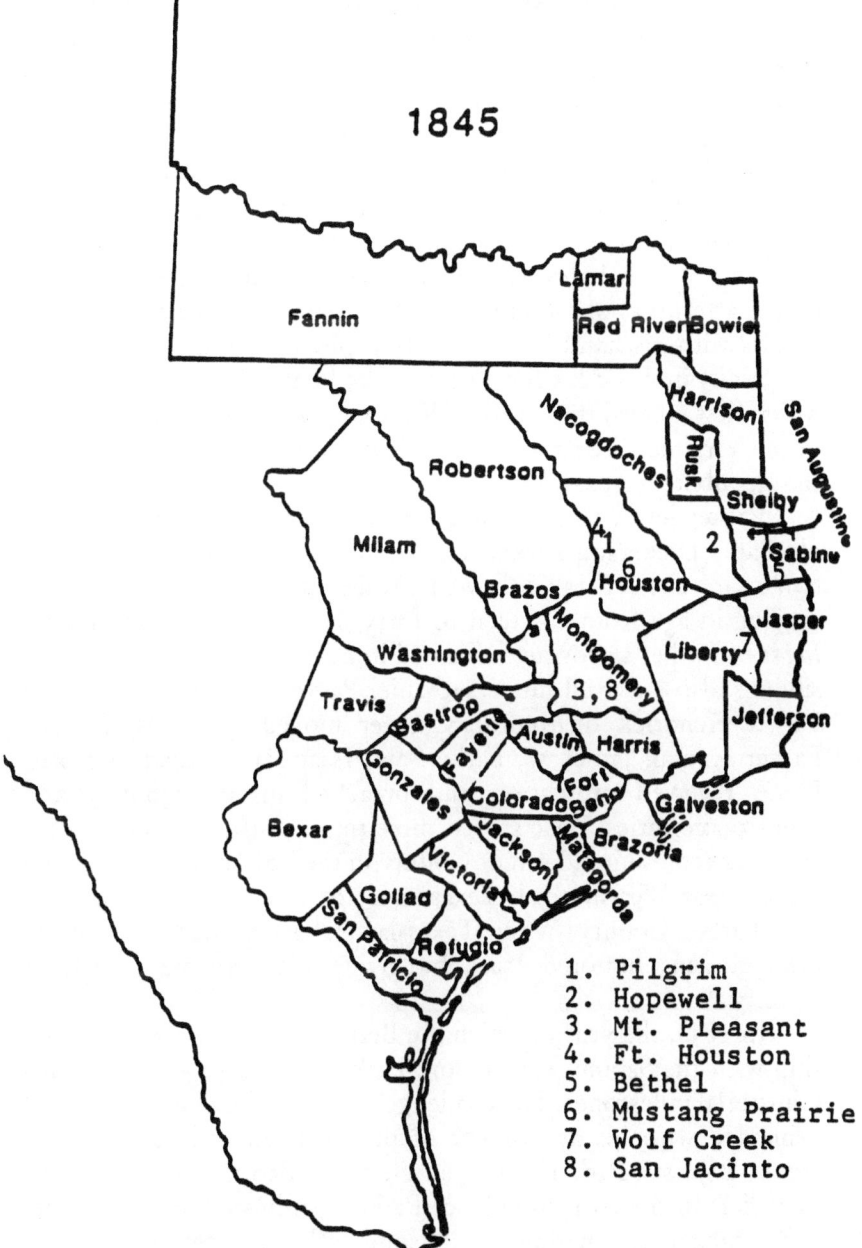

Figure 4. Churches organized by Parker. Based on Historical Atlas of Texas by Ray A. Stephens and William Holmes.

fulfilled his duties as moderator. Less than two weeks later, Parker meticulously tallied a debt which had been owed to him for smith work, corn, and bacon. Yet his strength ebbed in the wake of increased physical distress. Near the end of November he became bedridden. With stoic demure Parker accepted the reality of imminent death. He calmly arranged personal and business affairs and instructed the attending physician to refrain from harsh medicines and procedures. He only requested treatment which would alleviate suffering. Shortly before death, his discomfort abated. Around 5:00 on the afternoon of December 3, 1844, the dying Parker closed his eyelids with his hands and serenely expired. The next day friends and family interred his remains near the Pilgrim Church. The body which first inhaled the breath of life along the Rappahannock Valley in the Virginia Piedmont rested a few yards from Boxe's Creek in the Republic of Texas.[72]

Parker left a large family. Survivors included sixty-one-year-old Patsy Dickerson Parker, his wife of forty-three years. Almost two years later, Patsy followed Daniel in death. Nine children, ranging in age from eighteen to forty-one, outlived their parents. Most of Parker's progeny remained in East Texas. Five of Daniel's siblings also survived him. Nathaniel Parker of Illinois and Mary Parker Kendrick of Kentucky never moved to Texas. Phoebe Parker Anglin, James W. Parker, and Isaac Parker died in Texas. James received ordination and preached in Montgomery and Houston counties. Isaac served three terms in the Texas Congress and later represented Tarrant County in the legislature. Isaac finally settled near Weatherford, Texas, west of Fort Worth, in what is now Parker County. When Texas lawmakers created the county, local citizens honored Isaac by giving his surname to Parker County.[73]

In 1843, the year in which the Bethel Church chose to fellowship with the Sabine Association, Parker paused to gaze upon his ministerial milestones. The challenge by the Sabine Association had coincided with his assessment of personal rank and significance among Baptists. Parker addressed a letter to Baptist historian David Benedict. In the correspondence Parker manifested his sentiments concerning denominational leadership. Parker asserted "the right of a showing among the baptists." Moreover, Parker trumpeted: "perhaps I have done as much in establishing the baptists in the faith which once delivered to the saints against the corruption of the mission errors, as any man west of the Blue Ridge. . . ."[74] But in Texas, as in Tennessee and Illinois, Parker failed to exercise complete control over Baptist affairs. Even as he penned these words, some of the flocks in Texas looked to other shepherds.

This development in part reflected trends among Evangelicals, especially Baptists and Methodists, throughout the South. In the 1840s schism had erupted over slavery. Following the American Revolution, many Baptists and Methodists in the South had opposed slavery. Composed of lower socio-economic groupings, these Evangelicals resented the economic and moral degradation which accompanied human bondage. Yet by the second quarter of the nineteenth century, opposition to slavery by southern Evangelicals had faded. This waning resulted from three causes. First, many seemed to recognize that slavery provided a foundation for the southern economy. This base prospered Evangelicals as well as other southerners. Second, the resultant economic boon placed some Baptists and Methodists on the rungs of the upper class. No longer did Evangelicals necessarily carry the opprobrium of backcountry, lower-class religionists. In cities and towns Methodist and Baptist congregations began to call educated pastors. Members may not have bowed to the god of wealth, but Mammon sat in their houses of worship. Well-built brick churches, furnished with expensive pews and organs, replaced crude meeting houses. Finally, southerners anesthetized the pricks of conscience by accepting slavery as a necessary evil. Slaveholders feared that the activities of abolitionists would expose whites to depredations at the hands of African-Americans. The overall good of society seemed to demand that southerners assumed the burden of protecting whites and civilizing blacks. Southerners therefore erected a moral facade around slavery. They justified slavery while condemning abolitionists as threats to a law-abiding Christian society.[75]

The efforts to protect southern churches against antislavery influences resulted in fissures in the national denominational structures of Baptists and Methodists. In 1844 the Baptist Foreign Mission Society refused to support a slaveholding missionary. Baptist congregations in the South responded by organizing the Southern Baptist Convention. The following year southern Methodist churches withdrew from the Methodist Episcopal Church over the ownership of slaves by bishops. The seceding Wesleyans formed the Methodist Episcopal Church, South.[76]

Southern society remained harshly rigid when it came to the institution of slavery. In Texas the fear of abolitionists prevented open criticism of slavery among Evangelicals. For example, ministers from the Methodist Episcopal church—or Northern Methodists as southerners termed it—continued to preach in Texas. Although these ministers dared not attack slavery, their refusal to affiliate with the Methodist Episcopal Church, South caused their neighbors to place them under scrutiny.[77] Southerners not only scrutinized antislavery advocates but kept close surveillance over the religious activities of slaves. Methodists, Presbyterians, Episcopalians, Cumberland Presbyterians, Disciples of Christ, and Baptists accepted slaves as members. From 1833 to 1859 the Pilgrim Predestinarian Regular Baptist Church recorded five African-American members.[78] Yet white congregations often prevented the formation of separate churches for African-Americans. Slaves either worshiped with their masters or attended separate services conducted under the watchful eyes of Anglos. Baptists allowed some ecclesiastical autonomy by black congregations but like other Evangelicals closely monitored the worship of slaves. In 1854 the Colorado Baptist Association accepted an African-American congregation into the association. But the following year, the missionary Union Baptist Association rejected an appeal for membership by an all African-American church.[79]

In addition to concerns over abolitionists, southern Evangelicals had arrived at a new-found level of social prominence. Texas Baptists, like their coreligionists across the South, had climbed the social and economic ladder. In 1854 Sam Houston, then United States senator from Texas, received immersion and joined the fellowship of the Independence Baptist Church.[80] Evidence of affluency appeared in the more settled areas east of the Trinity River. Trappings of urban society appeared in Marshall, Huntsville, Galveston, and Houston. From the mid-1840s to the 1850s Texas Baptists, most of whom had aligned with promissionary churches, reflected their growing wealth by heavy investments in denominational work. They began to support missionaries, a state paper, and several academies.[81] The growth of these churches and the decline of pro-Parker congregations reflected these broad socio-economic developments.

Daniel Parker had secured a permanent place in the history of Texas Baptists. Parker had planted the first Baptist church in Texas. Through his efforts, a Baptist seed had taken root in eastern Texas. Under the Lone Star, Parker had pursued his yearn for ecclesiastical leadership. At the same time, his desire to purify Baptists served to disqualify rival churchmen. Yet by the time of his death, the broader context of human bondage and the wealth which accompanied an agrarian economy supported by slavery influenced most Texas Baptists to identify with a more centralized denominational alliance.

Chapter 6

Conclusion: "A Man of War"

IN THE EARLY YEARS of his ministry Daniel Parker compared himself to an Old Testament warrior. A self-described "man of war," Parker exuded zeal.[1] He also evoked positive and negative reactions in others. For Parker life became a struggle. He represented the first generation of Americans to reach adulthood in the years that followed the American Revolution. Like many frontiersmen, he strove to claim the promise of egalitarianism which had accompanied the Revolutionary experience. His struggle occurred in the religious and political arenas. Yet the efforts of Parker in both realms took on an ambiguous nature.

The most glaring contradiction of his ministry centered around the conflict over Arminianism. For many Americans the Revolution had confirmed the hope of social and political equality. Arminian free will complemented the self-reliance and individualism of Jeffersonianism and Jacksonian democracy. The sentiments of independence quickly emerged in American Christianity. The camp meetings of the Second Great Awakening broadcast democratic soteriology, the spiritual counterpart to political freedom, across the backwoods. Juxtaposed against free will, Calvinism, with its arbitrary God and determinism, seemed antithetical to the American spirit of individual initiative and action. Across the Union churchmen sought to resolve this apparent contradiction. In New England, Unitarianism disputed orthodox Congregationalism. Unitarians heralded a message based on rationality and universal salvation. But the most intense rivalry emerged on the frontier. Backwoodsmen responded favorably to Arminian precepts. In Tennessee and Kentucky, Cumberland Presbyterians modified the strictures of election. The whosoever-will theme of Alexander Campbell and Barton Stone jolted the Baptist Church in the Ohio and Mississippi valleys. Although these movements proved challenging, the most serious competition came from Methodism. Frontiersmen flocked to the Methodist fold. In the face of these inroads, Baptists sometimes mitigated or compromised their stand on election.

The free will of Arminianism likewise prompted a struggle in the psyche of Parker. The spiritual stirrings of the Second Great Awakening had swept across the Georgia backwoods. This phenomenon produced conversions that circumvented the prolonged soul searching which often characterized Calvinism. Witnessing the emotional crest of camp meetings, teen-aged Daniel Parker pondered the efficacy of Arminian doctrine.[2] But external conditions along with personal experiences and convictions had welded Parker to Calvinistic tenets. Particular Baptists, the ecclesiastical forebears of Parker, had cherished election. The principles of total depravity, unconditional election, limited atonement, irresistible grace, and the perseverance of the saints illuminated their understanding of divine grace. Frontiersmen, who thought of themselves as the elect, found solace in election. Calvinism thus blanketed backwoodsmen —exposed to death, sickness, hardship, and sorrow—with eternal security. Rather than helpless pawns of nature, the elect had a place in the predestined counsel of God. Although socially and economically impoverished, the frontiersman, if numbered among the elect, would ultimately experience heavenly bliss.

The resistance of Parker to the Arminian challenge echoed his desire for self-assertion. The Revolution had imbued Americans with a patriotism which bordered on religious fervor. Out of all nations of the then modern world, "Providence had assigned a world mission to the American nation."[3] The former colonists had received a sacred trust. Americans became the guardians of liberty for the world. In this vein, Parker sought to protect the Union against perfidy and simultaneously to defend the doctrinal purity of Baptists. Parker believed that the Baptist Church existed as the only true Church.⁴ But Arminian leaven threatened to corrupt the Baptist message. Parker therefore felt responsible to resist the doctrine as an assault on the true Church.

As a defender of the faith, the ministry had endowed Parker with a degree of prominence among frontier Baptists. Under republican ideals, the commoner could enjoy political, social, and economic benefits. Through his standing as a minister, Parker had the opportunity to reap respect and a position of leadership. Yet the Arminian challenge threatened him with disgrace. If Arminianism proved true, the elect did not occupy a special place in the plan of God. Consequently, if his message encountered defeat, the ministerial credentials of Parker stood in jeopardy.⁵ Also, Baptist desertions to Methodist and Christian Reformer folds stiffened the competitive bid for members on the frontier. Parker therefore chose to resist perceived Arminian encroachments on his denomination, doctrine, honor, and opportunities for social advancement.

Ecclesiastical innovations, which seemed to advance Arminianism, posed another danger. Parker deemed that societies for missions and benevolence imperiled the authority of local Baptist churches. The republican impulse undergirded Baptist commitment to congregational self-government. Parker proclaimed that the autonomy of the local church should not suffer compromise. Thus challenged, Parker chose "to draw the sword and fight."⁶

The missions controversy virtually obsessed Parker. The scripture, "The zeal of thine house hath eaten me up," appeared on the title pages of the *Church Advocate*.⁷ But the missions controversy did not originate with Parker. Others had voiced earlier protests. Opposition to centralized benevolence first appeared in the East. As early as 1805 the Hopewell Baptist Church in Mercer County, New Jersey, refused to collect funds for missionary or educational purposes.⁸ In the 1820s and early 1830s Joshua Lawrence in North Carolina and Gilbert Beebe in New York championed antimissionism in the East. Parker assumed that he had been the first American Baptist to take up the pen against missionary societies. He based his claim on the June or July 1820 publication of *A Public Address*, his first antimissions essay.⁹ But he erred in this assumption. Before Parker had published his work, westerner John Taylor already had decried missionary societies. In October 1819 sixty-seven-year-old Taylor, a Kentucky minister, had written *Thoughts on Missions*. In this antimissions composition Taylor denounced salaried missionaries as "sponges."[10]

The opposition to institutionalized missions and benevolence soon took on a quasi-denominational nature. In September 1832 representatives from antimissions churches in Maryland, Pennsylvania, New Jersey, Delaware, New York, and Virginia assembled at the Black Rock Church near Baltimore, Maryland. These messengers issued the Black Rock Address. This statement disavowed tract societies, Sunday schools, Bible societies, missionary societies, revival meetings, and theological schools as ostentatious, unscriptural, and man-made supplantations of sovereign grace. The churches that agreed with the Black Rock Address called themselves Old School or Primitive Baptists.[11] Although these churches did not embrace a centralized denominational structure, they rejected promissions Baptists as doctrinally unsound.

Parker did not participate personally in the Black Rock convention. Yet Parker exercised such a profound influence on the antimissions cause that he has been portrayed erroneously as a founder of Old School Baptists. As early as 1839 John Mason Peck wrote that Parker in the West and North Carolinian Joshua Lawrence cofounded "this sect."[12] In his zeal to discredit Parker and Lawrence, Peck overstated their significance. Although Parker and Lawrence polarized opposition to missions, neither man established the Primitive Baptist Church. Rather than a formally organized denomination, the group took on the nature of a loosely knit fellowship. Furthermore, the tenets of Old School Baptists predated Parker and Lawrence. The emphases of Primitive Baptists on congregational polity, associational participation, and election had appeared among the English Particular Baptists in the seventeenth and eighteenth centuries.

But more than any other figure Parker coalesced the prevailing sentiments of antimissionism in the West. Tennessee, the home of the missionary Southern Baptist Convention, felt the overpowering influence of Parker. Regardless of the influence of the Southern Baptist Convention, many Tennessee Baptists came to reject missionism. In 1845 Dr. Robert Boyte Crawford Howell, pastor of the First Baptist Church of Nashville and a leading figure in the Southern Baptist Convention, credited the stiff resistance to Parker. Howell alleged that in the early nineteenth century the majority of

Tennessee Baptist congregations initially had favored missionary societies. Yet the Arminian-disposed Methodists and Cumberland Presbyterians had rivaled Baptists. According to Howell, Parker used this challenge to mount a defense of election. In the process Parker anathematized missionary societies as the tool of Arminians. In so doing, he gained favor among Volunteer State Baptists and "set in motion the means that overthrew missions in Tennessee."[13]

In his struggle against missionary societies, Parker touted as virtually sacred the principle of congregational autonomy. But his espousal of independent church polity unveiled another contradiction. Although Parker professed allegiance to congregational self-government, at times he breached this principle. In Tennessee he incited discord in the Concord Association. Through his influence, Parker threatened to implement schism among the churches of the association. After becoming involved in the missions controversy in Illinois, he pushed to oust the Maria Creek Church from the Wabash District Association. Maria Creek had not fallen into doctrinal error. The congregation merely had allowed its membership the discretion to support the Baptist Board of Foreign Missions. Because of the mutual associational adherence to congregational autonomy, the decision by Maria Creek should not have evoked disciplinary action by other member churches. The attempt of the association to compel uniformity resulted in division. The ensuing rancor sparked personal rivalries over associational leadership. Before the controversy peaked, Parker had incorporated the missions issue into attacks on political foes.

The second religious controversy that whirled around Parker concerned Two Seedism. The doctrine provoked division among western Baptists, including Parker's Old School brethren. Yet Parker never anticipated that his hermeneutic would create such a stir.[14] He initially formulated the doctrine as a defense against political opponents and ecclesiastical advocates of the missions system. Satan proved a convenient scapegoat for Parker. Instead of conceding personal shortcomings, frontier preachers such as Parker often claimed that "the Devil had camped on his trail and had undone his work."[15] But Parker did not confine his scapegoating to a local congregation. His paper, the *Church Advocate*, disseminated Two Seedism over much of the South and West. As early as 1831 the doctrine, also known as Parkerism, seemed synonymous with the ministry of Daniel Parker. Any positive contributions of Parker became clouded by Two Seedism.[16]

Shortly after publication of the doctrine in 1826, Baptists in Illinois, Indiana, Kentucky, Tennessee, Mississippi, and Louisiana began to divide over the controversial theology. By 1834 a Two-Seed congregation in southeastern Louisiana had endorsed "the eternal existence of the Devil."[17] In 1842 the Cumberland Baptist Association in Tennessee officially condemned Two Seedism. This association included some of the churches in Dickson County which had been acquainted with the early ministry of Parker. A year after Cumberland censored Parkerism, the Stone's River Association, also in Tennessee, disavowed Two Seedism.[18]

By the eve of the Civil War, the proponents of Two Seedism particularly troubled many Old School Baptists. In 1860 Elder John M. Watson, who had ministered in the Stone's River Association in 1844, published a refutation of Parkerism. Watson confessed that Two-Seed adherents had caused "great excitement at this time."[19] Moreover, he lamented that Parkerism had taken on a genuinely heretical bent. Watson twined the origin of the heterodoxy to Manichaeanism, a third-century dualistic heresy with roots in Persia. Manichaeanism taught the existence of two opposing but eternal forces—the king of light and the king of darkness. The soul of man linked him to the kingdom of light. Yet man could be liberated only by a mystical exposure to the light of Christ.

Alexander Campbell initially seems to have charged Parker with Manichaean heresy. In 1830 Campbell tied Two Seedism with Manichaean dualism and Zoroastrian concepts of good and evil. Campbell referred to Parker as "the author of American Manichaeanism, and teacher of Persian Predestination."[20] This assertion overstated Parker's understanding of church history. With limited education, Daniel Parker had little or no knowledge of ancient heresies when he published *Views on the Two Seeds*. Parker later admitted that he initially "knew nothing of 'Manichean.'"[21] But after being informed of the Manichaean dualism, Parker conceded that he agreed with "some points" of Manichaean doctrine.[22] Parker did not divulge these areas of agreement. Yet over the next thirty years, those who had imbibed the Parkerian hermeneutic compounded Two Seedism into a more complex metaphysic. Their expansion of Parkerism did mirror dualistic elements of Gnosticism and Manichaeanism. First-century Gnosticism, influenced by Greek philosophy, posited a docetic view of matter. The material world remained corrupt. Only spiritual beings could experience salvation. Hence, liberated spirits could not become corrupted by association with the physical. In a similar vein, more radical Two Seeders held that death liberated the spirits of the elect and nonelect. The elect would return to God. Conversely, the nonelect would revert to Satan. In either case, only the soul had consequence. Because the spirit remained the essence of being, the promise of resurrection only applied to spirits rather than bodies. Hence, some Two Seeders denied the literal bodily resurrection of the righteous.[23]

Parkerism never became an accepted dogma among Old School Baptists. Yet a lack of consensus existed among Primitive Baptists concerning the position of Two Seedism as an orthodox doctrine. Some Baptists openly repudiated the teaching and others took a middle-of-the-road position and tolerated Parkerism as a theological quirk. While not endorsing its tenets, moderates did not make the doctrine a test of orthodoxy. But in some areas Two Seedism drew a receptive following. By the 1860s many Primitive Baptist ministers in southern Illinois, the area where Parker first published his doctrine, strongly held to Two Seedism.[24]

With the passage of time, most Old School Baptists rejected Two Seedism. Increasingly, they questioned the scriptural basis for Parkerism. Even Benjamin Parker, a son of Daniel and successor to the Pilgrim Baptist Church pulpit, refused to countenance Two Seedism. In 1876 the Texas Union Association of Regular Predestinarian Baptists, founded by Daniel Parker in 1840, officially condemned Two Seedism.[25] In the 1870s and 1880s certain Primitive Baptist authors issued strong caveats against Two Seedism. The arguments evidently proved effectual. By the early twentieth century, Parkerian dualism had fallen into general disfavor among Primitive Baptists.[26] Over the course of the twentieth century, the supporters of Two Seedism dwindled. In 1893 Two-Seed congregations reported 9,932 in membership, yet by 1975 only two known Two-Seed congregations survived. These churches, a congregation near Greencastle, Indiana, and another near Jacksboro, Texas, totaled eighty-four members.[27]

At first glance, the Two-Seed doctrine appears to have been little more than a theological anomaly. Written in self-defense, the interpretation had been formulated to bolster Parker's maligned reputation. *Views on the Two Seeds,* published in the same year that Parker sought reelection to the Illinois Assembly, refuted attacks against him. Yet at a deeper level, Two Seedism evidenced his desire for self-assertion as a backwoods theologian and politician.

In religion and politics Parker evidenced a distaste for opulence and privilege. Of yeoman stock, he had endured labor and privation on the Georgia, Tennessee, and Illinois frontiers. Like many subsistence farmers in the Upper South, Parker competed against the cultural hegemony of the slaveholding planter class. Without formal education and social polish, his initial participation in politics had been limited. But opportunities for political leadership in newly formed Illinois allowed him to enter political life. Perhaps Parker's initial impetus for entering politics had been influenced by the missions' issue. An illusion in *A Public Address* revealed this concern. Parker feared that the encroachments of the missions system might corrupt "our republican government," resulting in "blessed liberty" being "snatched from us."[28] Parker possibly felt that a legislative post would provide leverage against attempted inroads into government by missionary societies. Perhaps such anxiety explains an allegation by Parker's political enemies concerning his 1822 candidacy for the Illinois Assembly.[29] According to them, Parker had boasted that he had been divinely called to legislate for the people.

But in spite of Parker's professed commitment to republicanism, his political life did not always coincide with these principles. To Parker, the location of Columbia College in the national capital and the work of salaried missionaries on governmentally operated Indian stations proved a dangerous liaison between church and state. Yet his abhorrence of a church-state link faded when personal opportunities for public office appeared. Parker's fear of mixing religion and government did not prevent him from claiming divine leadership in campaigning for office in Illinois. Moreover, in Texas Parker sought public office even though his candidacy violated the law.

This apparent inconsistency regarding church and state appeared in the writings of Parker. His publications merged politics and religion. In one of the few references to earlier Baptists, Parker extolled the writings of Baptist minister John Leland. Leland had been reared in New England, where an established church had received tax support. Leland remained convinced that established religion and coercive contributions violated principles of political and religious conscience. After moving to Virginia in 1776, Leland spearheaded opposition to an established church among his Old Dominion brethren. Moreover, Leland had pushed for guarantees of religious freedom in the Bill or Rights.[30] Parker cited "A Blow at the Roots," a sermon by Leland printed in 1805, in the *Church Advocate*.[31] In his sermon Leland expressed an open admiration for republicanism and Thomas Jefferson. Leland referred to Jefferson as "the Man of the People," "a defender of the rights of man," and his "hero."[32]

But Parker exceeded the advocacy of Leland for freedom of conscience. Echoing the Jacksonian animosity for overarching agencies, Parker aimed his political pen at the eastern missionary societies. In August 1831 Parker observed: "and the time has now come when the honest politician who will not sell the rights of his country for the friendship of the mission supporters, may expect to fall under their displeasure. . . ."[33] Financially strapped because of publishing costs, Parker nevertheless thought it prudent to publish an extra edition of the *Church Advocate*. In this final publication, Parker expressly reprinted a Fourth of July sermon by Joshua Lawrence. Lawrence warned that professional clergy and missions societies intended to entrench themselves within the national government. Once there, the would-be despots would form a church-state link that promised to destroy hard-won freedoms. The article decried the loss of "civil and religious liberty" and the republican form of government if the danger continued unabated.[34]

Another political ambiguity concerned slavery. In Illinois the political baptism of Parker accompanied the struggle for the legalization of slavery. The contest against human bondage underscored his disdain for the planter class. Parker charged that affluent slaveholders obtained wealth from the lash-bloodied backs of black bondsmen.[35] In 1824 Illinoisans balloted their preferences on the issue of a proposed constitutional convention. If approved, the convention would have allowed the electorate to vote on legalized slavery. Parker sided with the legislative minority who opposed the convention.[36]

But after Parker had immigrated to Texas, he muffled personal opposition to human bondage. Political, economic, and social issues influenced his opposition to slavery in Illinois. Under the Lone Star these same concerns pulled him toward the opposite pole. In Texas Parker still identified with the "labouring class of men."[37] In so doing, he resented the excessive influence and perversion of justice by professional politicians, lawyers, and large land speculators. Economic survival on the Texas frontier proved tenuous in the early 1840s. Caught in the grip of a national depression, yeomen landowners struggled to maintain solvency. A large number of Anglo-Texan landholders viewed slavery as a necessary ingredient for economic prosperity. By the 1840s Parker owned several thousand acres of Texas land, and his economic future thus became linked to the continued exploitation of African-Americans.

Parker was not a political chameleon. He did not allow political whims to alter his position. At the same time, he recognized political reality. Perhaps the reticence of Parker resulted more from his fear of the potential social unrest wrought by abolitionists than from his personal support for slavery. Yet Parker's purse strings and opportunities for advancement remained tied to slavery. In Illinois large landowners such as Ninian Edwards and Edward N. Cullom had prospered from the sale of large amounts of land. Parker evidently hoped to do the same in Texas. But the Panic of 1837 set in motion economic repercussions which reached Texas. Declining land prices coupled with high prices for consumer goods dashed his hopes for quick wealth. The abolition of slavery might have resulted in decreased immigration and exacerbated economic woes. Moreover, the backlash of public sentiment against suspected abolitionists would have dimmed preacher Parker's chances for ministerial influence among the fledgling Baptist churches in Texas.

Rivalry, contention, and faction characterized Daniel Parker. But Parker represents more than a factious malcontent. He reflects the turbulent nature of post-Revolutionary frontier America. As a result of the Louisiana Purchase of 1803, the extended borders of the United States included the Mississippi River and its tributaries. The survival of the United States during the War of 1812, pinnacled by the accompanying victory of United States troops over the British army at New Orleans, stirred nationalism among Americans. Settlers, anxious to partake of economic opportunities, streamed toward the western frontier. In the process, they boosted a demand for goods, transportation, and an expansion of capital. Bankers, merchants, manufacturers, and entrepreneurs sought to profit from this boom.

In such a climate Parker assimilated the democratic spirit of Jeffersonian republicanism. The social and political oppression of Baptists in Virginia in the 1770s had influenced his aversion to established churches. One of the primary factors that fueled the opposition of Parker to missionary societies concerned the fear that local churches and associations might forfeit their independence. In Illinois and Texas he entered the political arena as a contender for the common citizen. In political and denominational circles he manifested a keen distaste for rank and privilege. Part of his antipathy remained rooted in sectional and class divisions.

Increased industrialization, an expanding economy, and a broadened transportation system exacerbated East-West differences. Sectional conflicts also carried religious overtones. New England remained a bastion of federalism. Many New England Protestant clergy, especially Congregationalists, favored federalism. But the Jeffersonian opposition to tax-supported churches threatened New England Congregational clergy. Federalists also distrusted the virtue and reason of ordinary men. Such political sentiments meshed with the philanthropic impetus of New England Protestant churchmen. Strongly influenced by Puritanism, many of these ministers remained convinced that the responsibility for a moral society rested on the elect. New England Protestants therefore felt impelled to save the West from profligacy and cultural decay. In the process they also wished to protect the West from unworthy men. Federalist churchmen equated Jeffersonian republicanism with deism, atheism, and agnosticism. Many New England clergy feared that the unrighteous might seize power and impede Christian society. By exporting education, benevolence, and evangelism, New England denominations hoped to exercise some degree of political and social control over the West.[38]

Although the battle cry had first been heard in the East, the struggle against missions reached its apex in the West. Frontier opposition to the missions system clearly manifested an antieastern bias. Around 1811 John Taylor had been offended by a visit from two New England fund-soliciting supporters of missions. Eight years later the venerable frontier Baptist recalled that their visit had caused him "to smell the *New England Rat.*"³⁹ Moreover, he commented that the so-called conversion of Luther Rice and Adoniram Judson to Baptist ranks had provided "no evidence of their religious or political principles being changed."⁴⁰ The publications of Parker likewise indicate an aversion to the East. In 1830 Richard N. Newport, the principal associate of Parker in Illinois, assailed the eastern ecclesiastical establishment in a letter to the *Church Advocate.*

> If we were to judge of the baptists in the eastern or old states, by the few *fleece hunters, time servers,* and *men pleasers,* whose motto is GIVE, GIVE, that have come among us from that quarter, it indeed would be very unfavorable. . . .⁴¹

Yet Newport did not hold all easterners responsible. He confessed that "there are precious sound baptists in and from the old states who are among the foremost in opposing these violators."⁴²

Negative sentiments toward the East also incorporated class resentment. Parker remained aware of the cultural and economic disparities that existed between East and West. He even faulted some eastern Old School Baptists, his antimissions brethren, for their alleged ostentations. In 1842 Parker countered an attack by Virginian Samuel Trott. Elder Trott, an Old School minister, had been critical of Two Seedism. He also had objected to some comments which Parker had made in favor of foot washing, a rite observed by many frontier Baptist churches.⁴³ Parker replied:

> . . . the exalted marks of distinction, too often manifested between the proposed followers of Christ are brought down. . . . Now, let some of the masters, or rich brethren in Virginia, or elsewhere, come to the black rusty feet of their Negro, or poor brother, (who perhaps are equally pious and beloved in Christ as themselves) and wash their feet as a disciple of the Saviour. . . .⁴⁴

But not all of Parker's opponents reveled in pomp and wealth. The Baptists who had received the brunt of his attacks lived in frontier Tennessee, Illinois, Indiana, and Texas. Furthermore, those western Baptists had social and theological foundations which reflected the background of Parker. William Polke and his Maria Creek brethren had roots in frontier Kentucky. Early Texan Isaac Reed hailed from Tennessee. Polke and Reed had been grounded in election. Moreover, affluence did not surround these coreligionists.

They did pose, however, a threat to Parker's leadership. Republicanism and the frontier had allowed rough-hewn Parker the opportunity to achieve a degree of eminence. But opponents threatened to deprive him of self-realized leadership. The resistance by Parker to Polke and Reed revealed a determination to claim his place in religion and politics.

In the effort to maintain church and doctrinal purity, Parker seems to have overstepped his authority. The penchant of Parker for faction and domination stands in sharp contrast to republican ideals. Because the excessive use of influence violated cardinal principles of republicanism, virtuous republicans regarded power seekers as dangerous to government and society. Republicans thought that self-serving despots used cabals and factions to accomplish their intrigues.[45] Although seemingly a gross violation of republicanism, Parker did not deem his actions to be a transgression of republican or Baptist principles. In his mind he had acted in the best interests of republicanism. Parker felt justified that he had protected Baptists against power-grasping missionary societies.

Shaped by Jeffersonian republicanism and seasoned in Jacksonian democracy, Parker engaged in conflict. He struggled to protect church and government against economic and social developments which challenged republicanism and opportunities for the common man. Similar to other self-made frontier churchmen, Parker favored the ancient practices of New Testament Christianity. His espousal of primitivism called for strict New Testament church polity. His panoramic view of the spiritual history of mankind extended from the dawn of Creation to the Second Coming. The Two-Seed doctrine transported the Church from the innocence of Eden to the apocalyptic consummation of the ages. He anxiously waited for the millennium, when God would intervene and destroy the enemies of righteousness. The new age would be marked by social justice and harmony.[46] Having kept the Church unstained, Parker could enjoy the fruits of his labor in the approaching millennium. Unfortunately, personal ambition tainted his efforts.

In terms of politics Parker was neither a perfect example of Jeffersonian republicanism nor Jacksonian democracy. Possessing traits of both ideologies, Parker emerges as a transitional figure. Reflecting the Revolutionary experience, Parker exalted republicanism. Yet his factious nature and desire for self-advancement did not cast him as a model of the virtuous citizenry that Jefferson had desired. Instead, in temperament and background Parker more nearly conformed to the Jacksonian mold. Parker and Jackson, both self-made and reared on the southern frontier, rose from poverty to achieve political prominence and material benefits. Instead of owning a small tract of land, Jackson became a large planter. By the time of his death, Parker also had amassed several thousand acres. Likewise, as men of war Parker and Jackson fiercely defended their individual realms and reputations. Jackson did so in the smoke of battle and with fists and dueling pistols. Parker launched his salvos from the pulpit.

But other aspects indicate that Parker was not a perfect Jacksonian. For example, backwoodsman Parker first voiced opposition to eastern missionary societies in 1816, several years before the Panic of 1819 and the ensuing sectional tensions which fueled the national political ascendancy of Jackson. Moreover, in Illinois Parker seemed not to have endorsed the party system which characterized the Jacksonian era. Rather, he appears to have campaigned more as an individual.

Early attention to Parker focused almost entirely on his schismatic effect on frontier Baptists. The salient aspect of this issue has been the missions controversy. With one brief exception, the political career of Parker has been ignored.[47] This book has sought to illuminate some previously unanalyzed or unknown aspects of the life and influence of Daniel Parker. First, Parker achieved political as well as religious importance. In certain respects he represented the republican characteristics of early nineteenth-century American Protestantism.[48] These attributes included the desire to elevate the self-taught theologian over the professional clergyman. Second, Parker played a significant political role in the contests over slavery in Illinois and the Republic of Texas. Particularly noteworthy in this regard is the manner in which political, social, and economic developments governed the response of Parker. Third, Parker provided valuable leadership for the government of Texas during the early days of the Revolution as a member of its Committee on State Affairs. In his role as a statesman and private citizen, Parker also attempted to influence Sam Houston in the critical period of Houston's first and second presidential terms. Finally, the reaction of Parker to the dynamics of local frontier politics offers insight into the tight web of church and community. For example, legal assaults by political challenger Wickliff Kitchell and disgruntled church members sparked the initial publication of his Two-Seed hermeneutic. Often, as in the case of William Polke and Thomas Kennedy, the fight against missionism had political overtones. The appearance of factions coupled denominational controversies with politics. Thus, Parker emerges not as a simple frontier preacher but rather as a significant religious and political leader in the West. While in those roles he helped to shape developments, he also felt the influence of social, economic, and political developments on the frontier.

Endnotes

NOTES TO INTRODUCTION
1. John Bond, *History of the Baptist Concord Association* (Nashville: Graves, Marks & Company, 1860), 28.
2. Charles True Goodsell, "The Baptist Anti-Missionary Movement in America" (M.A. diss., University of Chicago, 1924); Carlos Ebilton Bezerra, "Sources and Early History of the Anti-mission Controversy in the United States" (Th.M. thesis, Southern Baptist Theological Seminary, 1956); Byron Cecil Lambert, "The Rise of the Anti-Mission Baptists: Sources and Leaders, 1800-1840 (Ph.D. diss., University of Chicago, 1957). Guy W. Small completed "The Life of Daniel Parker at East Texas Baptist College in 1954. This sometimes inaccurate and unclear thesis simply narrates the life of Parker. Perhaps the most complete examination of Parker's dualism is "Daniel Parker's Doctrine of the Two Seeds" by O. Max Lee. Written as a Th.M. thesis at Southern Baptist Theological Seminary in 1962, the author concluded that Parker published the doctrine as an apology to the critics of election.

CHAPTER 1: GEORGIA AND TENNESSEE: THE FORMATIVE YEARS
1. *Church Advocate*, 2 (September 1831), 268.
2. W[illiam] H[enry] Perrin, A. A. Graham, and D. M. Blaim, comps., *The History of Coles County, Illinois* (Chicago: Wm. Le Baron, Jr., 1879; reprint, Evansville, Ind.: Unigraphic, 1969), 290; Kenneth Coleman, ed., *A History of Georgia* (Athens: University of Georgia, 1977), 106.
3. Robert E. Corlew, *Tennessee: A Short History* (Knoxville: University of Tennessee, 1981), 92.
4. Parker Genealogy File, Palestine Public Library, Palestine, Texas.
5. *Church Advocate*, 259.
6. Ibid., 263.
7. Daniel Parker Family Bible, Elkhart State Bank, Elkhart, Texas.
8. Sydney E. Ahlstrom, *A Religious History of the American People* (New Haven: Yale, 1972), 365.
9. John B. Boles, *The Great Revival, 1787-1805* (Lexington: University of Kentucky, 1972), 19-20; Wesley M. Gewehr, *The Great Awakening in Virginia, 1740-1790* (Durham: Duke University, 1930), 173.
10. Ahlstrom, *Religious History*, 433.

162   *FRONTIER RELIGION*

11. Ibid., 433-36.
12. Boles, *Great Revival,* 82.
13. *Minutes of the Georgia Baptist Association, 1803* (Augusta, Geo.: William J. Bunce, [1804]), no pagination.
14. *Church Advocate,* 267.
15. John Asplund, *The Universal Register of the Baptist Denomination in North America* (Boston: John W. Folsom, 1794; reprint, New York: Arno, 1980), 54 (page reference is to re-print edition).
16. Turnbull Baptist Church Minutes, Oct. 1806. Manuscript Division, Tennessee State Archives, Nashville.
17. Merrill E. Gaddis, "Religious Ideas and Attitudes in the Early Frontier," *Church History* 2 (1933), 167.
18. Robert E. Corlew, *A History of Dickson County, Tennessee* (Nashville: Tennessee Historical Commission, 1956), 19.
19. *Impartial Review,* July 4, 1807.
20. Turnbull Minutes, April 1806.
21. Ibid., May 1806. Daniel Parker, Sr. remained in Dickson County and had died by April 6, 1818. See Majorie Hood Fischer, comp. *Tennessee Tidbits,* 1778-1914, vol. 1 (Easley, S.C.: Southern Historical Press, 1986), 291.
22. Ordination qualified itinerants for a pastorate. But ordination did not necessarily convey an automatic invitation to pastoral leadership of the ordaining congregation.
23. Turnbull Minutes, September 1807.
24. Ibid., September 1806-April 1807.
25. Mill Creek Baptist Church Records, 1797-1814, June 30, 1804; April 18, 1807, Manuscript Division, Tennessee State Archives, Nashville. Two women, "Sary Parker, Junr." and "Sary Parker, Sen'r" are included among those present at the organizational meeting of the Turnbull Church in April 1806. "Sary Parker, Sen'r" became a bona fide member of Turnbull and eventually received a letter of dismissal from that congregation. The events surrounding the other "Sary" are unknown. "Sary, Junr." may have been the "Sally" referred to by the Mill Creek Church. If so, she possibly had not been officially dismissed from the Mill Creek Church when the charter members of Turnbull gathered. See Turnbull Church Minutes, April 1806.
26. Turnbull Minutes, April 7, 1809.
27. The Turnbull minutes fail to explain his absence. The document simply states that the church, without a pastor, chose "brother murvel" as Daniel's successor. See Turnbull Minutes, May 1807.
28. Ibid.
29. *Church Advocate,* 269.
30. Dickson County Deed Book, A:283-84, Clerk of Court, Charlotte, Tenn.
31. Walter T. Durham, *The Great Leap Westward* (Gallatin, Tenn.: Sumner County Public Library, 1969), 129.
32. Arthur M. Schlesinger, Jr., *The Age of Jackson* (Boston: Little, Brown, 1945), 126.
33. Glyndon G. Van Deusen, *The Life of Henry Clay* (Boston: Little, Brown, 1937), 111.

34. *Church Advocate*, 270.

35. Ibid., 275; James Winchester and William Cage Account Books, September 28, 1811. m.f. 180, Tennessee State Archives, Nashville.

36. Dickson County Deed Book, A:283-84.

37. Ibid., 355-56.

38. Sumner County Deed Book, 6:27-28, Tennessee State Archives, Nashville.

39. *Church Advocate*, 270.

40. Deane Porch, ed. *Sumner County, Tennessee Marriage Records* (Franklin, Tenn.: Louise G. Lynch, n.d.), 5; Sumner County Inventories, November 1816, 319, Tennessee State Archives, Nashville. Parker family genealogist Jane Parker Brown, 32785 Genoa Rd., Genoa, Illinois, suggests that Nathaniel Parker was the grandfather of Daniel Parker, Jr. Proof has not been definitely documented. It seems likely, however, that kinship existed. The children of Nathaniel Parker bore first names remarkably similar to the children of John Parker. John and Nathaniel Parker had roots in the same general areas of northern Virginia and Maryland. Although Nathaniel Parker's family were loyal Methodists, Richard, one of his sons, had by 1816 joined a church pastored by Daniel Parker. See Minutes of the Concord Association, 1816, Southern Baptist Historical Commission, Nashville.

41. Jay Guy Cisco, *Historic Sumner County, Tennessee* (n.p.: By the author, 1909), 287.

42. *Church Advocate*, 269-70.

43. Ibid., 295, 361.

44. *Democratic Clarion and Tennessee Gazette*, January 7, 1812; *Carthage Gazette*, February 8, 1812.

45. W. P. Strickland, ed., *Autobiography of Peter Cartwright* (Cincinnati: L. Swormstedt & A. Poe, 1860), 180.

46. *Minutes of the Concord Association, 1812* (Nashville: M. & J. Norvell, [1812]), 2; John Bond, *History of the Baptist Concord Association* (Nashville: Graves, Marks & Company, 1860), 20.

47. McFerrin, *History of Methodism*, 2:262.

48. *Minutes of the Concord Association, 1812*, 2.

49. Walter T. Durham, *Old Sumner: A History of Sumner County, Tennessee From 1805 to 1861* (Gallatin, Tenn.: Sumner County Public Library, 1972), 12.

50. J. H. Grime, *History of Middle Tennessee Baptists* (Cave City, Ky.: By the author, 1902), 330-31.

51. John B[erry] McFerrin, *History of Methodism in Tennessee*, vol. 1 (Nashville: A. H. Redford, 1875), 296.

52. Robert G. Torbet, *A History of the Baptists*, 3d ed. (Valley Forge, Pa.: Judson, 1963), 34-42, 223.

53. Gaddis, "Religious Ideas," 152-170.

54. Rhys Isaac, "Evangelical Revolt: The Nature of the Baptists' Challenge to the Traditional Order in Virginia, 1765 to 1775," *The William and Mary Quarterly* 31 (July 1974): 354-55.

55. Jude 3.

56. Torbet, *History of the Baptists*, 225-34.

57. Thomas F. O'Dea, *Sociology and the Study of Religion: Theory, Research, Interpretation* (New York: Basic Books, 1970), 211.

58. McFerrin, *History of Methodism*, 2:192.

59. Ibid., 265-67.

60. *Church Advocate*, 270.

61. Ibid., 272.

62. Ibid., 273; Parker Family Papers, "Biography of Daniel Parker," item 141, Center for American History, University of Texas, Austin; McFerrin, *History of Methodism*, 1:263-64.

63. *Church Advocate*, 273; Samuel King was a Methodist minister in the Nashville District around 1812. See McFerrin, *History of Methodism*, 3:74. Another noted Sumner County preacher by the same name cofounded the Cumberland Presbyterian denomination near Charlotte, Tennessee, in 1810. The Cumberland Presbyterians, much like the Methodists, rejected the traditional Presbyterian doctrine of strict election and limited atonement. See W.P.A. Church Records, 1785-1942, Acc. 1072, Box 7, File 3, Tennessee State Archives, Nashville.

64. "Biography of Daniel Parker."

65. *Church Advocate*, 274.

66. *Minutes of the Concord Association, 1812*, 1-2.

67. Bond, *Concord Association*, 23-25.

68. *Minutes of the Red River Baptist Association, 1816* (Russellville, Ky.: H. C. Sleight, [1816]), 1-6; *Minutes of the Red River Baptist Association, 1817* (Russellville, Ky.: George B. Crutcher, [1817]), 1-6.

69. Bond, *Concord Association*, 27-28.

70. James Ross, ed., *Life and Times of Elder Reuben Ross* (Philadelphia: Grant, Faires & Rodgers, n.d.; reprint, Nashville: McQuiddy, 1977), 145.

71. John Mason Peck, "Historical Sketches of the Baptist Denomination in Indiana, Illinois, and Missouri," *The Baptist Memorial and Monthly Chronicle* (15 July 1842), 198.

72. William G. McLoughlin, *New England Dissent, 1630-1833*, vol. 1 (Cambridge: Harvard, 1971), 340-49, 421-39.

73. David Benedict, *A General History of the Baptist Denomination in America* (New York: Lewis Colby, 1848), 821; Ahlstrom, *Religious History*, 320. Parker was aware of Kentucky Baptist affairs. In 1812 representatives from three Kentucky associations visited the Concord Association. See *Minutes of the Concord Association, 1812*.

74. Testament Baptist Church Minutes, Testament Baptist Church, Lafayette, Tenn.

75. Daniel Parker, *A Public Address* (Vincennes, Ind.: Stout & Osborn, 1820; reprint, Hamilton, Ill.: Hamilton Press, 1988), 50 (page reference is to reprint edition); Letter from Corbly Martin to Isaac McCoy, November 6, 1822, Isaac McCoy Papers [microfilm], Bracken Library, Ball State University, Muncie, Ind.; original at Kansas State Historical Society, Topeka; Daniel Parker, *The Second Dose of Doctrine on the Two Seeds* (Vincennes, Ind.: Elihu Stout, 1826 [1827]), 44-46.

76. Clifford S. Griffin, *Their Brothers' Keepers: Moral Stewardship in the United States, 1800-1865* (New Brunswick: Rutgers, 1960), 24.

77. Benedict, *General History*, 440.

78. B[enajah] H[arvey] Carroll, *The Genesis of American Anti-Missionism* (Louisville: Baptist Book Concern, 1902), 42-51; Torbet, *History of the Baptists*, 250.

79. Bond, *Concord Association*, 24-25.

80. *Minutes of Concord Association, 1816;* Daniel Parker, *The Author's Defence* (Vincennes, Ind.: E. Stout, 1824), 4.

81. Ibid.

82. Ibid.

83. Bond, *Concord Association*, 26.

84. *Minutes of Concord Association, 1816.*

85. *Latter Day Luminary*, 1 (May 1818), 119.

86. John Taylor, *Thoughts on Missions* (n.p., 1820), 9.

87. *Minutes of the Concord Association, 1817,* Southern Baptist Historical Commission, Nashville; Parker, *Author's Defence*, 4.

88. The Concord Minutes, 1817 do not indicate such a collection. They do record the appointment of two committees, one on finance and one on unfinished business. It is likely that the recommendation was an unofficial suggestion by one of these committees or an associational leader. Whitsitt and Wiseman, leaders in the promissions faction, served on the finance committee.

89. Bond, *Concord Association*, 27.

90. Ibid., 16.

91. Ibid., 20-23.

92. *Minutes of Concord Association, 1816–1817.*

93. Parker, *Author's Defence*, 4. The 1817 Concord Minutes contain no reference to Tilman or any alleged offense. Tilman and Arrington's Creek, his pastorate, are inexplicably absent from the list of member churches and messengers. The minutes of the Arrington's Creek Church, later known as Wilson's Creek, indicate that Tilman fell under the censure of the church. Tilman became involved in a difficulty with Patrick Mooney, another minister in the congregation. The church withdrew the preaching credentials of Tilman. In 1820 Tilman apologized to the congregation and had his credentials restored. See Wilson's Creek Minutes, 20 October, 24 November, 14 December 1816; 16 September 1820, Tennessee State Archives, Nashville.

94. Parker, *Author's Defence*, 4.

95. Bond, *Concord Association*, 26.

96. Grime, *History of Middle Tenn. Baptists*, 191-95.

97. Testament Minutes, January 8, 1815.

98. *Democratic Clarion and Tennessee Gazette*, June 25, 1811.

99. J. J. Burnett, *Sketches of Tennessee's Pioneer Baptist Preachers* (Nashville: Marshall & Bruce, 1919; reprint, Johnson City, Tenn.: Overmountain Press, 1985), 529-32.

100. William D. Sprague, *Annals of the American Baptist Pulpit* (New York: Robert Carter, 1860), 845-51; Norman Wade Cox, ed., *Encyclopedia of Southern Baptists* (Nashville: Broadman, 1958), s.v. "Tennessee Baptist Convention," pt. 2, by Charles Wesley Pope.

101. *Minutes of Concord Association, 1816.*

102. Ibid.; *Carthage Gazette*, October 1, 1813, July 1, 1817.

103. Parker used this advantage in 1816. All three of his pastorates voted al-

166 FRONTIER RELIGION

most unanimously against affiliation with the Baptist Board. See Parker, *Author's Defence,* 4.

104. Daniel White and John Turner, Whitsitt's co-councilmen, had remained in the Cumberland Association.

105. Turnbull Minutes, June 20, October 20, 1812.

106. Testament Minutes, March 5, 1814.

107. Sumner County Deeds, 7:150-151; James W. Parker, *Narrative of the Perilous Adventures, Miraculous Escapes, and Sufferings of Rev. James W. Parker* (Louisville: Louisville Morning Courier, 1844), 5.

108. *Church Advocate,* 277.

109. Theodore Calvin Pease, *The Frontier State, 1818-1848,* vol. 2, *The Centennial History of Illinois* (Springfield: Centennial Commission, 1918), 23.

110. Crawford County Original Land Entry Book, 28. Clerk of Court, Robinson, Ill.

111. *Church Advocate,* 277.

112. Crawford County Original Land Entry Book, 16, 29; Clark County Land Grant Records Book, 1:37 in Mazie M. Garver, ed. *Clark County, Illinois Land Grant Records* (Marshall, Ill.: Clark Co. Genealogical Society, 1973), 20, typewritten.

113. Grime, *History of Middle Tenn. Baptists,* 331.

114. Churches which observed Sunday worship once monthly customarily assembled for church business and preaching on Saturday preceding the Sunday preaching service.

115. *Church Advocate,* 277.

116. Corlew, *Tennessee: A Short History,* 212; Chase C. Mooney, "Some Institutional and Statistical Aspects of Slavery in Tennessee," *Tennessee Historical Quarterly 1* (September 1942): 227-28; William Barney, *The Road to Secession: A New Perspective on the Old South* (New York: Praeger, 1972), 38.

117. Richard H. Niebuhr, *The Social Sources of Denominationalism* (n.p.: Henry Holt, 1929; reprint, Cleveland: World Publishers, 1957), 139 (page reference is to reprint edition).

118. Daniel Parker, *Author's Defence,* 5.

CHAPTER 2:   THE ILLINOIS YEARS: POLITICAL LIFE

1. Robert P. Howard, *Illinois: A History of the Prairie State* (Grand Rapids: Eerdmans, 1972), 68-73, 85.

2. Solon Justus Buck, *Illinois in 1818* (Chicago: A. C. McClurg, 1918), 93.

3. Albert J. Beveridge, *Abraham Lincoln, 1809-1818,* vol. 1 (Boston: Houghton Mifflin, 1928), 71.

4. George W[ashington] Smith, *History of Illinois and Her People,* vol. 2 (Chicago: American Historical Society, 1927), 80; John Reynolds, *My Own Times* (Chicago: Chicago Historical Society, 1879), 163; Buck, *Illinois in 1818,* 93, 97.

5. Chase C. Mooney, *Slavery in Tennessee* (Bloomington: Indiana University, 1957), 37-38.

6. Eugene H. Berwanger, *The Frontier Against Slavery: Western Anti-Negro*

Prejudice and the Slavery Extension Controversy (Urbana, Ill.: University of Illinois, 1971), 18.

7. *Illinois Intelligencer,* 7 June 1823; *Republican Advocate,* July 24, 1823.

8. Berwanger, *Frontier Against Slavery,* 20.

9. Ibid., 24.

10. Charles M. Franklin, comp., *Indiana Territorial Pioneer Records, 1801-1820,* vol. 3 (Indianapolis: Heritage House, 1985), 17.

11. *Senate Journal,* 3d Assy., 1st sess., 1822 (Vandalia, Ill.: Blackwell & Berry, 1823), 30.

12. In the early 1820s at least two cotton gins operated in southern Illinois. William Henry Perrin, ed., *History of Crawford and Clark Counties* (Chicago: O. L. Baskin, 1883), 134; *Republican Advocate,* January 8, 1824; *The Western Sun,* March 30, 1822.

13. Buck, *Illinois in 1818,* 140; *Republican Advocate,* July 24, 1823.

14. Buck, *Illinois in 1818,* 60-61; Gregory A. Parrott, "U.S. Rangers of Fort LaMotte" *The Robinson Argus,* April 6, 1984; *The Western Sun,* April 18, 1818; Perrin, *History of Crawford and Clark Counties,* 143.

15. *Minutes of the Wabash District Association, 1822* (Vincennes, Ind.: E. Stout, 1822); Joseph Chambers, "Short History of the Wabash District Association And union associations." Original manuscript typewritten and published as *Maria Creek Church Papers* (Vincennes, Ind.: Lewis Historical Library, 1969), 44-45; Grand Prairie Church Minutes, January 20, 1821, Primitive Baptist Library, Carthage, Ill.

16. Perhaps the increase partially reflects an influx of newcomers. Land sales boomed in southeastern Illinois in 1822. In 1821 the United States Land Office in Palestine recorded $954 in sales. The following year it entered $16,474. See Theodore Calvin Pease, *The Frontier State, 1818-1848,* vol. 2, *The Centennial History of Illinois* (Springfield: Illinois Centennial Commission, 1918), 176.

17. Because of the traditional Baptist advocacy of believer's baptism and the soul searching encountered under hyper-Calvinism, baptismal candidates were commonly either adults or in their late teens.

18. *Minutes of the Wabash District Association 1822; Minutes of the Wabash District Association, 1823* (Vincennes, Ind.: E. Stout, 1823).

19. Ibid.

20. Crawford County Commissioners Record Book, 1816-1824, 179, 184, Clerk of Court, Robinson, Ill.

21. Theodore Calvin Pease, ed., *Illinois Election Returns, 1818-1848,* vol. 28, *Collections of the Illinois State Historical Library* (Springfield: Illinois State Historical Library, 1923), 185; Buck, *Illinois in 1818,* 301.

22. Pease, *Frontier State,* 130; Thomas Ford, *A History of Illinois, from its Commencement as a State in 1818 to 1847* (Chicago: S. C. Griggs, 1854), 284.

23. Pease, *Illinois Election Returns,* 159, 194, 204, 214, 229, 239, 250, 262, 280, 459; Reynolds, *My Own Times,* 167; W. P. Strickland, ed., *Autobiography of Peter Cart-wright* (Cincinnati: L. Swormsteadt & A. Poe. 1860), 169, 262.

24. Ford, *History of Illinois,* 40.

25. Charles Sellers, *The Market Revolution: Jacksonian America, 1815-1846* (New York: Oxford University, 1991), 131-36.

26. Pease, *Frontier State*, 93.
27. Ibid., 96-97.
28. Ibid., 93.
29. *The Western Sun*, November 1, 1817; *Republican Advocate*, July 17, 1823.
30. Howard, *Illinois: A History*, 121-24.
31. Pease, *Frontier State*, 41.
32. Joel Barlor v. Joseph A. Parker, Isaac Parker, and Daniel Parker, Box 1, Case 12, Crawford County Circuit Court, Robinson, Illinois
33. Pease, *Frontier State*, 10-11, 41.
34. Robert M. Sutton, "Edward Coles and the Constitutional Crisis in Illinois, 1822-1824," *Illinois Historical Journal* 82 (Spring 1989): 37.
35. Howard, *Illinois: A History*, 130.
36. N. Dwight Harris, *The History of Negro Servitude in Illinois* (Chicago: A. C. McClurg, 1904), 55-56; Howard, *Illinois: A History*, 130-31; Charles Boewe, ed., *Prairie Albion: An English Settlement in Pioneer Illinois* (Carbondale, Illinois: Southern Illinois University, 1962), 268.
37. Ibid., 130-31; Margaret Cross Norton, ed., *Illinois Census Returns, 1820*, vol. 26, *Collections of the Illinois State Historical Library* (Springfield: Illinois State Historical Library, 1934), passim.
38. Buck, *Illinois in 1818*, 200; Howard, *Illinois: A History*, 132.
39. Reynolds, *My Own Times*, 142.
40. Buck, *Illinois in 1818*, 140; Donald S. Spencer, "Edward Coles: Virginia Gentleman in Frontier Politics," *Journal of the Illinois State Historical Society* 61 (Spring 1968): 152-53.
41. Spencer, "Edward Coles: Virginia Gentleman," 153.
42. Kurt E. Leichtle, "The Rise of Jacksonian Politics in Illinois," *Illinois Historical Journal* 82 (Summer 1989): 95, 97.
43. Sutton, "Edward Coles," 35.
44. Pease, *Election Returns*, 14-15.
45. Edward H. Piper to Elias Kent Kane, June 9, 1820; Joseph Kitchell to Elias Kent Kane, December 10, 1828; David McGahey to Elias Kent Kane, February 16, 1832, Elias Kent Kane Papers, Chicago Historical Society, Chicago.
46. Pease, *Election Returns*, 14-15, 19.
47. Ford, *History of Illinois*, ed. Milo Milton Quaife, Lakeside Classics ed., vol. 1 (Chicago: R. R. Donnelley, 1945), 117.
48. Buck, *Illinois in 1818*, 300.
49. Ibid., 280.
50. Perrin, *History of Crawford and Clark Counties*, 41.
51. Crawford County Commissioners Record Book, 1816-1824, 1, 183, Clerk of Court, Robinson, Ill.
52. Frank D. Henderson, John R. Rea, and Jane Dowd Dailey, comps. *The Official Roster of the Soldiers of the American Revolution Buried in the State of Ohio* (Columbus: F. J. Heer, 1929), 216.
53. Crawford County Original Land Entry Book, 16, 17, 21, 27, 29, Clerk of Court Office, Robinson, Ill.
54. E. B. Washburne, ed., *The Edwards Papers*, vol. 3, *Chicago Historical Society's Collection* (Chicago: Fergus, 1884), 149-50.

55. *The Biographical Encyclopedia of Illinois of the Nineteenth Century* (Philadelphia: Galaxy Publishing, 1875), 467; Crawford County Commissioners Record Book 1816-1824, 40, 53; *Assembly Journal* 1st Assy., 2d sess., 1819 (Kaskaskia, Ill.: Blackwell & Berry, 1819), 212; Louis B. Ewbank and Dorothy L. Riker, eds., *The Laws of Indiana Territory, 1809-1816* (Indianapolis: Indiana Historical Bureau, 1934), 846.

56. Joseph Kitchell to Elias K. Kane, 10 December 1828, Elias Kent Kane Papers.

57. Pease, *Frontier State,* 48.

58. United States Manuscript Census, Crawford County, Ill., 1820, 1830, passim [microfilm], Mahon Public Library, Lubbock, Tex.

59. Joseph E. Suppiger, "Amity to Enmity: Ninian Edwards and Jesse B. Thomas," *Journal of the Illinois State Historical Society* 67 (April 1974): 210.

60. Clye Gaddis, "'Pioneer Day' Labor Day Celebration Calls Attention to Historical Spots," *Robinson Daily News,* August 26, 1967.

61. John Mason Peck to Isaac McCoy, June 13, 1822, Isaac McCoy Papers, Bracken Library, Ball State University, Muncie, Ind.

62. Executive Record, 1818-1832, 1:35-36, Illinois State Archives, Springfield.

63. Pease, *Election Returns,* 14-15.

64. Ibid., 196.

65. Crawford County Commissioners Record Book, 1816-1824, 38.

66. Pease, *Frontier State,* 41.

67. *Illinois Intelligencer,* December 21, 28, 1822; January 4, 25; February 15, 1823; December 16, 1824; January 19, 1826; *Republican Advocate,* January 24, 1823; *Illinois Senate Journal,* 3d Assy., 1st sess., 63, 220, 224, 262; *Senate Journal,* 4th Assy., 1st sess., 1824 (Vandalia, Ill.: Robert Blackwell, 1824), 32, 46.

68. *Senate Journal,* 3d Assy., 1st sess., 3, 18-31.

69. Sutton, "Edward Coles," 40; Pease, *Frontier State,* 85-86.

70. Norton, *Illinois Census Returns,* 26-48.

71. Daniel Parker, "A Public Address" (Vincennes, Ind.: Stout & Osburn, 1820); reprint, Hamilton, Ill.: Hamilton Press, 1988, 51 (page reference is to reprint edition).

72. Frank M. Masters, *A History of Kentucky Baptists* (Louisville: Kentucky Baptist Historical Society, 1953), 60; John M[ason] Peck, "Kentucky Baptists," *The Baptist Memorial and Monthly Chronicle* (February 1, 1842): 44.

73. Myron D. Dillow, "A History of Baptists in Illinois" (Th.D. diss., Southwestern Baptist Theological Seminary, 1965), 135-36.

74. *Minutes of the Wabash District Association, 1824.*

75. *Senate Journal,* 3d Assy., 1st sess., 33.

76. Ibid., 43.

77. Ibid., 58.

78. Parker may have partially intended his motion as a diversionary tactic. Anticonvention and proconvention supporters divided equally over Parker's prayer motion. Those who favored postponement included seven proconvention and three anticonvention senators. Three proconvention and two anticonvention delegates opposed postponement. Ibid., 130, 163.

79. *Illinois Intelligencer,* February 1, 1823.
80. Ibid.
81. Ibid., January 25, 1823
82. *Senate Journal,* 3d Assy., 1st sess., 182.
83. *Illinois Intelligencer,* February 1, 1823.
84. Harris, *History of Negro Servitude,* 37.
85. Ibid., 34.
86. Ibid., 35-39.
87. *The Western Sun,* April 22, 1823.
88. Harris, *History of Negro Servitude,* 42.
89. *Illinois Intelligencer,* June 14, 1823.
90. Reynolds, *My Own Times,* 153.
91. Ibid., 155.
92. Wickliff Kitchell to Daniel Parker, February 20, 1825, Daniel Parker v. Wickliff Kitchell, Box 7, Case 59, Crawford County Circuit Court, Robinson, Ill; Daniel Parker Family Bible, Elkhart State Bank, Elkhart, Tex. Sarah Parker died July 28, 1825.
93. Pease, *Election Returns,* 14.
94. Reynolds, *My Own Times,* 155.
95. Crawford County returns indicated 134 ballots in favor of the convention and 262 against the proposal. Clark Countians rejected the issue by 116 to 31. In Edgar only 3 out of 237 voted in favor. Pease, *Election Returns,* 27.
96. *Senate Journal,* 4th Assy., 1st sess., 183; *Senate Journal,* 4th Assy., 2d sess., 1826 (Vandalia, Ill.: Robert Blackwell, 1826), 24-25, 28; *Illinois Intelligencer,* November 19, December 31, 1824.
97. *Senate Journal,* 4th Assy., 2d sess., 135.
98. *Illinois Intelligencer,* June 5, 1823.
99. *Senate Journal,* 3d Assy., 1st sess., 95; *Wabash District Association Minutes, 1822;* Grand Prairie Baptist Church Minutes, November 18, 1821.
100. *Senate Journal,* 3d, Assy., 1st sess., 211.
101. Pease, *Illinois Election Returns,* 196; *Frontier State,* 37-38.
102. Crawford County Commissioners Book, 1816-1824, 153; *Illinois Intelligencer,* February 15, 1823.
103. Little Village Baptist Church Minutes, June 24, 1820, Primitive Baptist Library, Carthage, Ill.
104. Harry L. Watson, *Jacksonian Politics and Community Conflict: The Emergence of the Second American Party System in Cumberland County, North Carolina* (Baton Rouge: Louisiana State University, 1981), 77.
105. Daniel Parker to Wickliff Kitchell, February 18, 1825, Daniel Parker v. Wickliff Kitchell, Box 7, Case 59.
106. Pease, *Election Returns,* 214.
107. Wickliff Kitchell to Daniel Parker, January 8, 1825, *Daniel Parker v. Wickliff Kitchell.*
108. *Laws Passed By the Legislative Council and House of Representatives of Illinois Territory,* 4th sess. (Kaskaskia, Ill. Territory, 1816), 78-79.
109. Robinson for Defendant, Daniel Parker v. Wickliff Kitchell.
110. *Wabash District Association Minutes,* 1824.

111. Robinson for Defendant, Daniel Parker v. Wickliff Kitchell. Parker had been in Tennessee in the summer of 1820 and also in December 1820. See William Polke to Isaac McCoy, June 20, 1820, Isaac McCoy Papers; Robertson County Deed Book, Q: 508, Tennessee State Archives, Nashville. See Wickliff Kitchell to Daniel Parker, February 20, 1825 and Robinson for Defendant, Daniel Parker v. Wickliff Kitchell.

112. David McGahey preached to a New Light congregation south of Palestine. McGahey became a follower of Alexander Campbell, the founder of the Disciples of Christ. Campbell held Arminian views. Edward Cullom affiliated with the Methodist Church. See Chris H. Bailey, "Old Crawford County," *The Robinson Argus,* October 7, 1971; Perrin, *History of Crawford and Clark Counties,* 143; Watson, *Jacksonian Politics,* 59, 73; *Church Advocate,* 2 ([October or November] 1831), 30, 107.

113. Parker, "A Public Address," 49.

114. Wickliff Kitchell to Daniel Parker, February 20, 1825, Daniel Parker v. Wickliff Kitchell.

115. Daniel Parker to Wickliff Kitchell, February 18, 1825, Daniel Parker v. Wickliff Kitchell.

116. "I hope you will Excuse me, for not asking your leve [sic], nor rendering and account of my business to you. Sir, but I will favour you, perhaps, with Information which may be Instructing to the aspiring mind which is in a state of Improvement, My wife has had two breeds [sic] of chickens this winter, the old pet hen, had ten chickens and the little speckeled [sic] hen had Eight. She is a good little hen for chickens, but I am sorry sir to have to informe [sic] you that she has lost all of hirn [sic] but one, the old pet hen has six alive yet, but poor little things they have sufferd [sic] in cold wether [sic]. I hope you will Excuse me for not giving you the number of piges [sic] my sowes [sic] has had this season, but they have dun [sic] very well." See Daniel Parker to Wickliff Kitchell, February 15, 1825, Daniel Parker v. Wickliff Kitchell.

117. Sixteen-year-old Abigail Parker, the second child of Daniel, had born a child out of wedlock in February 1821. See Daniel Parker Family Bible. Kitchell referred to the animated pulpit style of Parker in his attempt to portray Parker as mentally deranged and morally unfit. "I can See you methinks after reading my letter. Your mind worked up into a State of delirum [sic]. Your features distorted into the entire likeness of your mind. Seizeing [sic] your Ears with both of your hands, Lowering them and rending your hair. Then passing your hands hastily to your rear. (There always appeared to be great Sympathy between your ends.) Then Stomping with your feet, Scratching and Crying "Tyrany [sic] and Persecution" till Suddenly your body and briches parting. Shame and nakedness brought you back to reflection. Then leasurely [sic] returning your briches over your center. You Set down completely exhausted with the Operation of the Spirit." See Wickliff Kitchell to Daniel Parker, February 20, 1825, Daniel Parker v. Wickliff Kitchell.

118. Daniel Parker v. Elijah Dodson, Box 2, Case 50, Crawford County Circuit Court, Robinson, Ill.

119. I Corinthians 6:1; Parker v. Dodson.

120. Crawford County Circuit Court Record Book, B:98, 139, Circuit Court, Robinson, Ill.; Robert Gill Summons, Daniel Parker v. Wickliff Kitchell.

Samuel Baker was a member of Little Village. See Little Village Minutes, March 22, 1818.

121. *Illinois Intelligencer,* July 21, 1823; Clark County Deed Book, A:64, Clerk of Court, Marshall, Ill.

122. Perrin, *History of Crawford and Clark Counties,* 227.

123. Pease, *Election Returns,* 196, 219; Daniel Parker, *A Short Hint* (Vincennes, Ind.: Elihu Stout, 1827), 39.

124. Pease, *Election Returns,* 219.

125. Ibid.

126. United States Manuscript Census, Lawrence County, Ill., 1830, passim [microfilm], Mahon Public Library, Lubbock, Tex.

127. Pease, *Election Returns,* 28.

128. Ellen M. Whitney, ed., *The Blackhawk War, 1831-32,* vol. 1, *Collections of the Illinois State Historical Library* (Springfield: Illinois State Historical Library, 1970), 438.

129. Pease, *Frontier State,* 161.

130. Little Village Church Minutes, September 24, 1825, February 25, 1832; North Fork Baptist Church Minutes, April 1821, Primitive Baptist Library, Carthage, Ill.

131. McGahey to Kane, February 16, 1832.

132. Pease, *Election Returns,* 32, 57, 80-81.

133. Ibid., 32, 80.

134. Ibid., 284.

135. Watson, *Jacksonian Politics,* 75.

136. *Illinois Intelligencer,* June 14, 1823.

137. *Assembly Journal,* 2d Assy., 1st sess., 1820 (Vandalia, Ill.: Browne & Berry, 1821), 75-76.

138. Illinois Election Returns, 2:34-40, Illinois State Archives, Springfield.

139. *Republican Advocate,* January 4, 1823.

140. *Illinois Intelligencer,* January 19, 1826.

141. John Clayton, *The Illinois Fact Book and Historical Almanac, 1673-1968* (Carbondale, Ill.: Southern Illinois University, 1970), 34.

142. Leichtle, "Rise of Jacksonian Politics," 105-07.

143. Harry L. Watson, *Liberty and Power: The Politics of Jacksonian America* (New York: Hill and Wang, 1990), 201.

CHAPTER 3: THE ILLINOIS YEARS: RELIGIOUS CONTROVERSY

1. William Henry Perrin, ed., *History of Crawford and Clark Counties, Illinois* (Chicago: O. L. Baskin, 1883), 204.

2. John B. Dillon, *A History of Indiana* (Indianapolis: Bingham & Doughty, 1859), 55.

3. Joseph Chambers, "Short History of the Wabash Association and Union Association." Original manuscript typewritten and published as *Maria Creek Church Papers* (Vincennes, Ind.: Lewis Historical Library, n.d.), 73; James Leaton, *History of Methodism in Illinois From 1793 to 1832* (Cincinnati: Walden & Stowe,

1883), 111; William Warren Sweet, *The Presbyterians*, vol. 2, *Religion on the American Frontier, 1783-1840* (New York: Cooper Square, 1964), 48.

4. *Maria Creek Papers*, 9.

5. Ibid., 14-15.

6. T. J. Wheeler, *History of Palestine Association of Baptists in Illinois* (n.p.: By the author, 1938), vi, 28. Wheeler gathered some of his information from the original records of La Motte Baptist Church.

7. *Maria Creek Papers*, 18.

8. *Latter Day Luminary*, 1 (November 1819), 511.

9. Frank M. Masters, *A History of Baptists in Kentucky* (Louisville: Baptist Historical Society, 1953), 61-62.

10. *Maria Creek Papers*, 16, 24.

11. Isaac McCoy License, Maria Creek Approval for Missionary Activity, March 16, 1816, Baptist Board of Foreign Missions Circular Letter, 1815. All in the Isaac McCoy Papers, Ball State University, Muncie, Ind.; Silver Creek Baptist Church Minutes, October 8, 1808, Indiana Division, Indiana State Library, Indianapolis.

12. *Maria Creek Papers*, 15, 18-19; Isaac McCoy, *History of Baptist Indian Missions* (Washington: William M. Morrison, 1840), 43-45; Walter N. Wyeth, *Isaac McCoy: Early Indian Missions* (Philadelphia: W. N. Wyeth, 1895), 9-18, 30; John F. Cady, "Isaac McCoy's Mission to the Indians of Indiana and Michigan," *Indiana History Bulletin* 17 (February 1939): 100-106.

13. James W. Parker, *Narrative of the Perilous Adventures, Miraculous Escapes, and Sufferings of Rev. James W. Parker* (Louisville: *Morning Courier*, 1844), 6.

14. Little Village Baptist Church Minutes, June 25, August 22, 1818, Primitive Baptist Library, Carthage, Ill.

15. Early records of the church do not indicate the presence of an official pastor. Tradition holds that Parker organized the church in the home of Thomas Mills in early 1817. See Little Village Minutes, typewritten addenda, 1955.

16. Little Village Minutes, August 22, 1818.

17. Daniel Parker, *The Author's Defence* (Vincennes, Ind.: E. Stout, [1824]), 5.

18. Ibid.; William Bruce to Isaac McCoy, September 2, 1818, Isaac McCoy Papers.

19. Little Village Minutes, September 26, 1818.

20. *Latter Day Luminary*, 1 (May 1819), 413.

21. Ibid., February 27, 1819.

22. Little Village Minutes, August 21, 1819.

23. *Maria Creek Papers*, 47.

24. In 1817 this association had sent messengers to the Wabash District Association. Minutes do not exist for 1818-1820. But by 1823 the Red River and Wabash District associations had resumed mutual correspondence. Sugg Fort held the office of clerk in the Red River Association. In August 1820 Fort communicated with Isaac McCoy concerning the opposition of Daniel Parker to missionary efforts. See *Minutes of the Red River Association, 1817* (Russellville, Ky.: George H. Crutcher, 1817) 3; *Minutes of the Red River Association, 1823* (Russellville, Ky.: Charles Rhea, 1823), nonpaginated; *Minutes of the Wabash District Association,*

1822 (Vincennes, Ind.: E. Stout, 1822), 4; Daniel Parker, *Author's Defence*, 5; Daniel Parker, "A Public Address" (Vincennes, Ind.: Stout & Osborn, 1820; reprint, Hamilton, Ill.: Hamilton Press, 1988), 1 (page references are to reprint edition); Sugg Fort to McCoy, August 18, 1820, Isaac McCoy Papers.

25. Daniel Parker, *A Public Address*, 38–49; William Polke to Isaac McCoy, June 20, 1820, Isaac McCoy Papers; Daniel 11:31; Matthew 24:15.

26. Daniel Parker, *A Public Address*, 48.

27. Fort to McCoy, August 18, 1820.

28. McCoy planned to publish the "Three Letters" but first intended on sending them to Daniel Parker. Polke likely meant to deliver the "Three Letters" to Parker by the hands of Thomas Kennedy on May 20, 1821. Yet Polke returned the "Letters" to McCoy in February 1822. Polke used the excuse that he had been unable to transcribe the manuscript. On the other hand, there may have been other reasons. Polke became a candidate for the office of lieutenant governor in 1822. It is possible that Polke did not wish to allow Parker additional cause for taking action against Polke or Maria Creek in a forthcoming special associational meeting in June 1822. See [Isaac McCoy], "Three Letters to Daniel Parker," American Baptist Collection, Manuscript Division, Illinois State Historical Library, Springfield; *Maria Creek Papers*, 31-33; William Polke to Isaac McCoy, February 24, 1822, Isaac McCoy Papers.

29. Daniel Parker, *A Public Address*, 7.

30. *The Western Sun*, September 27, 1817.

31. William Polke to Isaac McCoy, December 3, 1821, Isaac McCoy Papers.

32. James Polke, "Some Memoirs of the Polke, Piety, McCoy, McQuaid, and Mathes Families," *Indiana Magazine of History* 10 (March 1914); reprint (New York: Kraus, 1967): 85-90 (page references are to reprint edition); William Polke Papers, Special Collections, Lilly Library, Indiana University, Bloomington; *Maria Creek Papers*, 73-75; *The Western Sun*, January 25, 1817, July 3, 1818, February 3, 1821.

33. *Maria Creek Papers*, 28-39. Aaron Frakes, the pastor of promissions Maria Creek and Prairie Creek churches, had died the previous February.

34. William Polke to Isaac McCoy, October 26, 1821, Isaac McCoy Papers.

35. Ibid.

36. *Maria Creek Papers*, 49-51.

37. John Mason Peck to Isaac McCoy, June 13, 1822, Isaac McCoy Papers.

38. William Polke to McCoy, February 24, 1822.

39. Ibid.

40. *Biblical Recorder and Southern Watchman* 6 (February 29, 1840), front page.

41. William Polke to McCoy, February 24, 1822.

42. Matthew Lawrence, *John Mason Peck: The Pioneer Missionary Preacher* (New York: Fortuny's, 1940), 21-24, 33-38.

43. John Mason Peck to Isaac McCoy, April 17, 1822, Isaac McCoy Papers; Rufus Babcock, ed., *Forty Years of Pioneer Life: Memoir of John Mason Peck, D.D.* (Philadelphia: American Baptist Publication Society, 1864; reprint, Carbondale, Ill.: Southern Illinois University, 1965), 173 (page references are to original edition).

44. Peck to McCoy, June 13, 1822.
45. James Polke, "Some Memoirs," 100.
46. Peck to McCoy, June 13, 1822; Babcock, 173-174.
47. Harris vacillated between the pro and antimissions factions. In 1823 the Wabash District Association had voted that Harris should deliver the annual message in 1824. Because Harris and his flock had joined the Union Association, Parker, without official authority, refused to permit Harris to preach at the 1824 Wabash District Association. Harris evidently reconsidered his allegiance. In 1825 Harris no longer appeared in the Union Association minutes. By 1830 Harris had evidently reconciled with Parker. For, Harris ministered to a church in the Wabash District Association. See *Minutes of the Union Association, 1824* (n.p., [1824]), 1; *Minutes of the Union Association, 1825* (Vincennes, Ind.: E. Stout, 1825), 1; *Minutes of the Union Association, 1827* (Vincennes, Ind.: E. Stout, 1827), 1; *Minutes of the Wabash District Association, 1830* (Vincennes, Ind.: Western Sun, 1830), 2.
48. Little Village sent two representatives.
49. Daniel, James W., a younger brother, and John, the Parker patriarch, attended.
50. *Minutes of the Wabash District Association, 1822*, 2.
51. Corbly Martin to Isaac McCoy, November 6, 1822, Isaac McCoy Papers.
52. Ibid.
53. *Wabash District Association Minutes, 1822*, 3.
54. United States Manuscript Census Returns, Crawford County, Ill., 1820, 33 [microfilm], Mahon Public Library, Lubbock, Tex.; William Polke to McCoy, December 3, 1821.
55. *Minutes of the Union Association, 1832* (Vincennes, Ind.: Vincennes Gazette, [1832]), 1.
56. William Polke to Isaac McCoy, December 2, 1822, Isaac McCoy Papers.
57. *Illinois Intelligencer,* 11, January 25, 1823.
58. Robert G. Torbet, *A History of the Baptists,* 3d ed. (Valley Forge, Pa.: Judson, 1973), 309-10; *The Debates and Proceedings,* 18th Congress, 1st sess., 1824, vol. 1 (Washington: Gales and Seaton, 1856), 1427, 1734.
59. Daniel Parker, *Plain Truth* (n.p., [1823]), 12.
60. Ibid.
61. McCoy, *History of Baptist Indian Missions,* 124.
62. Daniel Parker, *Plain Truth,* 13.
63. *Maria Creek Papers,* 52-53; *Minutes of the Wabash District Association, 1823* (Vincennes, Ind.: E. Stout, [1823]), 5, 7.
64. *Minutes of the Union Association, 1824,* 1.
65. Prairie Creek and Mount Pleasant accounted for the two additional churches. Mount Pleasant had joined the Wabash District Association in 1823 but did not vote on the Maria Creek dispute. The clerk of the Wabash District Association included Prairie Creek Church as an official member. At the request of its messengers, this church received a letter of dismission from the Association.
66. *Minutes of the Wabash District Association, 1824,* 2.
67. *Minutes of the White River Association* (Bloomington: J. C. Carlton, 1856), 17.
68. *Biblical Recorder and Southern Watchman,* 6 (February 29, 1840), front

page; *Minutes of the White River Association,* 16; Daniel Parker, *The Second Dose of Doctrine on the Two Seeds* (Vincennes, Ind.: Elihu Stout, 1826 [1827]), 52.

69. Minutes of the Illinois Association, 1824, American Baptist Collection, Manuscript Division, Illinois State Historical Library, Springfield; *Minutes of the Wabash District Association, 1825* (Vincennes, Ind.: E. Stout, [1825]), 2-4.

70. Daniel Parker, *Second Dose,* 56; *Minutes of the Little Pigeon Association of United Baptists, 1824* (n.p.: Brundon & Co., [1824]), 2.

71. Daniel Parker v. Wickliff Kitchell, Box 7, Case 53, Crawford County Circuit Court, Robinson, Ill.

72. Crawford County Circuit Court Book, B:94, Circuit Court, Robinson, Ill.; Crawford County Deed Book, A:280-81, Clerk of Court, Robinson, Ill.; Edgar County Deed Book, 1:44, Clerk of Court, Paris, Ill.

73. Daniel Parker v. Wickliff Kitchell, Box 7, Case 53.

74. *Illinois Intelligencer,* November 4, 1825, December 29, 1825.

75. Daniel Parker, *Views,* 4.

76. *Church Advocate,* 2 (September 1831), 279.

77. Torbet, *History of the Baptists,* 267.

78. *Minutes of the Cumberland Baptist Association, 1816* (Franklin, Tenn.: I. N. Henry, [1816]), 8-29.

79. Daniel Parker, *A Short Hint* (Vincennes, Ind.: E. Stout, 1827), 47.

80. Daniel Parker, *Second Dose,* 6-11.

81. Daniel Parker, *Views,* 18.

82. Ibid., 19.

83. Ibid., 36.

84. Daniel Parker, *Second Dose,* 77.

85. Ibid.

86. Daniel Parker, *Short Hint,* 15-16.

87. Ibid., 8.

88. Daniel Parker, *A Supplement or Explanation of My Views on the Two Seeds,* in *Views on the Two Seeds* (Vandalia, Ill.: Robert Blackwell, 1826), 8.

89. Ibid., 3.

90. Ibid., 8.

91. Daniel Parker, *Short Hint,* 40.

92. Thomas Kennedy v. Abraham Taylor and Benjamin Parker, Box 5, Case 70, Crawford County Circuit Court, Robinson, Ill. The suit concerned the official capacity of Kennedy as treasurer of Crawford County. Taylor had sued for the recovery of a bond posted on September 7, 1819 while he had been a constable in Crawford County. Benjamin Parker had cosigned with Taylor.

93. Thomas Kennedy Summons, Daniel Parker v. Wickliff Kitchell, Box 7, Case 53; Affidavit for Witness Fees, Daniel Parker v. Wickliff Kitchell, Box 7, Case 59.

94. Daniel Parker, *Short Hint,* 32.

95. Daniel Parker, *Second Dose,* 59-60.

96. Crawford County Commissioners Record Book, 1816-1824, 2, Clerk of Court, Robinson, Ill.; Illinois Election Returns, 2:38, Illinois State Archives, Springfield.

97. Daniel Parker, *Short Hint,* 46.

98. The structure measured approximately 26 by 36 feet. See Wheeler, *History of Palestine Association*, 15.

99. Daniel Parker, *Second Dose*, 60; Little Village Minutes, August 1826.

100. Daniel Parker, *Short Hint*, 27-29.

101. *Minutes of the Wabash District Association, 1826* (Vincennes, Ind.: E. Stout, [1826]), 1.

102. *Church Advocate*, 1 (April 1830), 162; 1 (June 1830), 216; 1 (September 1830), 265; 2 (December 1830), 72; 2 (March 1831), 144.

103. *Minutes of the Wabash District Association, 1830*, 2, 7-8; *Minutes of the Wabash District Association, 1829* (Vincennes, Ind.: E. Stout, [1829]), 2; *Minutes of the Blue River Association, 1830* (n.p., [1830]), 2; *Minutes of the Eel River Association of Baptists, 1830* (Lafayette, Ind.: J. B. Semans, 1830), 4, 6; Robert Louis Webb, *Walk About Zion* (n.p.: By the author, 1976), 24; Union Primitive Baptist Church Minutes, November 9, 1827, Primitive Baptist Library, Carthage, Ill.

104. *Minutes of the Wabash District Association, 1826, 1830,* 2 respectively.

105. B[enajah] H[arvey] Carroll, *The Genesis of American Anti-Missionism* (Louisville: Baptist Book Concern, 1902), 204-211.

106. *Church Advocate*, 2 (July 1831), 221.

107. Ibid.

108. Daniel Parker, *Author's Defence*, 28-29.

109. *Church Advocate*, 2 ([October or November] 1831), 130.

110. Little Village Minutes, July 26, 1832.

111. LaMire Holden Moore, *Southern Baptists in Illinois* (Nashville: Benson, 1957), 26.

112. James W. Parker, *Narrative*, 5.

113. *The Clarion*, April 27, 1819.

114. People v. William Kilbuck, Box 5, Case 39, Crawford County Circuit Court Record Book, A:11-14, Circuit Court, Robinson, Ill.; McCoy, *History of Baptist Indian Missions*, 55; "Palestine Murder Trial Brings Hanging Verdict But Killer Breaks Jail." *Robinson Daily News,* December 28, 1961.

115. Daniel Parker, *Plain Truth*, 13; Daniel Parker, *Second Dose*, 53-54; Daniel Parker, "A Public Address," 8–9.

116. Charles True Goodsell, "The Baptist Anti-Missionary Movement in America" (M.A. thesis, University of Chicago, 1924); Byron Cecil Lambert, "The Rise of the Anti-Mission Baptists: Sources and Leaders, 1800-1840" (Ph.D. diss., University of Chicago, 1957).

117. Corbly Martin to Isaac McCoy, March 2, 1823, Isaac McCoy Papers.

118. Ibid., April 15 1823.

119. Ibid., March 7, 1823.

120. *Church Advocate*, 2 ([October or November] 1831), 92.

121. *The Western Baptist*, 1 (October 1830), 12.

122. *Biblical Recorder and Southern Watchman*, 6 (February 29, 1840), front page.

123. Unless Parker employed a redactor, it is doubtful that he wrote the letter. The literary flair and command of Latin demonstrated a hand other than Parker's.

124. Daniel Parker, *A Public Address*, 35.

125. Clark County Land Book, A:64, Clerk of Court, Marshall, Ill.; Mazie M. Garver, ed., *Clark County, Illinois Land Grant Records* (Marshall, Ill.: Clark County Genealogical Society, 1973), 20; Crawford County Original Land Entry Book, 18, 29, Clerk of Court, Robinson, Ill.

126. Daniel Parker, *Short Hint*, 39.

127. Isaac McCoy and William Bruce were brothers-in-law of William Polke. Thomas Piety was the first cousin of William and Charles Polke. George W. Lindsay, a son-in-law of William Polke, practiced law in western Indiana sometime between 1816 and 1833. See James Polke, "Some Memoirs," 83-109; "Ancient Reminiscences," William Price Manuscript, Indiana Division, Indiana State Library, Indianapolis.

128. *Minutes of the Wabash District Association, 1822-1825*, passim.

129. *Minutes of the Wabash District Association, 1824*, 4-5.

130. Out of thirty-six promissions messengers to the 1824 Wabash District Association and known contributors to the McCoy mission only Polke and Rose owned slaves. See William Polke to McCoy, December 3, 1821; United States Manuscript Census Returns, Indiana, Harrison, Jefferson, Gibson, Knox, Posey, Randolph, Sullivan, and Vigo counties, Ind., 1820, passim [microfilm], Mahon Public Library, Lubbock, Tex.

131. *Knox County Indiana: Early Land Records and Court Indexes, 1783-1815*, vol. 3 (Chicago: Genealogical Services, 1973), 29.

132. William Polke to Isaac McCoy, June 1, 1823, Isaac McCoy Papers.

133. *Maria Creek Papers*, 79-80.

134. Peck to McCoy, June 13, 1822.

135. *Church Advocate*, 2 (July 1831), 280.

136. Daniel Parker, *Short Hint*, 15.

137. Ibid., 31.

138. Ibid., 32.

139. Daniel Parker, *A Public Address*, 5.

140. Bertram Wyatt-Brown, "The Antimission Movement in the Jacksonian South: A Study in Regional Folk Culture," *The Journal of Southern History* 36 (November 1970): 505.

141. Richard T. Hughes and C. Leonard Allen, *Illusions of Innocence: Protestant Primitivism in America, 1630-1875* (Chicago: University of Chicago, 1988), 90-91.

142. Nathan O. Hatch, *The Democratization of American Christianity* (New Haven: Yale, 1989), 9; Gordon S. Wood, "Ideology and the Origins of Liberal America," The William and Mary Quarterly 44 (July 1987): 627-40.

143. Hughes and Allen, *Illusions*, 2.

144. Harry L. Watson, *Liberty and Power: The Politics of Jacksonian America* (New York: Hill and Wang, 1990), 47.

145. *Church Advocate*, 2 (August 1831), 251.

CHAPTER 4: THE TEXAS YEARS: PIONEER AND POLITICAL LEADER

1. William] H[enry] Perrin, A. A. Graham, and D. M. Blaim, comps., *The History of Coles County, Illinois* (Chicago: William Le Baron, Jr., 1879), 337; Mal-

colm D. McLean, ed., *Papers Concerning Robertson's Colony in Texas*, vol. 7 (Arlington, Tex.: University of Texas at Arlington, 1980), 491-93; G. D. Ayres, "Texas," *Jeffersonian Republican* (Jefferson, Mo.), May 10, 1834, 2. Although the Parker party has been placed on the White River in Arkansas when the meteorite shower occurred, it is more likely that the group had just crossed into Texas.

2. McLean, *Papers*, 9:308; United States Manuscript Census, Crawford County, Illinois, 1830, 6 [microfilm], Mahon Public Library, Lubbock, Tex.; Parker Genealogy File, Palestine Public Library, Palestine, Tex.; "Records of an Early Texas Baptist Church," *The Quarterly of the Texas State Historical Association 11* (October 1907): 89-92.

3. *The Western Sun*, August 12, 1820.

4. H[enderson] [K.] Yoakum, *History of Texas*, vol. 1 (New York: Redfield, 1855), 218.

5. *Illinois Intelligencer*, November 1, 1823, August 13, 1824. By 1824 Austin had settled 300 families.

6. Ibid., February 9, 1826.

7. Ernest Wallace, ed. *Documents of Texas History* (Lubbock, Tex.: Texas Tech Library, 1963), 53.

8. *Illinois Intelligencer*, February 16, 1826.

9. James W. Parker, *Narrative of the Perilous Adventures, Miraculous Escapes, and Sufferings of Rev. James W. Parker* (Louisville: Morning Courier, 1844), 6.

10. Jacob Harlan to Edward Muncy, October 9, 1826, Harlan-Sargent Papers, Illinois State Historical Library, Springfield.

11. United States Manuscript Census, Conway County, Arkansas, 1830, 150 [microfilm], Arkansas State Library, Little Rock. James bought a trunk in Crawford County on August 21, 1830. See Minutes of the Pilgrim Predestinarian Baptist Church [original manuscript], Center for American History, University of Texas, Austin.

12. McLean, *Papers*, 8:74.

13. James W. Parker, *Narrative*, 6; McLean, *Papers*, 7:256-57; Conway County Deed and Mortgage Index, A:196, Arkansas State Library, Little Rock.

14. McLean, *Papers*, 7:183-189.

15. H[ans] P[eter] N[ielson] Gammel, comp. *The Laws of Texas, 1822-1897*, vol. 1 (Austin: Gammel Book, 1898), 126, 424.

16. McLean, *Papers*, 7:187.

17. Ibid., 256.

18. Ibid.

19. James Robert Parker, Interview by author, 16 July 1993, Elkhart, Tex. James Robert Parker, direct descendant of Daniel Parker, related that James approached Daniel about coming to Texas. Daniel responded that if God wanted him to go then he needed divine confirmation. James assured his brother that perhaps God had sent him as a sign.

20. *Illinois Intelligencer*, October 19, 1822.

21. Ibid., August 5, 1825.

22. *Minutes of the Blue River Association, 1832* (n.p.: n.p.[1832]), 2.; *Minutes of the Salem Association, 1832* (New Harmony, Ind.: Richard Beck, 1832), 3-4.

23. The 1832 minutes of the Wabash District Association have not been preserved.

24. Church records in Illinois conspicuously lack mention of Daniel from late 1832 until May 1833. See Minutes of the Little Village Baptist Church, December 24, 1831-May 25, 1833, Primitive Baptist Library, Carthage, Ill.

25. Wallace, *Documents*, 97; Villamae Williams, ed. *Stephen F. Austin's Register of Families* (Austin: By the editor, 1984), 35.

26. "Records of an Early Texas Baptist Church," 89.

27. Ibid., 91-92; Grace Jackson, *Cynthia Ann Parker* (San Antonio: Naylor, 1959), 8; Villamae Williams, *Register*, 96. The likely route taken by the Parker party would have led through Marion County in southern Illinois. The train then crossed the Mississippi River at St. Genevieve, Missouri. Turning southward, the party passed through Batesville, Little Rock, and Washington, all in the Arkansas Territory. At Washington, or nearby, they took the road to Natchitoches, Louisiana. James W. Parker, *Narrative*, 94; *The Western Predestinarian Baptist*, [February 1] 1842, 10.

28. James W. Parker, *Narrative*, 7.

29. In 1875 Ben Parker, a son of Daniel, related information concerning the early days of the family in Texas. See *A Memorial and Biographical History of Navarro, Henderson, Anderson, Limestone, Freestone and Leon Counties, Texas* (Chicago: Lewis Publishing, 1893), 234-35; Nacogdoches Archives, 75:187, Center for American History, University of Texas, Austin.

30. John Parker, a "licensed minister of the gospel" performed a wedding ceremony in Edgar County, Illinois, as late as September 20, 1834. Benjamin Parker transacted land sales in Coles County, Illinois, in April and November 1835. Theodore Calvin Pease, ed., *Illinois Election Returns, 1818-1848*, vol. 18, *Collections of the Illinois State Historical Library* (Springfield: Illinois State Historical Library, 1923), 274; *A Memorial and Biographical History*, 235; Marriage Record, A:93, Clerk of Court, Edgar County, Paris, Ill.; Coles County Deed Book, B:98, 259, Clerk of Court, Charleston, Ill.

31. Robert A. Calvert and Arnoldo De Leon, *The History of Texas* (Arlington Heights, Ill.: Harlan Davidson, 1990), 55-66.

32. Yoakum, *History of Texas*, 2:854-55.

33. Ibid.

34. Amelia W. Williams and Eugene C. Barker, eds., *The Writings of Sam Houston*, vol. 1 (Austin: University of Texas, 1938), 302-03.

35. Thirteen days later Parker had arrived in San Felipe. "Records of an Early Texas Baptist Church," 99.

36. Gammel, *Laws*, 1:507-10.
37. Ibid., 512.
38. Ibid.
39. Ibid., 520.
40. Ibid., 526-28.
41. Ibid., 522.
42. Ibid., 534, 538.
43. Ibid., 582, 589-90, 600, 610.

44. Joe E. Ericson and Carolyn Ericson, *Spoiling for a Fight: John S. Roberts and Early Nacogdoches* (Waco, Tex.: Texian, 1989), 95-96.

45. Paul D. Lack, *The Texas Revolutionary Experience: A Political and Social History, 1835-1836* (College Station, Tex.: Texas A&M, 1992), 64-65.

46. Gammel, Laws, 1:632.

47. Randolph B. Campbell, *An Empire for Slavery: The Peculiar Institution in Texas, 1821-1865* (Baton Rouge: Louisiana State University, 1989), 10-19.

48. Ibid., 27-31.

49. Ibid., 41.

50. Merton L. Dillon, "Benjamin Lundy in Texas," *The Southwestern Historical Quarterly* 63 (July 1959): 46-57.

51. William C. Binkley, ed., *Official Correspondence of the Texas Revolution, 1835-1836*, vol. 1 (New York: D. Appleton-Century, 1936), 161.

52. At his death in 1838 Barrett owned five slaves. The 1840 Census of Texas records that Menifee had seven slaves. At least seven of the thirteen councilmen on December 30, 1835 owned slaves in 1840. Only two, Daniel Parker and John McMullen, did not own slaves. Census data for the remaining four members is not available. See Eugene C. Barker, "Don Carlos Barrett," *The Southwestern Historical Quarterly* 20 (July 1916-April 1917): 145; Gifford White, ed., *The 1840 Census of the Republic of Texas* (Austin: Pemberton, 1966), 28, passim.

53. Gammel, *Laws*, 1:721-22.

54. Campbell, *Empire*, 31.

55. John H. Jenkins, ed., *The Papers of the Texas Revolution, 1835-1836*, vol. 3 (Austin: Jay A. Matthews, 1973), 447.

56. Ibid.

57. Gammel, *Laws*, 1:704.

58. Ibid., 722.

59. Ibid., 633.

60. Llerena Friend, *Sam Houston: The Great Designer* (Austin: University of Texas, 1954), 65; M. K. Wisehart, *Sam Houston: American Giant* (Washington; Luce, 1962), 144-45.

61. Gammel, *Laws*, 1:634.

62. Jenkins, *Papers of the Texas Revolution*, 3:237-39.

63. Gammel, *Laws*, 1:697.

64. Authorization for the procurement of supplies, Captain Teal, January 25, 1836 and Silas W. Parker, December 18, 1835. See Joseph A. Parker, Republic of Texas Audited Claims, Comptroller of Public Accounts Records (RG 304), Archives Division, Texas State Library, Austin, Tex.

65. Jenkins, *Papers of the Texas Revolution*, 3:447.

66. Louis Wiltz Kemp, *The Signers of the Texas Declaration of Independence* (Houston: Anson Jones Press, 1944), 309-11.

67. "Records of an Early Texas Baptist Church," 100.

68. James T. De Shields, *Tall Men with Long Rifles* (San Antonio: Naylor, 1971), 123. Fort Houston, two miles west of present Palestine, Texas, had been plotted in late 1835. Enclosed by pickets, the wall measured 150 by 80 feet. It contained two rows of log houses. See Edward Stiff, *The Texan Emigrant* (Cincinnati: George Conclin, 1840), 108; Edna McDonald Wylie, "The Fort Houston Settle-

ment" (M.A. thesis, Sam Houston State Teachers College, 1958), 10.; Baldwin Parker, "Life of Quanah Parker, Comanche Chief," 1-2, [as recorded and edited by J. Evetts Haley], August 29, 1930, Center for American History, University of Texas, Austin.

69. McLean, *Papers*, 7:41, 10:41-49; James T. De Shields, *Border Wars of Texas* (Tioga, Tex.: Herald, 1912; reprint, Waco, Tex.: Texian, 1976), 124-33 (page references to reprint edition).

70. According to the information received by the Indian informant, Daniel Parker, Junior related that 500 Indians composed the war party. Rachel Parker Plummer, one of the captives, was eighteen at the time of the attack. She recorded in 1839 that the attackers numbered "something not far from eight hundred." Such large numbers did not usually compose raiding parties. Besides the possibility of exaggeration, there are several possible explanations. Raiding deep into Anglo territory, the Comanches wished to increase the number of warriors. At least two contingents of Comanches had united previous to the raid. Also, Caddoes, normally agrarian and less nomadic than the Comanches, wished to even the score for an Anglo attack on a Caddoan village. For this reason, representatives from some Caddo tribes had joined the party. Finally, when Comanche war parties broke camp for extended raids, Comanche women often accompanied warriors as equipment bearers. Rachael may have included some of the women in her estimate. See Daniel Parker, Jr., "The Defeat of Fort Parker by Daniel Parker," June 18, 1836, in handwriting of Daniel Parker, Sr., Daniel Parker Papers, Center for American History, University of Texas, Austin; Rachel Lofton, Susie Hendrix, and Jane Kennedy, eds., *The Rachel Plummer Narrative* (n.p.: By the editors, 1926), 15, 92; Ernest Wallace and E. Adamson Hoebel, *The Comanches: Lords of the South Plains* (Norman, Okla.: University of Oklahoma, 1952), 253-54, 287.

71. James W. Parker, *Narrative*, 9, 14; Lofton, Hendrix, and Kennedy, *Plummer Narrative*, 92-93. By 1844 all of the captives with the exception of Cynthia Ann Parker, had been rescued. Cynthia, a daughter of Silas, lived with the Comanches until her recapture in 1860. James W. Parker to Mirabeau Buonaparte Lamar, February 3, 1844, in Charles Adams Gulick, Jr. and Winnie Allen, eds. *The Papers of Mirabeau Buonaparte Lamar* (Austin: Von Boeckmann-Jones, 1924), 38.

72. James, W. Parker, *Narrative*, 15.

73. "Defeat of Parker's Fort," Daniel Parker Papers. The document is signed "Daniel Parker, Jun." but is plainly in the hand of Daniel Parker. In his early years in Tennessee Daniel Parker had been known as Daniel Parker, Jr. But after leaving Dickson County, Tennessee, and with a son named after him, the elder Daniel Parker had become known as Daniel Parker, Sr. Perhaps Daniel, Sr. wrote the account while son Daniel returned with the burial party. The senior Daniel Parker seems to have been the unofficial secretary for the Fort Houston community.

74. Williams and Barker, *Writings of Sam Houston*, 1:446.

75. Daniel Parker request for reimbursement, May 24, 1837. See Daniel Parker, Republic of Texas Audited Claims, Comptroller of Public Accounts Records (RG 304), Archives Division, Texas State Library, Austin.

76. Sam Houston to Michael Cosbey, September 16, 1836, #542, Andrew Jackson Houston Papers, Archives Division, Texas State Library, Austin.

77. Daniel Parker to Houston, January 25, 1837, #804, Andrew Jackson Houston Papers.
78. Williams and Barker, *Writings of Sam Houston*, 2:53-54.
79. J. W. Wilbarger, *Indian Depredations in Texas* (Austin: Pemberton, 1967), 347-48.
80. Armistead Albert Aldrich, *The History of Houston County, Texas* (San Antonio: Naylor, 1943), ix-x; Wylie, "The Fort Houston Settlement," 44-45.
81. "Records of an Early Texas Baptist Church," 101, 105, 123, 127.
82. G. Lusk Statement, October 31, 1839. See John Houston, claims seat in Congress held by Daniel Parker, June 19, 1839, Memorials & Petitions Series, Legislative Records (RG 100), Archives Division, Texas State Library, Austin.
83. Gammel, Laws, 1:1057.
84. The writer did not establish the familial relation of John Houston to Sam Houston. In his youth in Tennessee, Sam Houston had an older brother named John. The writings of Sam Houston omit any reference to this sibling in Texas. It is possible that John, the electoral contestant, was a distant relative. On the other hand, John may have been unrelated. Several Houstons resided in Shelby County in 1840.
85. John Houston to House of Representatives, November 12, 1839. See John Houston, claims seat in Congress held by Daniel Parker, June 19, 1839.
86. Samuel Todd Statement, November 1, 1839. See John Houston, claims seat in Congress held by Daniel Parker, June 19, 1839.
87. *Austin City Gazette* (Austin, Tex.), November 27, 1839.
88. Report of Second Auditor for House of Representatives, November 22, 1839, Daniel Parker, Republic of Texas Audited Claims, Comptroller of Public Accounts (RG 304), Archives Division, Texas State Library, Austin.
89. Daniel Parker Papers; Receipt for Lumber Bill, July 14, 1841. Also see Parker family papers in possession of Ron Parker, Groesbeck, Texas.
90. Seymour V. Connor, *The Peters Colony of Texas* (Austin: The Texas State Historical Association, 1959), 5.
91. William Ransom Hogan, *The Texas Republic: A Social and Economic History* (Austin: University of Texas, 1969), 93.
92. Daniel Parker Appeal for Division of Estate of James Madden, undated, Daniel Parker Papers; James W. Parker, *Narrative*, 55.
93. Houston County Tax List, 1843, Archives Division, Texas State Library, Austin.
94. Wisehart, *Sam Houston*, 306-13.
95. William Kennedy, *Texas: The Rise, Progress, and Prospects of the Republic of Texas* (London: n.p., 1841; reprint, Fort Worth: Molyneaux Craftsmen, 1925), 730-31 (page references are to reprint edition).
96. Hogan, *Texas Republic*, 82-100.
97. Z[acharius] N. Morrell, *Flowers and Fruits in the Wilderness* 3d ed. (St. Louis: Commercial Printing, 1872; reprint, Irving, Tex.: Griffin Graphic Arts, 1966), 93 (page references are to reprint edition).
98. Hogan, *Texas Republic*, 82-86.
99. Houston County Tax List, 1843.

184   FRONTIER RELIGION

100. Daniel Parker to Sam Houston, June 28, 1842, #2524, Andrew Jackson Houston Papers.
101. Hogan, *Texas Republic,* 260-62.
102. Ibid., 11
103. Connor, *Peters Colony,* 25, 27, 39, 49.
104. Ibid., 16-17.
105. Leroy P. Graf, "Colonizing Projects in Texas South of the Nueces, 1820-1845," *The Southwestern Historical Quarterly* 50 (April 1947): 445.
106. Daniel Parker to Sam Houston, July 29, 1842, #2597, Andrew Jackson Houston Papers.
107. Archie P. McDonald, ed., *Hurrah for Texas: The Diary of Adolphus Sterne, 1838-1851* (Waco, Tex.: Texian, 1969), 186; Daniel Parker to Sam Houston, December 29, 1843, #3206, Andrew Jackson Houston Papers.
108. James W. Parker to Texas Congress, November 4, 1840. See James W. Parker, asks aid to fight Indians and rescue prisoners, November 9, 1840, Memorials & Petitions Series, Legislative Records (RG 100), Archives Division, Texas State Library, Austin.
109. James W. Parker to Sam Houston, March 14, 1843, #2975, Andrew Jackson Houston Papers.
110. Daniel Parker to Houston, December 29, 1843.
111. Ibid.
112. Gammel, *Laws,* 1:522.
113. Daniel Parker to Houston, July 29, 1842.
114. Ibid.
115. Zoie Odom Newsome, "Antislavery Sentiment in Texas, 1821-1861" (M.A. thesis, Texas Tech University, 1968), 44.
116. Gammel, *Laws,* 1:1079.
117. Campbell, *Empire,* 68.
118. Ibid., 67.
119. Houston County Tax List, 1838.
120. By 1838 Isaac Parker owned one slave. James W. owned three in 1840. Possibly for the speculative purposes, John Parker invested in nine slaves. In 1855 Bennett paid $400 for a young female slave and her infant. See Houston County Tax Rolls, 1838; White, *1840 Census of Texas,* 115; Bill of Sale, James P. Dumas to John Parker, April 18, 1854, Daniel Parker Papers; Bill of Sale, Eli A. Bower to Miles Bennett, September 1, 1855, in possession of Ron Parker.
121. "Records of an Early Texas Baptist Church," *The Quarterly of the Texas State Historical Association* 12 (July 1908): 32.
122. David T. Bailey, *Shadow on the Church: Southwestern Evangelical Religion and the Issue of Slavery, 1783-1860* (Ithaca, N.Y.: Cornell University, 1985), 95-99, 139.
123. Daniel Parker, *A Public Address* (Vincennes, Ind.: Stout & Osborn, 1820; reprint, Hamilton, Ill.: Hamilton Press, 1988), 51-52 (page references are to reprint edition).
124. Bailey, *Shadow on the Church,* 125-26.
125. Campbell, *Empire,* 70.
126. Ibid., 31, 55-56. The Texas census in 1847 reported 38,753 bondsmen

out of a total population of 142, 009. Three years later the United States census showed a population total of 212,592 and 58,161 slaves.

127. Isaac Parker to Sam Houston, February 28, 1844, #3372, Andrew Jackson Houston Papers.

CHAPTER 5: THE TEXAS MINISTRY

1. Z[acharius] N. Morrell, *Flowers and Fruits in the Wilderness*, 3d ed. (St. Louis: Commercial Printing, 1872; reprint, Irving, Tex.: Griffin Graphic Arts, 1966), 29 (page references are to reprint edition); Lewis M. Edgar, *A History of the Primitive Baptists, in the Western Districts of Tennessee & Kentucky* (Paris, Tenn.: Intelligencer, 1881), 43; *Church Advocate*, 1 (June 1830), 215.

2. Morrell, *Flowers and Fruits*, 20-21.

3. Edward S. Ellis, *The Life of David Crockett* (Philadelphia: Porter & Coates, 1884), 181-84.

4. Morrell, *Flowers and Fruits*, 32.

5. W[illiam] B[luford] DeWees, *Letters From An Early Settler of Texas* (Waco, Tex.: Texian, 1968), 16, 137.

6. Howard Miller, "Stephen F. Austin and the Anglo-Texan Response to the Religious Establishment in Mexico, 1821-1836," *Southwestern Historical Quarterly* 91 (January 1988), 286.

7. Ibid., 287. Miller states that only two parish priests remained.

8. Winnie Allen, "The History of Nacogdoches, 1691-1830" (M.A. thesis, University of Texas, 1925), 90, 90a, 91-96.

9. Miller, "Response to the Religious Establishment," 303.

10. H[ans] P[eter] N[ielson] Gammel, comp., *The Laws of Texas, 1822-1897*, vol. 1 (Austin: Gammel Book, 1898), 72, 424.

11. Ibid., 126.

12. Miller, "Response to the Religious Establishment," 286.

13. Ibid., 287.

14. Gammel, *Laws*, 1:248.

15. David Woodman, Jr. *Guide to Texas Emigrants* (Boston: M. Hawes, 1835), 35.

16. William Stuart Red, *The Texas Colonists and Religion, 1821-1836* (Austin: E. L. Shettles, n.d.), 82.

17. Nacogdoches Archives, 77:91, Center for American History, University of Texas, Austin.

18. Gammel, *Laws*, 1:26.

19. Miller, "Response to the Religious Establishment," 290.

20. H[enderson] [K.] Yoakum, *History of Texas*, vol. 2 (New York: Redfield, 1855), 536–38, 542; Red, *Texas Colonists*, 83.

21. Ben J. Parker, "Early Times in Texas and History of the Parker Family," *Palestine (Tex.) Daily Herald*, February 12, 1935.

22. Malcolm D. McLean, ed., *Papers Concerning Robertson's Colony in Texas*, vol. 7 (Arlington, Tex.: University of Texas at Arlington, 1980), 256.

23. Eugene C. Barker, *The Life of Stephen F. Austin* (Austin: Texas State Historical Association, 1949), 348-61.

24. *Kaskaskia Republican*, November 6, 1824.
25. Miller, "Response to the Religious Establishment," 292-93.
26. Church records record "Saturday, January 20th 1834." The church clerk evidently assigned the wrong date to the meeting. In that year, January 20 fell on Monday. See "Records of an Early Texas Baptist Church," *The Quarterly of the Texas State Historical Association* 11 (October 1907): 92.
27. Ibid., 96-100.
28. Church records do not record any services at the old location until July 3, 1841. By then the church lay in the recently created Houston County. By 1841 several of the membership evidently had moved back to their old homes. Ibid., 123.
29. Ibid., 98-105.
30. The first Baptist church constituted in Texas seems to have been a congregation organized by Elder Abner Smith near the Colorado River in 1834. Like Daniel Parker, Smith held strong antimissionary views. See Robert A. Baker, *The Blossoming Desert* (Waco, Tex.: Word Books, 1970), 50; Morrell, *Flowers and Fruits*, 72.
31. S. F. Sparks, "Recollections of S. F. Sparks," *The Quarterly of the Texas State Historical Association* 12 (July 1908): 77.
32. A. J. Holt, "A Brief History of Union Baptist Church, Nacogdoches County, Texas." Original compiled 18 December 1911. (Typewritten nonpaginated copy of original at A. Webb Roberts Library, Southwestern Baptist Theological Seminary, Fort Worth, Tex.) Union Baptist, presently known as Old North Church, is the oldest extant missionary Baptist congregation in Texas. The church is affiliated with the Southern Baptist Convention.
33. "Records of an Early Texas Baptist Church," 108-09.
34. Ibid., 109. In 1844 Parker explained that Bryant had "no ordained or legal authority to administer the ordinances of the gospel." See *The Baptist*, 1 (April 12, 1845), 532.
35. "Records of an Early Texas Baptist Church," 108-110.
36. Ibid., 110.
37. Samuel B. Hesler, "Old North (Union) Baptist Church, 1838-1984" (Research paper, Southwestern Baptist Theological Seminary, 1985), 8-9.
38. Morrell, *Flowers and Fruits*, 77.
39. *The Union Baptist Association: Centennial History, 1840-1940* (Brenham, Tex.: Banner-Press, n.d.), 8-9.
40. *Minutes of the Union Baptist Association, 1840* (Houston: Telegraph Press, 1840), 16.
41. Ibid., 118.
42. Cushing Biggs Hassell and Sylvester Hassell, *History of the Church of God* (Middletown, N.Y.: Gilbert Beebe's Sons, 1886; reprint, Atlanta: Turner Lassetter, 1948), 913-14 (page references are to reprint edition); United States Manuscript Census, East Feliciana Parish, La., 1840, 257. Some discrepancy exists concerning the organizational date of the Union Association of Regular Predestinarian Baptists. The early associational officers apparently wished to assert the preeminence of the predestinarian Union Association over missionary Baptists in Texas. In 1848 Baptist historian David Benedict wrote that the predestinarian Union Association had been organized in 1838. Benedict based his information on the

1843 minutes of this association, which had been sent to him by Daniel Parker. The 1854 minutes recorded that year's meeting as the fifteenth annual assembly. If so, the first annual convention of the Union Association of Regular Predestinarian Baptists occurred in 1839. This insinuates that an organizational session, presumably in 1838, predated the first meeting of the constituted body. Yet the Pilgrim Church minutes plainly listed 1840 as the organizational date. Also, in January or February 1842 the first edition of *The Western Predestinarian Baptist,* an antimissionary paper edited by Parker ally Richard N. Newport, dated the second associational assembly as 1841. Possibly the early clerks of the Association traced the informal beginning to 1838. This was the year after the Hopewell Church formed. Moreover, in 1838 the Pilgrim Church in Shelby County began holding separate services. One group of members met approximately ten miles northeast of San Augustine. A second arm met eight miles east of the settlement. See David Benedict, *A General History of the Baptist Denomination in America and Other Parts of the World* (New York: Lewis Colby & Co., 1848), 787; *Minutes of the Union Association of Regular Predestinarian Baptists* (Palestine, Tex.: Trinity Advocate, 1854), title page, A. Webb Roberts Library, Southwestern Baptist Theological Seminary, Fort Worth, Tex.); *The Western Predestinarian Baptist,* [February 1] 1842; "Records of an Early Texas Baptist Church," 103; W[illiam] E[dward] Paxton, *A History of the Baptists of Louisiana* (St. Louis: C. R. Barnes, 1888), 365.

43. *Minutes of the Mississippi Baptist Association, 1834* (Clinton, La.: H. Rogers, 1835), 4; Glen Lee Greene, *House Upon a Rock: About Southern Baptists in Louisiana* (Alexandria, La.: Louisiana Baptist Convention, 1973), 142-43. Paxton had led the Natalbany Baptist Church, near present Hammond, Louisiana, into the Two-Seed fold. Because of this position by the congregation, more orthodox Baptists in the area regarded the Natalbany church as heretical. In February 1829 Paxton preached Two Seedism at his Mount Nebo pastorate in Tangipahoa Parish. In the 1830s the Mount Nebo Church excluded him.

44. *Western Predestinarian Baptist,* [February 1] 1842, 13.

45. Ibid.

46. Ibid., March 1, 1842, 17.

47. Daniel Parker, *Views on the Two Seeds* (Vandalia, Ill.: Robert Blackwell, 1826), 4.

48. *Western Predestinarian Baptist,* March 15, 1842, 38.

49. Daniel Parker, *The Second Dose of Doctrine on the Two Seeds* (Vincennes, Ind.: Elihu Stout, 1826 [1827]), 23.

50. *Western Predestinarian Baptist,* March 1, 1842, 28.

51. Ibid., October 25, 1843, 271.

52. Ibid., May 8, 1844, passim.

53. Daniel Parker to Sam Houston, January 25, 1837, #804, Andrew Jackson Houston Papers, Archives Division, Texas State Library, Austin.

54. William Ransom Hogan, *The Texas Republic: A Social and Economic History* (Austin: University of Texas, 1969), 147-48.

55. George Louis Crockett, *Two Centuries in East Texas* (Dallas: Southwest Press, 1932), 307.

56. Baker, *Blossoming Desert,* 84-85.

57. Edna McDonald Wylie, "The Fort Houston Settlement" (M.A. thesis, Sam Houston State Teachers College, 1958), 72-75.
58. Baker, Blossoming Desert, 81.
59. Ibid., 88; Morrell, *Flowers and Fruits,* 189.
60. "Records of an Early Texas Baptist Church," 145.
61. Ibid., *The Baptist,* 532.
62. "Records of an Early Texas Baptist Church," 145.
63. Ibid.
64. *Western Predestinarian Baptist,* April 15, 1843, 220.
65. Benedict, *General History,* 788; "Records of an Early Texas Baptist Church," 102, 118-19, 121, 125, 133, 139, 144.
66. Boggy Bayou organized as a promissions church on February 15, 1855. See Minute Book of Boggy Bayou Baptist Church. Typewritten copy in the Louisiana Room, Shreve Memorial Library, Shreveport, La.
67. The Mount Pleasant congregation dissolved in 1844 and formed the nucleus for the San Jacinto Church. See "Records of an Early Texas Baptist Church," 144-45.
68. Daniel Parker Will, Typewritten copy at A. Webb Roberts Library, Southwestern Baptist Theological Seminary, Fort Worth, Tex.
69. James W. Parker, "Biography of Daniel Parker," Daniel Parker Papers, Center for American History, University of Texas, Austin.
70. Daniel Parker Family Bible, Elkhart State Bank, Elkhart, Tex.
71. Morrell, *Flowers and Fruits,* 190.
72. James W. Parker, "Biography"; *The Baptist,* 531-32; E. Powel due D. Parker, Daniel Parker Papers.
73. Parker Genealogy File, Palestine Public Library, Palestine, Tex.; H. Smythe, *Historical Sketch of Parker County and Weatherford, Texas* (St. Louis: Louis C. Lavat, 1877; facsimile edition, Waco, Tex.: W. M. Morrison, 1973), 1-2; Genealogical information furnished by Mary Reaves Dees, 4340 N. W. Twelfth St., Oklahoma City, Okla.
74. Benedict, *General History,* 787.
75. Donald G. Mathews, *Religion in the Old South* (Chicago: University of Chicago, 1977), 81-90, 151-57.
76. Sydney E. Ahlstrom, *A Religious History of the American People* (New Haven: Yale University, 1972), 660-64.
77. Randolph B. Campbell, *An Empire for Slavery: The Peculiar Institution in Texas, 1821-1865* (Baton Rouge: Louisiana State University, 1989), 220.
78. "Records of an Early Texas Baptist Church," 94-95.
79. Campbell, *Empire,* 172-73.
80. Morrell, *Flowers and Fruits,* 342.
81. Baker, *Blossoming Desert,* 98-112.

CHAPTER 6: CONCLUSION: "A MAN OF WAR"
1. *Church Advocate,* 2 (September 1831), 272.
2. Ibid., 264.

3. Sydney E. Ahlstrom, *A Religious History of the American People* (New Haven: Yale University, 1972), 383.
4. Daniel Parker, *Views on the Two Seeds* (Vandalia, Ill.: Robert Blackwell, 1826), 18.
5. *Church Advocate*, 2 (September 1831), 271.
6. Ibid.
7. John 2:17.
8. Cushing Biggs Hassell and Sylvester Hassell, *History of the Church of God* (Middletown, N.Y.: Gilbert Beebe's Sons, 1886; reprint, Atlanta: Turner Lassetter, 1948), 556 (page reference is to reprint edition).
9. Daniel Parker, *A Public Address* (Vincennes, Ind.: Stout & Osborn, 1820; reprint, Hamilton, Ill.: Hamilton Press, 1988), 1 (page reference is to reprint edition).
10. John Taylor, *Thoughts on Missions* (n.p., 1820), 6.
11. Julieta Haynes, "A History of the Primitive Baptists" (Ph.D. diss., University of Texas, 1959), 58-59, 318-331. In many respects Primitive Baptists still adhere to the principles of the Black Rock Address. The denomination has no centralized agency, publication, or Bible institute. Services are held once weekly or monthly. Sunday schools are not part of the educational ministry. Many churches reject musical instruments of any kind for worship services. Evangelism, mostly in the form of pastoral sermons, is accomplished entirely under the auspices of individual congregations.
12. *The Biblical Recorder and Southern Watchman*, 5 (September 7, 1839), [front page].
13. R[obert Boyte Crawford] Howell, "Missions and Anti-missions in Tennessee," *The Baptist Memorial and Monthly Record* 4 (November 1845): 305-06.
14. Daniel Parker, *The Second Dose of Doctrine on the Two Seeds* (Vincennes, Ind.: Elihu Stout, 1826 [1827]), 59.
15. Merrill E. Gaddis, "Religious Ideas and Attitudes in the Early Frontier," *Church History* 2 (1933): 164-65.
16. John Mason Peck, "Dangerous Errors Abroad," *The Western Baptist* 1 (May 1831): 69-70.
17. *Minutes of the Mississippi Baptist Association, 1834* (Clinton, La.: H. Rogers, 1835), 4; David Benedict, *A General History of the Baptist Denomination in America* (New York: Lewis Colby & Co., 1848), 770, 830, 869; Robert Louis Webb, *History of the Spoon River Association of Regular Baptists* (Carthage, Ill.: Primitive Baptist Library, n.d.), [15]; *Minutes of the Salem Association, 1834* (Vincennes, Ind.: Elihu Stout, [1834]), 4; *Eel River Association* (Franklin, Ind.: Franklin College, n.d.), 4 (typewritten).
18. *Minutes of the Cumberland Baptist Association, 1842* (n.p., [1842]), passim, Samuel Colgate Historical Library, American Baptist Historical Commission, Rochester, N.Y.); Minutes of the Stone's River Association, 1844 (Nashville: B. R. McKennie, [1844]), 4.
19. John M. Watson, *The Old Baptist Test* (Nashville: Republican Banner, 1860), 60.
20. *The Christian Baptist*, 7 (1 March 1830), 207; reprint, Nashville: Gospel Advocate, 1956 (page reference is to reprint edition).

21. *Church Advocate*, 1 (May 1830), 178.
22. Ibid.
23. Watson, *Old Baptist Test*, 99.
24. Lemuel Potter, *Labors and Travels of Elder Lemuel Potter, as an Old School Baptist Minister* (Evansville, Ind.: Keller Printing, 1894; reprint, Carthage, Ill.: Primitive Baptist Library, n.d.), 262-67.
25. *Minutes of the Union Association of Regular Predestinarian Baptists, 1876* (Palestine, Tex.: R. H. & J. T. Small, 1876), 4. Ben pastored the Pilgrim Predestinarian Church from 1864 to 1896. See *Minutes of Union Association of Regular Predestinarian Baptists, 1897* (n.p., [1897]), passim.
26. George Y. Stipp, *A Refutation of the Doctrine Called "Two Seeds"* (Majority Point, Ill.: Cumberland Democrat, 1879; reprint, Carthage, Ill.: Primitive Baptist Library, n.d.), [27-29] (page references are to nonpaginated reprint); Lemuel Potter, *Unconditional Election Stated and Defined* (Carmi, Ill.: Courier Stream Book, 1880; reprint, Carthage, Ill.: Primitive Baptist Library, n.d.), passim; W. R. Mattox, "The 'Two-Seed' Doctrine," *Primitive Monitor* 27 (May 1912): 194-201, 27 (June 1912): 251-61; J. S. Newman, *Who Are the Primitive Baptists* (Bonham, Tex.: Baptist Trumpet, 1903), 51-59; C. H. Cayce, *Hot Shot for Campbellites, for Any Arminian, for Two Seeders and Soul Sleepers* (Martin, Tenn.: Cayce's & Turner, 1915), 14-20.
27. Justin A. Smith, *A History of the Baptists in the Western States* (Philadelphia: American Baptist Publication Society, 1896), 131; Terry E. Miller, "Otter Creek Church, Indiana: Lonely Bastion of Daniel Parker's 'Two-Seedism,'" *Foundations: A Baptist Journal of History and Theology* 18 (October 1975): 368.
28. Parker, *A Public Address*, 49.
29. Wickliff Kitchell to Daniel Parker, 20 February 1825, Daniel Parker v. Wickliff Kitchell, Box 7, Case 59, Crawford County Circuit Court, Robinson, Ill.
30. Andrew M. Manis, "Regionalism and a Baptist Perspective on Separation of Church and State," *American Baptist Quarterly* 2 (September 1983): 213-227.
31. *Church Advocate*, 1 (May 1830), 187.
32. L. F. Greene, ed., *The Writings of John Leland* (New York: Arno Press & The New York Times, 1969), 255.
33. *Church Advocate*, 2 (August 1831), 250.
34. *Church Advocate*, 2 ([November or December] 1831), 4.
35. Parker, *A Public Address*, 51-51.
36. Theodore Calvin Pease, ed., *Illinois Election Returns, 1818-1848*, vol. 28, *Collections of the Illinois State Historical Library* (Springfield: Illinois State Historical Library, 1923), 27.
37. Daniel Parker to Sam Houston, July 29, 1842, #2597. Andrew Jackson Houston Papers, Archives Division, Texas State Library, Austin, Tex.
38. Ahlstrom, *Religious History*, 425-26; Clifford S. Griffin, *Their Brothers' Keepers: Moral Stewardship in the United States, 1800-1865* (New Brunswick: Rutgers University, 1960), 9-13; Charles I. Foster, *An Errand of Mercy: The Evangelical United Front, 1790-1837* (Chapel Hill: University of North Carolina, 1960), 223.
39. Taylor, *Thoughts*, 6.
40. Ibid.

41. *Church Advocate*, 2 (December 1830), 60.

42. Ibid.

43. Foot washing remained a common practice among frontier Baptists. Although most did not regard it as a church ordinance, many Baptists thought that it encouraged humility.

44. *The Western Predestinarian Baptist*, (March 15, 1842), 40.

45. Harry L. Watson, *Liberty and Power: The Politics of Jacksonian America* (New York: Hill and Wang, 1990), 6.

46. *Church Advocate*, 2 (April 1831), 150-64.

47. Donald F. Tingley, "Illinois Days of Daniel Parker, Texas Colonizer," *Journal of the Illinois State Historical Society* 51 (Winter 1958): 388-402.

48. Nathan O. Hatch, *The Democratization of American Christianity* (New Haven: Yale University , 1989), passim; Gordon S. Wood, "Ideology and the Origins of Liberal America," *The William and Mary Quarterly* 44 (July 1987): 627-40.

Bibliography

Primary

Manuscripts

Joseph Chambers Manuscript. Vincennes University Archives, Vincennes, IN. Compiled into typewritten version and published as *Maria Creek Church Papers*. Vincennes, Ind. Lewis Historical Library, n.d.

Harlan-Sargent Papers. Illinois State Historical Library, Springfield, Ill.

Holt, A. J. "A Brief History of Union Baptist Church, Nacogdoches County, Texas." Original compiled December 18, 1911. Typewritten nonpaginated copy of original at A. Webb Roberts Library, Southwestern Baptist Theological Seminary, Fort Worth, Tex.

Andrew Jackson Houston Papers. Archives Division, Texas State Library, Austin, Tex.

Elias Kent Kane Papers. Chicago Historical Society, Chicago, Ill.

Isaac McCoy Papers. Microfilm edition at Ball State University, Muncie, Ind. (original at Kansas State Historical Society, Topeka, Kans.)

[McCoy, Isaac]. "Three Letters to Daniel Parker." American Baptist Collection, Manuscript Division, Illinois State Historical Library, Springfield, Ill.

Daniel Parker Family Bible. Elkhart State Bank, Elkhart, Tex. Contains notes about the Parker family in the handwriting of Daniel Parker.

Daniel Parker Papers. Center for American History, University of Texas, Austin, Tex.

Daniel Parker Will. Typewritten copy at A. Webb Roberts Library, Southwestern Baptist Theological Seminary, Fort Worth, Tex.

Parker family papers in possession of Ron Parker, Groesbeck, Tex.

William Polke Papers. Lilly Library, Indiana University, Bloomington.

William Price. "Ancient Reminiscences." Indiana Division, Indiana State Library, Indianapolis, Ind.

James Winchester and William Cage Account Books. Tennessee State Archives, Nashville, TN. Microfilm.

Government Documents

United States
United States Congress. *The Debates and Proceedings.* 18th Cong., 1st sess., vol. 2. Washington: Gales and Seaton, 1856.
United States Manuscript Census, Conway County, Arkansas, 1830. On microfilm at Arkansas State Library, Little Rock, Ark.
United States Manuscript Census, Crawford County, Ill.,1820, 1830. On microfilm at Mahon Public Library, Lubbock, Tex.
United States Manuscript Census, East Feliciana Parish, LA., 1840. On microfilm at Mahon Public Library, Lubbock, Tex.
United States Manuscript Census, Lawrence County, Ill., 1830. On microfilm at Mahon Public Library, Lubbock, Tex.
United States Manuscript Census Returns, Crawford County, Ill. 1820. On microfilm at Mahon Public Library, Lubbock, Tex.
United States Manuscript Census Returns, Indiana, Harrison, Jefferson, Gibson, Knox, Posey, Randolph, Sullivan, and Vigo counties, Ind., 1820. On Microfilm at Mahon Public Library, Lubbock, Tex.

State

Illinois
Executive Record, 1818-1832, vol 1. Illinois State Archives, Springfield, Ill.
Illinois Election Returns, vol 2. Illinois State Archives, Springfield, Ill.
State of Illinois. *Assembly Journal.* 2d Assy., 1st sess., 1820. Vandalia, Ill.: Browne & Berry, 1821.
State of Illinois. *Assembly Journal.* 1st Assy., 2d sess., 1819. Kaskaskia, Ill.: Blackwell & Berry, 1819.
State of Illinois. *Senate Journal.* 4th Assy., 1st sess., 1824. Vandalia, Ill.: Robert Blackwell, 1824.
State of Illinois. *Senate Journal.* 4th Assy., 2d sess., 1826. Vandalia, Ill.: Robert Blackwell, 1826.
State of Illinois. *Senate Journal.* 3d Assy., 1st sess., 1822. Vandalia, Ill.: Blackwell & Berry, 1823.
Territory of Illinois. *Legislative Council and House of Representatives Journal.* 4th sess., 1816. Kaskaskia, Illinois Territory, 1816.

Texas
Legislative Records. Archives Division, Texas State Library, Austin, Tex.
Republic of Texas Audited Claims. Comptroller of Public Accounts Records, Archives Division, Texas State Library, Austin, Tex.

County

Arkansas
Conway County Deed and Mortgage Index, vol. A. Arkansas State Library, Little Rock, Ark. Microfilm.

Illinois
Clark County Deed Book, vol. A. Clerk of Court, Marshall, Ill.
Clark County Land Book, vol. A. Clerk of Court, Marshall, Ill.
Coles County Deed Book, vol. B. Clerk of Court, Charleston, Ill.
Crawford County Circuit Court Book, vol. B. Circuit Court, Robinson, Ill.
Joel Barlor v. Joseph A. Parker, Isaac Parker, and Daniel Parker. Box 1, Case 12. Crawford County Circuit Court, Robinson, Ill.
Thomas Kennedy v. Abraham Taylor and Benjamin Parker. Circuit Court Record Book, A:124, Crawford County Circuit Court, Robinson, Ill.
Daniel Parker v. Elijah Dodson. Box 2, Case 50. Crawford County Circuit Court, Robinson, Ill.
Daniel Parker v. Wickliff Kitchell. Box 7, Case 53. Crawford County Circuit Court, Robinson, Ill.
Daniel Parker v. Wickliff Kitchell. Box 7, Case 59. Crawford County Circuit Court, Robinson, Ill..
People v. William Kilbuck. Box 5, Case 39. Circuit Court Record Book, vol. A:11-14, Crawford County Circuit Court, Robinson, Ill.
Crawford County Commissioners Record Book, 1816-1824. Clerk of Court, Robinson, Ill.
Crawford County Deed Book, vol. A. Clerk of Court, Robinson, Ill.
Crawford County Original Land Entry Book. Clerk of Court, Robinson, Ill.
Edgar County Deed Book, vol. 1. Clerk of Court, Paris, Ill.
Edgar County Marriage Records, vol. A. Clerk of Court, Paris, Ill.

Tennessee
Dickson County Deed Book, vol. A. Clerk of Court, Charlotte, TN.
Robertson County Deed Book, vol. Q. Tennessee State Archives, Nashville, TN. Microfilm.
Sumner County Deed Book, vols. 6-7. Tennessee State Archives, Nashville, TN. Microfilm.
Sumner County Inventories. Tennessee State Archives, Nashville, TN. Microfilm.

Texas
Houston County Tax List, 1838-1881. Archives Division, Texas State Library. Microfilm.
Nacogdoches Archives. Center for American History, University of Texas, Austin, Tex.

CHURCH RECORDS

Minutes of the Blue River Association, 1830, 1832. n.p., [1830]; n.p., [1832]. On microfilm at the Primitive Baptist Library, Carthage, Ill.
Minute Book of Boggy Bayou Baptist Church. Louisiana Room, Shreve Memorial Library, Shreveport, La. Typewritten copy of original manuscript.
Minutes of the Concord Association, 1812. Nashville: M. & J. Norvell, [1812]. Located at Samuel Colgate Historical Library, American Baptist Historical Society, Rochester, N.Y.

196   FRONTIER RELIGION

Minutes of the Concord Association, 1816-1817. Microfilm of manuscript at Southern Baptist Historical Commission, Nashville, Tenn.

Minutes of the Cumberland Baptist Association, 1816, 1842. Franklin, Tenn.: I. N. Henry, [1816]; n.p., 1842. Located at Samuel Colgate Historical Library, American Baptist Historical Society, Rochester, N.Y.

Minutes of the Eel River Association of Baptists, 1830. Lafayette, Ind.: J. B. Semans, 1830. Located at Samuel Colgate Historical Library, American Baptist Historical Society, Rochester, N.Y.

Minutes of the Georgia Baptist Association, 1803. [Augusta, GA.: William J. Bunce, 1804]. On microfilm at Special Collections Library, Mercer University, Macon, Ga.

Grand Prairie Church Minutes. Primitive Baptist Library, Carthage, Ill.

Minutes of the Illinois Association, 1824. American Baptist Collection, Manuscript Division, Illinois State Historical Library, Springfield, Ill.

Minutes of the Little Village Baptist Church, 1817-1845. Primitive Baptist Library, Carthage, Ill.

Minutes of the Little Pigeon Association of United Baptists, 1824. n.p.: Brundon & Co., [1824]. Located at Samuel Colgate Historical Library, American Baptist Historical Society, Rochester, N.Y.

Mill Creek Baptist Church Records, 1797-1814. Manuscript Division, Tennessee State Archives, Nashville, Tenn.

Minutes of the Mississippi Baptist Association, 1834. Clinton, LA.: H. Rogers, 1835. Located at Southern Baptist Historical Commission, Nashville, Tenn.

North Fork Baptist Church Minutes. Primitive Baptist Library, Carthage, Ill.

Minutes of the Pilgrim Predestinarian Baptist Church. Center for American History, University of Texas, Austin, Tex. Manuscript.

Minutes of the Red River Baptist Association, 1816-1817, 1823. Russellville, Ky.: H. C. Sleight, [1816]; George B. Crutcher, [1817]; Charles Rhea, 1823. Located at Samuel Colgate Historical Library, American Baptist Historical Commission, Rochester, N.Y.

Minutes of the Salem Association, 1832, 1834. New Harmony, Ind.: Richard Beck, 1832; Vincennes, Ind.: Elihu Stout, [1834]. Photocopies at Primitive Baptist Library, Carthage, Ill.

Silver Creek Baptist Church Minutes. Indiana Division, Indiana State Library, Indianapolis, Ind. Manuscript.

Minutes of the Stone's River Association, 1844. Nashville: B. R. McKennie, [1844]. Located at Samuel Colgate Historical Library, American Baptist Historical Commission, Rochester, N.Y.

Testament Baptist Church Minutes. Testament Baptist Church, Lafayette, Tenn.

Turnbull Baptist Church Minutes. Manuscript Division, Tennessee State Archives, Nashville, Tenn.

Minutes of the Union Association (Illinois), 1824-1825, 1827, 1832. Vincennes, Ind.: Elihu Stout, 1824-1825, 1827, 1832. Located at Samuel Colgate Historical Library, American Baptist Historical Commission, Rochester, N.Y.

Minutes of the Union Association of Regular Predestinarian Baptists, 1876, 1897. Palestine, Tex.: R. H. & T. J. Small, 1876; n.p., [1897]. On microfilm at A. Webb Roberts Library, Southwestern Baptist Theological Seminary, Fort Worth, Tex. Microfilm.

Minutes of the Union Baptist Association (Texas, promissions), 1840. Houston: Telegraph Press, 1840. Located at Southern Baptist Historical Commission, Nashville, Tenn.
Union Primitive Baptist Church Minutes. Primitive Baptist Library, Carthage, Ill.
Minutes of the Wabash District Association, 1822-1831. Vincennes, Ind.: Elihu Stout, 1822-1831. Microfilm and photocopies located Primitive Baptist Library, Carthage, Ill.
Minutes of the White River Association. Bloomington: J. C. Carlton, 1856. Photocopy at Primitive Baptist Library, Carthage, Ill.
Wilson's Creek Baptist Church Minutes. Manuscript Division, Tennessee State Archives, Nashville, Tenn.
W.P.A. Church Records, 1785-1942. Box 7, File 3. Tennessee State Archives, Nashville, Tenn. Microfilm.

NEWSPAPERS

Illinois
Illinois Intelligencer, 1822-1826. (Vandalia)
Kaskaskia Republican, 1824.
Republican Advocate, 1823-1824. (Kaskaskia)

Indiana
The Western Sun, 1817-1823. (Vincennes)

Tennessee
Carthage Gazette, 1811-1817.
Clarion and Tennessee Gazette, 1813-1821. (Nashville)
Democratic Clarion and Tennessee Gazette, 1809-1813. (Nashville)
Impartial Review, 1805-1809. (Nashville)

Texas
Austin City Gazette, 1839.

RELIGIOUS PERIODICALS

The Baptist, 1 (12 April 1845).
Baptist Chronicle, 1 (November 1830).
The Biblical Recorder and Southern Watchman, 5 (7 September 1839); 6 (29 February 1840).
The Christian Baptist, 1823-1830. Reprint, Nashville: Gospel Advocate, 1956.
Church Advocate, 1829-1831.
Columbian Star, 1 (21 November 1829).
Latter Day Luminary, 1819.
The Western Baptist, 1 (October 1830).
The Western Predestinarian Baptist, 1842-1844.

Books

Asplund, John. *The Universal Register of the Baptist Denomination in North America.* Boston: John W. Folsom, 1794; reprint, New York: Arno, 1980.
Beecher, Lyman. *A Plea for the West.* 3d ed. Cincinnati: Truman & Smith, 1836.
Babcock, Rufus, ed., *Forty Years of Pioneer Life: Memoir of John Mason Peck, D.D.* Philadelphia: American Baptist Publication Society, 1864; reprint, Carbondale, Ill.: Southern Illinois University, 1965.
Benedict, David. *A General History of the Baptist Denomination in America, and other Parts of the World.* 2 vols. Boston: Lincoln & Edwards, 1813.
Benedict, David. *A General History of the Baptist Denomination in America and Other Parts of the World.* New York: Lewis Colby & Co., 1848. Although entitled the same as the 1813 work, the contents justify its inclusion as a separate source.
Binkley, William C., ed. *Official Correspondence of the Texas Revolution, 1835-1836.* 2 vols. New York: D. AppletonCentury, 1936.
Boewe, Charles, ed. *Prairie Albion: An English Settlement in Pioneer Illinois.* Carbondale, Ill.: Southern Illinois University, 1962.
Bond, John. *History of the Baptist Concord Association.* Nashville: Graves, Marks & Company, 1860.
DeWees, W[illiam] B[luford]. *Letters From An Early Settler of Texas.* Waco, Tex.: Texian, 1968.
Edwards, Morgan. *The Customs of Primitive Churches.* n.p., n.d.
Eel River Association. Franklin, Ind.: Franklin College, n.d. Typewritten.
Ewbank, Louis B. and Dorothy L. Riker, eds. *The Laws of Indiana Territory, 1809-1816.* Indianapolis: Indiana Historical Bureau, 1934.
Ford, Thomas. *A History of Illinois, from its Commencement as a State in 1818 to 1847.* Chicago: S. C. Griggs, 1854; Lakeside Classics ed. Edited by Milo Milton Quaife. 2 vols. Chicago: R. R. Donnelley, 1945.
Franklin, Charles M., comp. *Indiana Territorial Pioneer Records, 1801-1820.* 3 vols. Indianapolis: Heritage House, 1985.
Gammel, H[ans] P[eter] N[ielson], comp. *The Laws of Texas, 1822-1897.* 10 vols. Austin: Gammel Book, 1898.
Garver, Mazie M., ed. *Clark County, Illinois Land Grant Records.* Marshall, Ill.: Clark Co. Genealogical Society, 1973. Typewritten.
Greene, L. F., ed. *The Writings of the Late Elder John Leland.* New York: G. W. Wood, 1845; reprint, New York: Arno Press, 1969.
Gulick, Charles Adams, Jr. and Winnie Allen, eds. *The Papers of Mirabeau Buonaparte Lamar.* 6 vols. Austin: Von Boeckmann-Jones, 1924.
Jenkins, John H., ed. *The Papers of the Texas Revolution 1835-1836.* 10 vols. (Austin: Jay A. Matthews, 1973.
Kennedy, William. *Texas: The Rise, Progress and Prospects of the Republic of Texas.* London: n.p., 1841; reprint, Fort Worth: Molyneaux Craftsmen, 1925.
Knox County Indiana: Early Land Records and Court Indexes 1783-1815. 3 vols. Chicago: Genealogical Services, 1973.
Lofton, Rachel, Susie Hendrix, and Jane Kennedy, eds. *The Rachel Plummer Narrative.* n.p.: By the editors, 1926.
McCoy, Isaac. *History of Baptist Indian Missions.* Washington: William M. Morrison, 1840.

———. *Remarks on the Practicability of Indian Reform Embracing Their Colonization.* Boston: Lincoln & Edmands, 1827.
McDonald, Archie P., ed. *Hurrah for Texas: The Diary of Adolphus Sterne, 1838-1851.* Waco, Tex.: Texian, 1969.
McLean, Malcolm D. ed. *Papers Concerning Robertson's Colony in Texas.* 19 vols. Arlington, Tex.: University of Texas at Arlington, 19741993.
Morrell, Z[acharius] N. *Flowers and Fruits in the Wilderness.* 3d ed. St. Louis: Commercial Printing, 1872; reprint, Irving, Tex.: Griffin Graphic Arts, 1966.
Muir, Andrew Forest, ed. *Texas in 1837.* Austin: University of Texas, 1958.
Norton, Margaret Cross, ed. *Illinois Census Returns, 1820.* Vol. 26, *Collections of the Illinois State Historical Library.* Springfield: Illinois State Historical Library, 1934.
Parker, Daniel. *The Author's Defence.* Vincennes, Ind.: E. Stout, [1824].
———. *A Public Address.* Vincennes, Ind.: Stout & Osburn, 1820; reprint, Hamilton, Ill.: Hamilton Press, 1988.
———. *The Second Dose of Doctrine on the Two Seeds.* Vincennes, Ind.: Elihu Stout, 1826 [1827].
———. *A Short Hint.* Vincennes, Ind.: Elihu Stout, 1827.
———. *A Supplement or Explanation of My Views on the Two Seeds.* In *Views on the Two Seeds.* Vandalia, Ill.: Robert Blackwell, 1826.
———. *Views on the Two Seeds.* Vandalia, Ill.: Robert Blackwell, 1826.
Parker, James W. *Narrative of the Perilous Adventures, Miraculous Escapes, and Sufferings of Rev. James W. Parker.* Louisville: *Morning Courier,* 1844.
Pease, Theodore Calvin, ed. *Illinois Election Returns 1818-1848.* Vol. 28, *Collections of the Illinois State Historical Library.* Springfield: Illinois State Historical Library, 1923.
Porch, Deane, ed. *Sumner County, Tennessee Marriage Records.* Franklin, Tenn.: Louise G. Lynch, n.d.
Reynolds, John. *My Own Times.* Chicago: Chicago Historical Society, 1879.
Ross, James, ed. *Life and Times of Elder Reuben Ross.* Philadelphia: Grant, Faires & Rodgers, n.d.; reprint, Nashville: McQuiddy, 1977.
Semple, Robert Baylor. *History of the Baptists in Virginia.* Rev. ed. n.p., 1810; reprint, Cottonport, La.: Polyanthos, 1972.
Stiff, Edward. *The Texan Emigrant.* Cincinnati: George Conclin, 1840.
Strickland, W. P., ed. *Autobiography of Peter Cartwright.* Cincinnati: L. Swormstedt & A. Poe, 1860.
Taylor, John. *Thoughts on Missions.* n.p., 1820.
Wallace, Ernest, ed. *Documents of Texas History.* Lubbock, Tex.: Texas Tech Library, 1963.
Washburne, E. B., ed. *The Edwards Papers.* 3 vols. Chicago: Fergus, 1884.
Watson, John M.. *The Old Baptist Test.* Nashville: *Republican Banner,* 1860.
White, Gifford, ed. *The 1840 Census of the Republic of Texas.* Austin: Pemberton, 1966.
Whitney, Ellen M., ed. *The Blackhawk War. 1831-32.* Vol. 1, *Collections of the Illinois State Historical Library.* Springfield: Illinois State Historical Library, 1970.
Williams, Amelia W. and Eugene C. Barker, eds. *The Writings of Sam Houston.* 8 vols. Austin: University of Texas, 1938.

Williams, Villamae, ed. *Stephen F. Austin's Register of Families.* Austin: By the editor, 1984.
Woodman, David, Jr. *Guide to Texas Emigrants.* Boston: M. Hawes, 1835.

JOURNALS AND ARTICLES

Ayres, G. D. "Texas." *Jeffersonian Republican,* 10 May 1834, 2.
Howell, R[obert Boyte Crawford]. "Missions and Anti-missions in Tennessee." *The Baptist Memorial and Monthly Record* 4 (November 1845): 305-09.
Peck, John Mason. "Historical Sketches of the Baptist Denomination in Indiana, Illinois, and Missouri." *The Baptist Memorial and Monthly Chronicle* 1 (15 July 1842): 197-210.
"Dangerous Errors Abroad." The Western Baptist 1 (May 1831): 69-70.
"Kentucky Baptists." *The Baptist Memorial and Monthly Chronicle* 1 (February 1842): 40-47.
Polke, James. "Some Memoirs of the Polke, Piety, McCoy, McQuaid, and Mathes Families." *Indiana Magazine of History* 10 (March 1914); reprint, New York: Kraus, 1967: 83-109.
"Records of an Early Texas Baptist Church." *The Quarterly of the Texas State Historical Association* 11 (October 1907): 85-156; 12 (July 1908): 1-60.
Sparks, S. F. "Recollections of S. F. Sparks." *The Quarterly of the Texas State Historical Association* 12 (July 1908) : 61-77.

SECONDARY

UNPUBLISHED

Allen, Winnie. "The History of Nacogdoches, 1691-1830." M.A. thesis, University of Texas, 1925.
Bezerra, Benilton Carlos. "Sources and Early History of the Anti-Mission Controversy in the United States, 1814-1840." Th.M. thesis, Southern Baptist Theological Seminary, 1956.
Dillow, Myron D. "A History of Baptists in Illinois." Th.D. diss., Southwestern Baptist Theological Seminary, 1965.
Goodsell, Charles True. "The Baptist Anti-Missionary Movement in America." M.A. thesis, University of Chicago, 1924.
Haynes, Julieta. "A History of the Primitive Baptists." Ph.D. diss., University of Texas, 1959.
Hesler, Samuel B. "Old North (Union) Baptist Church, 1838-1984." Research paper, Southwestern Theological Seminary, 1985.
Lambert, Byron Cecil. "The Rise of the Anti-Mission Baptists: Sources and Leaders, 1800-1840." Ph.D. diss., University of Chicago, 1957.
Lee, O. Max. "Daniel Parker's Doctrine of the Two Seeds." Th.M. thesis, Southern Baptist Theological Seminary, 1962.

Newsome, Zoie Odom. "Antislavery Sentiment in Texas, 1821-1861." M.A. thesis, Texas Tech University, 1968.
Parker, Baldwin. "Life of Quanah Parker, Comanche Chief." Recorded and edited by J. Evetts Haley, 29 August 1930. Center for American History, University of Texas, Austin, Tex.
Parker Genealogy Charts. Furnished by Mary Reaves Dees, 4340 N. W. Twelfth St., Oklahoma City, Okla. and Jane Parker Brown, 32785 Genoa.Rd., Genoa, Ill.
Parker Genealogy File. Palestine Public Library, Palestine, Tex.
Parker, James Robert. Interview by author, 16 July 1993, Elkhart, Tex.
Scott, Lorine Maud. "Daniel Parker and the First Baptist Church in Texas." M.A. thesis, University of Chicago, 1931.
Small, Guy W. "The Life of Daniel Parker." M.A. thesis, East Texas Baptist College, 1954.
Wylie, Edna McDonald. "The Fort Houston Settlement." M.A. thesis, Sam Houston State Teachers College, 1958.

BOOKS

Ahlstrom, Sydney E. *A Religious History of the American People.* New Haven: Yale University, 1972.
Aldrich, Armistead Albert. *The History of Houston County Texas.* San Antonio: Naylor, 1943.
Bailey, David T. *Shadow on the Church: Southwestern Evangelical Religion and the Issue of Slavery, 1783-1860.* Ithaca, N.Y.: Cornell University, 1985.
Baker, Robert A. *The Blossoming Desert.* Waco, Tex.: Word Books, 1970.
Barker, Eugene C. *The Life of Stephen F. Austin.* Austin: Texas State Historical Association, 1949.
Barney, William. *The Road to Secession: A New Perspective on the Old South.* New York: Praeger, 1972.
Beveridge, Albert J. *Abraham Lincoln, 1809-1818.* 6 vols. Boston: Houghton Mifflin, 1928.
The Biographical Encyclopedia of Illinois of the Nineteenth Century. Philadelphia: Galaxy Publishing, 1875.
Boles, John B. *The Great Revival, 1787-1805.* Lexington: University of Kentucky, 1972.
Buck, Solon Justus. *Illinois in 1818.* Chicago: A. C. McClurg, 1918.
Burnett, J. J. *Sketches of Tennessee's Pioneer Baptist Preachers.* Nashville: Marshall & Bruce, 1919; reprint, Johnson City, Tenn.: Overmountain Press, 1985.
Cady, John F. *The Origin and Development of the Missionary Baptist Church in Indiana.* Franklin, Ind.: Franklin College, 1942.
Calvert, Robert A. and Arnoldo De Leon. *The History of Texas.* Arlington Heights, Ill.: Harlan Davidson, 1990.
Campbell, Randolph B. *An Empire for Slavery: The Peculiar Institution in Texas, 1821-1865.* Baton Rouge: Louisiana State University, 1989.
Carroll, B[enajah] H[arvey]. *The Genesis of American Anti-Missionism.* Louisville: Baptist Book Concern, 1902.

Carroll, J[ames] M[ilton]. *A History of Texas Baptists*. Dallas: *Baptist Standard*, 1923.
Cayce, C. H. *Hot Shot for Campbellites, for Any Arminian for Two Seeders and Soul Sleepers*. Martin, Tenn.: Cayce's & Turner, 1915.
Cisco, Jay Guy. *Historic Sumner County, Tennessee*. n.p.: By the author, 1909.
Clayton, John. *The Illinois Fact Book and Historical Almanac, 1673-1968*. Carbondale, Ill.: Southern Illinois University, 1970.
Coffey, Achilles. *A Brief History of the Regular Baptists, Principally of Illinois*. Paducah, Ky.: Martin, 1877.
Coleman, Kenneth, ed. *A History of Georgia*. Athens: University of Georgia, 1977.
Connor, Seymour V. *The Peters Colony of Texas*. Austin: The Texas State Historical Association, 1959.
Corlew, Robert E. *A History of Dickson County, Tennessee*. Nashville: Tennessee Historical Commission, 1956.
———. *Tennessee: A Short History*. Knoxville: University of Tennessee, 1981.
Cox, Norman Wade, ed. *Encyclopedia of Southern Baptists*. 2 vols. Nashville: Broadman, 1958. S.v. "Tennessee Baptist Convention," pt. 2, by Charles Wesley Pope.
Crockett, George Louis. *Two Centuries in East Texas*. Dallas: Southwest Press, 1932.
De Shields, James T. *Border Wars of Texas*. Tioga, Tex.: Herald, 1912; reprint, Waco, Tex.: Texian, 1976.
———. *Tall Men with Long Rifles*. San Antonio: Naylor, 1971.
Dillon, John B. *A History of Indiana*. Indianapolis: Bingham & Doughty, 1859.
Durham, Walter T. *The Great Leap Westward*. Gallatin, Tenn.: Sumner County Public Library, 1969.
———. *Old Sumner: A History of Sumner County Tennessee From 1805 to 1861*. Gallatin, Tenn.: Sumner County Public Library, 1972.
Edgar, Lewis M. *A History of the Primitive Baptists in the Western Districts of Tennessee & Kentucky*. Paris, Tenn.: Intelligencer, 1881.
Edwards, Ninian W[irt]. *Life and Times of Ninian Edwards*. Springfield: Illinois State Journal, 1870; reprint, New York: Arno Press, 1975.
Ellis, Edward S. *The Life of David Crockett*. Philadelphia: Porter & Coates, 1884.
Ericson, Joe E. and Carolyn Ericson. *Spoiling for a Fight: John S. Roberts and Early Nacogdoches*. Waco, Tex.: Texian, 1989.
Esarey, Logan. *History of Indiana: From its Exploration to 1822*. 3 vols. Dayton: Dayton Historical Publishing, 1923.
Fischer, Majorie Hood, comp. *Tennessee Tidbits, 1778-1914*. 2 vols. Easley, S.C.: Southern Historical Press, 1986.
Foster, Charles I. *An Errand of Mercy: The Evangelical United Front, 1790-1837*. Chapel Hill: University of North Carolina, 1960.
Friend, Llerena. *Sam Houston: The Great Designer*. Austin: University of Texas, 1954.
Gewehr, Wesley M. *The Great Awakening in Virginia 1740-1790*. Durham: Duke University, 1930.
Greene, Glen Lee. *House Upon a Rock: About Southern Baptists in Louisiana*. Alexandria, LA.: Louisiana Baptist Convention, 1973.

Griffin, Clifford S. *Their Brothers' Keepers: Moral Stewardship in the United States 1800-1865.* New Brunswick: Rutgers, 1960.

Grime, J. H. *History of Middle Tennessee Baptists.* Cave City, Ky.: By the author, 1902.

Harris, N. Dwight. *The History of Negro Servitude in Illinois.* Chicago: A. C. McClurg, 1904.

Hassell, Cushing Biggs and Sylvester Hassell. *History of the Church of God.* Middletown, N.Y.: Gilbert Beebe's Sons, 1886; reprint, Atlanta: Turner Lassetter, 1948.

Hatch, Nathan O. *The Democratization of American Christianity.* New Haven: Yale, 1989.

Henderson, Frank D., John R. Rea, and Jane Dowd Dailey, comps. *The Official Roster of the Soldiers of the American Revolution Buried in the State of Ohio.* Columbus: F. J. Heer, 1929.

The History of Edgar County, Illinois. Chicago: Wm. Le Barron, 1879; reprint, Evansville, Ind.: Edgar County Sesquicentennial Committee, 1968.

Hogan, William Ransom. *The Texas Republic: A Social and Economic History.* Austin: University of Texas, 1969.

Howard, Robert P. *Illinois: A History of the Prairie State.* Grand Rapids: Eerdmans, 1972.

Hughes, Richard T. and C. Leonard Allen. *Illusions of Innocence: Protestant Primitivism in America, 1630-1875.* Chicago: University of Chicago, 1988.

Isaac, Rhys. *The Transformation of Virginia, 1740-1790.* Chapel Hill: University of North Carolina, 1982.

Jackson, Grace. *Cynthia Ann Parker.* San Antonio: Naylor, 1959.

Keith, Ben F., ed. *History of Maria Creek Church.* Vincennes, Ind.: A. V. Crotts, 1889.

Kemp, Louis Wiltz. *The Signers of the Texas Declaration of Independence.* Houston: Anson Jones Press, 1944.

Lack, Paul D. *The Texas Revolutionary Experience: A Political and Social History, 1835-1836.* College Station, Tex.: Texas A & M, 1992.

Lawrence, Matthew. *John Mason Peck: The Pioneer Missionary Preacher.* New York: Fortuny's, 1940.

Leaton, James. *History of Methodism in Illinois From 1793 to 1832.* Cincinnati: Walden & Stowe, 1883.

Masters, Frank M. *A History of Kentucky Baptists.* Louisville: Kentucky Baptist Historical Society, 1953.

Mathews, Donald G. *Religion in the Old South.* Chicago: University of Chicago, 1977.

McFerrin, John B[erry]. *History of Methodism in Tennessee.* Vol. 1 Nashville: A. H. Redford, 1875; Vols. 2-3 Nashville: Southern Methodist Publishing House, 1872, 1879.

McLoughlin, William G. *New England Dissent, 1630-1833.* 2 vols. Cambridge: Harvard, 1971.

Miyakawa, T. Scott. *Protestants and Pioneers: Individualism and Conformity.* Chicago: University of Chicago, 1964.

Mooney, Chase C. *Slavery in Tennessee.* Bloomington: Indiana University, 1957.

Moore, LaMire Holden. *Southern Baptists in Illinois.* Nashville: Benson, 1957.

Nave, Orville J. and Anna Seamans Nave, eds. *Nave's Study Bible.* n.p.: By Orville J. Nave, 1907; reprint, n.p.: Southwestern Company, 1978.
Newman, J. S. *Who Are the Primitive Baptists.* Bonham, Tex.: Baptist Trumpet, 1903.
Niebuhr, Richard H. *The Social Sources of Denominationalism.* n.p.: Henry Holt, 1929; reprint, Cleveland: World Publishers, 1957.
O'Dea, Thomas F. *Sociology and the Study of Religion Theory, Research, Interpretation.* New York: Basic Books, 1970.
Paxton, W[illiam] Edward]. *A History of the Baptists of Louisiana.* St. Louis: C. R. Barns, 1888.
Pease, Theodore Calvin. *The Frontier State, 1818-1848.* Vol. 2, *The Centennial History of Illinois.* Springfield Centennial Commission, 1918.
Perrin, William Henry, ed. *History of Crawford and Clark Counties, Illinois.* Chicago: O. L. Baskin, 1883.
Perrin, W[illiam] H[enry], A. A. Graham, and D. M. Blaim, comps. *The History of Coles County, Illinois.* Chicago: William Le Baron, Jr., 1879.
Pittman, R. H. *Biographical History of Primitive or Old School Baptist Ministers of the United States.* Anderson, Ind.: Herald Publishing; n.d..
Posey, Walter Brownlow. *The Baptist Church in the Lower Mississippi Valley, 1776-1845.* Lexington: University of Kentucky, 1957.
Potter, Lemuel. *Labors and Travels of Elder Lemuel Potter, as an Old School Baptist Minister.* Evansville, Ind.: Keller Printing, 1894; reprint, Carthage, Ill.: Primitive Baptist Library, n.d.
———. *Unconditional Election Stated and Defined.* Carmi, Ill.: Courier Stream Book, 1880; reprint, Carthage, Ill.: Primitive Baptist Library, n.d.
Red, William Stuart. *The Texas Colonists and Religion, 1821-1836.* Austin: E. L. Shettles, n.d.
Remini, Robert V., ed. *The Jacksonian Era.* Columbia, S.C.: University of South Carolina, 1972.
Schlesinger, Arthur M., Jr. *The Age of Jackson.* Boston: Little, Brown, 1945.
Sellers, Charles. *The Market Revolution: Jacksonian America. 1815-1846.* New York: Oxford University, 1991.
Smith, George W[ashington]. *History of Illinois and Her People.* 6 Vols. Chicago: American Historical Society, 1927.
Smith, Justin A. *A History of the Baptists in the Western States.* Philadelphia: American Baptist Publication Society, 1896.
Smythe, H. *Historical Sketch of Parker County and Weatherford, Texas.* St. Louis: Louis C. Lavat, 1877; facsimile reprint, Waco, Tex.: W. M. Morrison, 1973.
Sprague, William D. *Annals of the American Baptist Pulpit.* New York: Robert Carter, 1860.
Stephens, A. Ray and William Holmes. *Historical Atlas of Texas.* Norman, Okla.: University of Oklahoma, 1984.
Stipp, George Y. *A Refutation of the Doctrine Called "Two Seeds."* Majority Point, Ill.: Cumberland Democrat, 1879; reprint, Carthage, Ill.: Primitive Baptist Library, n.d.
Sweet, William Warren. *The Baptists.* Vol. 1, *Religion on the American Frontier, 1783-1840.* New York: Cooper Square, 1964.

---. The Presbyterians. Vol. 2, *Religion on the American Frontier, 1783-1840.* New York: Cooper Square, 1964.
Torbet, Robert G. *A History of the Baptists.* 3d ed. Valley Forge, Pa.: Judson, 1973.
Turner, Frederick Jackson. *The Significance of the Frontier in American History.* Edited by Harold P. Simonson. New York: Continuum, 1991.
The Union Baptist Association: Centennial History, 1840-1940. Brenham, Tex.: Banner-Press, n.d.
Van Deusen, Glyndon G. *The Life of Henry Clay.* Boston: Little,Brown, 193-7.
Wallace, Ernest and E. Adamson Hoebel. *The Comanches: Lords of the South Plains.* Norman, Okla.: University of Oklahoma, 1952.
Watson, Harry L. *Jacksonian Politics and Community Conflict The Emergence of the Second American Party System in Cumberland County, North Carolina.* Baton Rouge: Louisiana State University, 1981.
---. *Liberty and Power: The Politics of Jacksonian America.* New York: Hill and Wang, 1990.
Webb, Robert Louis. *History of the Spoon River Association of Regular Baptists.* Carthage, Ill.: Primitive Baptist Library, n.d.
---. *Walk About Zion.* n.p.: By the author, 1976.
Webb, Walter Prescott, ed. *The Handbook of Texas.* 2 vols. Austin: Texas State Historical Association, 1952.
Weber, Max. *The Protestant Ethic and the Spirit of Capitalism.* New York: Schribers's, 1930.
Wheeler, T. J. *History of Palestine Association of Baptists in Illinois.* n.p.: By the author, 1938.
Wilbarger, J. W. *Indian Depredations in Texas.* Austin: Pemberton, 1967.
Wisehart, M. K. *Sam Houston: American Giant.* Washington; Luce, 1962.
Wood, Gordon S. "The Democratization of Mind in the American Revolution." In *Leadership in the American Revolution.* By the Third Library of Congress Symposium on the American Revolution. Washington: Library of Congress, 1974: 63-89.
Wyeth, Walter N. *Isaac McCoy: Early Indian Missions.* Philadelphia: W. N. Wyeth, 1895.

JOURNALS AND ARTICLES

Bailey, Chris H. "Old Crawford County." *The Robinson (Ill.) Argus,* 7 October 1971.
Banner, Lois W. "Religious Benevolence as Social Control: A Critique of an Interpretation." *The Journal of American History* 60 (June 1993): 23-41.
Barker, Eugene C. "Don Carlos Barrett." *The Southwestern Historical Quarterly* 20 (July 1916-April 1917): 139145.
Cady, John F. "Isaac McCoy's Mission to the Indians of Indiana and Michigan." *Indiana History Bulletin* 17 (February 1939): 100-113.
Dillon, Merton L. "Benjamin Lundy in Texas." *The Southwestern Historical Quarterly* 63 (July 1959): 4662.
Gaddis, Clye. "'Pioneer Day' Labor Day Celebration Calls Attention to Historical Spots." Robinson (Ill.) *Daily News,* 26 August 1967.

Gaddis, Merrill E. "Religious Ideas and Attitudes in the Early Frontier." *Church History* 2 (1933): 152-70.
Graf, Leroy P. "Colonizing Projects in Texas South of the Nueces, 1820-1845." *The Southwestern Historical Quarterly* 50 (April 1947): 431-48.
Isaac, Rhys. "Evangelical Revolt: The Nature of the Baptists' Challenge to the Traditional Order in Virginia, 1765 to 1775." *The William and Mary Quarterly* 31 (July 1974): 345-68.
Leichtle, Kurt E. "The Rise of Jacksonian Politics in Illinois." *Illinois Historical Journal* 82 (Summer 1989): 93-107.
Manis, Andrew M. "Regionalism and a Baptist Perspective on Separation of Church and State." *American Baptist Quarterly* 2 (September 1983): 213-227.
Mattox, W. R. "The 'Two-Seed' Doctrine." *Primitive Monitor* 27 (May 1912): 194-201; 27 (June 1912): 251-61.
Miller, Howard. "Stephen F. Austin and the Anglo-Texan Response to the Religious Establishment in Mexico, 1821-1836." *Southwestern Historical Quarterly* 91 (January 1988): 283316.
Miller, Terry E. "Otter Creek Church, Indiana: Lonely Bastion of Daniel Parker's 'Two-Seedism.'" *Foundations: Baptist Journal of History and Theology* 18 (October 1975): 358-76.
Mode, Peter G. "The Second Great Awakening as Organizational Process, 1780-1830: An Hypothesis." *American Quarterly* 21 (Spring 1969): 23-43.
Mooney, Chase C. "Some Institutional and Statistical Aspects of Slavery in Tennessee." *Tennessee Historical Quarterly* 1 (September 1942): 195-228.
"Palestine Murder Trial Brings Hanging Verdict But Killer Breaks Jail." *Robinson (Ill.) Daily News*, 28 December 1961.
Parker, Ben J. "Early Times in Texas and History of the Parker Family." *Palestine (Tex.) Daily Herald*, 12 February 1935.
Parrott, Gregory A. "U.S. Rangers of Fort LaMotte." *The Robinson (Ill.) Argus*, 6 April 1984.
Spencer, Donald S. "Edward Coles: Virginia Gentleman in Frontier Politics." *Journal of the Illinois State Historical Society* 61 (Spring 1968): 150-163.
Suppiger, Joseph E. "Amity to Enmity: Ninian Edwards and Jesse B. Thomas." *Journal of the Illinois State Historical Society* 67 (April 1974): 201-11.
Sutton, Robert M. "Edward Coles and the Constitutional Crisis in Illinois, 1822-1824." *Illinois Historical Journal* 82 (Spring 1989) : 33-46.
Tingley, Donald F. "Illinois Days of Daniel Parker, Texas Colonizer." *Illinois Historical Journal* 51 (Spring 1958): 388-402.
Wood, Gordon S. "Ideology and the Origins of Liberal America." *The William and Mary Quarterly* 44 (July 1987): 627-40.
Wyatt-Brown, Bertram. "The Antimission Movement in the Jacksonian South: A Study in. Regional Folk Culture." *The Journal of Southern History* 36 (November 1970): 501-529.

Index

Adams, John Quincy, xiii, 51, 52
Age of Jackson, The, xiv
Alamo, 106
Allen, C. Leonard, xv
Almonte, Juan N., 102
American Baptist Historical Society, v
American Baptist Home Mission Society, 134
American Board of Commissioners for Foreign Missions, 17
American Particular Baptists, 12
Anglin, Elisha, 97
Anglin, Phoebe Parker, 142
Archer, William B., 49, 50, 51, 52
Arkansas State Library, v
Arminianism, 4, 11, 14, 17, 23, 24, 48, 133, 146, 147, 148
Arrington's Creek Baptist Church, 18
Asbury, Francis, 11
Austin Colony, 95, 130
Austin, Moses, 92, 131
Austin, Stephen F., 92, 93, 94, 98, 102, 130, 131
Author's Defence, The, x, 85

Bank of the United States, xiii
Baptist Banner and Western Pioneer, The, 134, 136
Baptist Board of Foreign Missions for the United States, 18, 19, 61, 69, 150
Baptist Foreign Mission Society, 143
Baptist Triennial Convention, 17
Baptists: and associations and/or churches, 11, 21, 58, 69, 71, 80, 81, 95, 134, 156; and church polity, 7; and their doctrine, xv, 16, 147; and the Great Awakening, 2, 4; influx of, 10, 17, 57, 94, 95, 129, 130, 145; and Parker, Daniel, ix, xviii, 74, 78, 85, 88, 90, 95, 130, 139, 145, 148, 150, 158, 159; and slavery, 41, 44, 123, 144; and Two-Seedism, 74, 135, 136, 137, 157
Barr, Alwyn, v
Barrett, Don Carlos, 103, 104, 105, 106
Baylor College, 138
Baylor University, 138
Bays, Joseph, 129
Beaumont Committee of Public Safety, 102
Beebe, Gilbert, 136, 148
Benedict, David, 21, 142
Bennett, Miles, 122
Bennett, William P., 46
Bethel, Cantrel, 18, 20, 21, 22
Bethel Church, 140, 142
Birkbeck, Morris, 44
Black, Moses, 4
Black Rock Address, 149
Blackburn, Rev. Gideon, vii
Blackhawk War, 51
Bledsoe, Col. Anthony, 10
Blue River Association, 71
Bond, John, 19
Bond, Shadrach, 33
Bowles, Chief, 114
Brown, Patsy, 97
Browne, Thomas C., 32, 33, 36, 38, 40
Bruce, William, 62, 70
Bryant, James L., 133
Buck Creek Baptist Church, 58
Buffalo Creek Baptist Church, 7
Burnet, David G., 117
Burnet Grant, 97

Burns, Jeremiah, 18
Busseron Baptist Church, 67

Cady, John F., ix
Calhoun, John C., 32
Calvinism, xvi, 2, 4, 24, 25, 12, 13, 16, 146, 147
Campbell, Alexander, xv, 56, 79, 88, 89, 147, 151
Carlson, Paul, v
Carroll, Benajah Harvey, ix
Carroll, James Milton, ix
Castro, Henri, 117
Catholicism, 97, 127, 128, 131
Center for American History at the University of Texas, v
Chambers, Joseph, 59, 62, 70
Cheek, Joel, 76
Cherokee Bill, the, 121
Chicago Historical Society, v
Christian Baptist, The, 79
Christian Reformer, 148
Christology, 74
Church Advocate, ix, x, 79, 81, 83, 87, 126, 148, 150, 154, 157
Claiborne Parish, 95
Clark, George Rogers, 34
Clay, Henry, xvii, 51, 52, 127
Coles, Edward, 28, 36, 40, 45, 55
Colonization Law of 1824, 93; of 1825, 93, 94
Colorado Baptist Association, 144
Columbia College, 69, 153
Committee of Privileges and Elections, 111
Committee on State Affairs and Judiciary, 101, 103, 104
Concord Association, 10-11, 15, 18, 19, 20, 21, 21, 23, 25, 150
Confederation Congress, 34
Congregational Church, 13
Congregationalism, xv, 2, 11, 146,-147, 156
Constitution of the Republic of Texas, 111, 121
Cook, Daniel Pope, 32, 37, 55
Cook, Rev. Valentine, 14
Cos, Martin Perfecto de, 98, 99
Council of the Provisional Government, 100

Cox, T. W., 134
Craig, H. T., 137
Crawford County Commissioners Court, 30
Crawford, William Harris, 32, 33
Crockett, David, 126, 127
Cryst, Stephen, 71-72
Cullom, Edward N., 30, 36, 37, 38, 47, 48, 53, 54, 68, 155
Culpeper County, Virginia, 2, 3
Cumberland Baptist Association, 73, 151
Cumberland Presbyterians, 144, 147, 150

Daniel Parker v. Wickliff Kitchell, 76
De las Piedras, Jose, 129
Democratization of American Christianity, The, xv
Denmon, William, 4
DeWees, William Bluford, 127
DeWitt, Green C., 93, 94
Dickson County, Tennessee, 6
Disciples of Christ, 144
Dixon's Creek Baptist Church, 21, 22
Dodson, Elijah, 46, 48, 49, 72
Dunkers, 39
Duty, Martha, 59
Duty, Solomon, 93
Dyer, Dwight, v

Eddy, Henry, 52
Edwards, Haden, 100
Edwards, Jonathan, 2
Edwards, Ninian Beal, 32, 37, 55, 155
Edwardsville Spectator, 44
1817 Concord Association, 19, 48
Elbert County, Georgia, 1
Elliot, Robert, 70
English Baptists, 17
English Particular Baptists, 12, 149
Episcopalians, 73, 144
Evangelicals, 143

Federalist Party, xi, xii, 31
Fields, Brice, 76
Foreign Missions, 17
Fort Houston, 107, 108, 109, 112, 116, 137, 138, 139
Fort Houston Church, 140

Index   209

Fort La Motte, 30
Fort Parker, 97, 106, 107, 108, 116
Fort Sugg, 61, 65
Fort Wayne, 68, 69
Foster, Richard C., vii
Foster, Robert C., 19, 21, 31
Fourth Assembly, 39, 45, 53
Franco-Texienne Bill, 117
Franklin County, Georgia, 5
Frost, Robert, 108
Frost, Samuel M., 108

Galveston Bay and Texas Land Company, 100, 112, 115
Gasper River Presbyterian Church, 3
General Missionary Convention of the Baptist Denomination in the United States for Foreign Missions, 17
Genesis of American Anti-Missionism, The, ix
Gill, Robert, 49
Glady Fork Baptist Church, 67, 76
Gnosticism, 151, 152
Grammer, John, 42, 43
Grand Prairie Church, 30, 48, 67
Great Awakening, 2, 3
Great Revival, 3, 4
Green River Association, 19
Greenwood, Garrison, 99, 107, 109, 132

Hamilton, Alexander, xi
Hanks, Wyatt, 104, 105
Hansen, Nicholas, 43
Hansford, John H., 111
Hargrave, Willis, 37, 38
Harris, Elder Tyre, 67
Harrison, William Henry, 62
Hartford Convention, xii
Hatch, Nathan O., xv
Highland Association, 71
Highsmith, William, 51
History of Texas Baptists, A, ix
Holmes, William, 110, 141
Hopewell Baptist Church, 10, 13, 15, 24, 132, 134, 135, 140, 148
Houston, John, 111
Houston, Sam, xviii, 98, 99, 104, 105, 107, 108, 109, 113, 115, 116, 117, 118, 119, 121, 125, 126, 137, 138

Howell, Robert Boyte Crawford, 149, 150
Hubbard, Adolphus Frederick, 45
Hughes, Richard T., xv

Illinois Assembly, ix, x, 41, 71, 95, 153
Illinois Intelligencer, 44, 68
Illinois Senate, viii
Illinois State Archives, v
Illinois State Historical Library, v
Illusions of Innocence: Protestant Primitivism in America, 1630-1875, xv
Independence Baptist Church, 144
Indiana Centinel, 84
Indiana State Library, v
Indiana University, v

Jackson, General Andrew, xiii, 51, 52, 159
Jacksonian Ear, The, xiv
Jacksonian Politics and Community Conflict: The Emergence of the Second American Party System in Cumberland County, North Carolina, xiv
Jefferson, Thomas, x, xi, xii, 88, 154
Jeffersonianism, x, 48
Jones, Anson, 117, 138
Judaism, xvi
Judson, Adoniram, 17, 157

Kane, Elias Kent, 33, 36, 38, 52
Kendrick, Mary Parker, 142
Kennedy, Joseph, 76
Kennedy, Thomas, 46, 47, 57, 60, 70, 72, 74, 75, 76, 77, 78, 85, 87, 88, 90, 160
Kilbuck, William, 81, 82
King, Rev. Samuel, 14
Kinney, William, 31
Kitchell, Joseph, 36, 37, 38, 47, 68
Kitchell, Wickliff, 36, 37, 38, 46, 48, 49, 50, 51, 52, 53, 54, 71, 72, 76, 160

La Motte Baptist Church, 46, 56, 57, 60, 62, 64, 67, 68, 69, 72, 76, 77, 78, 85, 87, 122
Lamar, Mirabeau Buonaparte, 113, 114, 117, 118, 119

Law of April 6, 1830, 97
Lawrence, Joshua, 83, 85, 148, 149, 154
Leadership in the American Revolution, xv
Leland, John, 153, 154
Lewis Historical Library, v
Liberty and Power: The Politics of Jacksonian America, xiv
Lilly Library, v
Lincoln, Abraham, 27
Lincoln, Thomas, 27
Lindsay, George W., 68
Little Flock Baptist Church, 67
Little, Lewis, 72
Little Village Baptist Church, 46, 58, 59, 60, 67, 77, 78, 95
Logan County, Kentucky, 3
Louisiana and Texas Regular Predestinarian Baptist Association, 140
Louisiana Purchase of 1803, 155
Lundy, Benjamin, 102

Mahon Public Library, v
Manichaeanism, 151-152
Maria Creek Baptist Church, 57, 58, 59, 60, 62, 63, 64, 65, 67, 68, 69, 70, 82, 83, 85, 86, 150, 157
Market Revolution, vii, xii
Market Revolution: Jacksonian America 1815 1846, The, xiv
Marshall, John, xi
Martin, Corbly, 68, 82, 83
Massachusetts Missionary Society, 66
McCall, Thomas, 81
McCoy, Isaac, 58, 59, 60, 61, 62, 63, 65, 66, 69, 81, 82, 85, 90
McGahey, David, 31, 36, 47, 48, 52
McGready, Rev. James, 3
McKendree, William, 11
McLean, John, 33
Menifee, William, 103, 105
Mercer, Jesse, 4
Mero District Association, 21
Methodists: and Arminianism, 4, 12, 16, 148, 150; and Parker, Daniel, 16, 23, 148; and Baptists, 11, 12, 13-14, 16, 41, 57, 143, 144, 148, 150; influx of, 10, 13, 23, 57, 131, 138, 143, 147, 148; and slavery, 41, 47, 143, 144
Methodist Episcopal Church, 143, 144
Mexican Army, 106, 107, 120
Mexican Congress, 128
Middle Tennessee Baptists, 12
Military Affairs Committee, 104, 105
Mill Creek Baptist Church, 7, 21, 67
Millerite, xiv
Monroe, James, 31
Morgan, Winnie, 139
Mormon church, xiv, 89
Morrell, Zacharius N., 134, 126, 127
Mount Pleasant Baptist Church, 134, 135, 139
Muir, Andrew Forest, 96
Mustang Prairie Church, 140

Nail's Creek Baptist Church, 5, 7
Nashville Democratic Clarion, 21
Nashville Impartial Review, 6
Neely, Charles, 46
New England Congregational, 156
New England Protestants, 156
New England Rat, 157
New Lights, 2, 3, 16
New Testament Christianity, xv, 158
Newcomb, Benjamin, v
Newport, Richard, 70, 73, 78, 157
Ninth Illinois General Assembly, 97
North Fork Baptist Church, 51
Northwest Ordinance, 34
Norton, Asa, 46, 70, 78
Noyes, John Humphrey, 88, 89

Old Lights, 2, 3, 16, 17
Old School Baptists, 136, 137, 139, 149, 151, 152, 157
Oneida Community, 88, 89
Origin and Development of the Missionary Baptist Church in India, The, ix

Palestine Land Office, 38
Panic of 1819, xiii, xiv, 32, 35, 159
Panic of 1837, 114, 123, 155
Parker, Aaron, 5
Parker, Abigail, 76
Parker, Benjamin, 76, 97, 108, 152

Parker, Cynthia Ann, 119
Parker, Daniel: and antimissionism, 148, 149, 150, 153, 156;——, in Georgia and Tennessee, 19, 25;———, in Illinois, 48, 56, 59, 61, 67, 69, 74, 81, 82, 88, 89, 90; ——, in Texas, 134, 135, 137; and Arminianism, 4, 10, 24-25, 48, 146, 147, 148; and associations and/or churches, 56, 77, 130, 131, 132, 133, 134, 138, 139, 140, 141, 145, 152; and the Baptist Board of Foreign Missions, 18, 19, 61, 82; and Calvinism, viii, 24-25, 56; and the Concord Association, 15, 19; as a councilman, 98-101, 103, 104, 105, 106; and the *Church Advocate*, 79, 83; death of, 119, 142; and the Fourth Assembly, 39, 45, 53-54; and Houston, Sam, 109, 115-116, 117, 118, 119, 125, 137; and illegal disputes, 46, 47, 48-49, 53, 72, 84, 111; as an Illinois senator, viii, 31, 37, 38-39, 40, 42, 43-44, 45, 46, 49, 53, 54; and Jacksonian democracy, x, xiv, xvii, 89, 90, 146, 158, 159; and Jeffersonian republicanism, viii, x, xvii, 53, 89, 125, 146, 156, 158, 159; and Kennedy, Thomas, 47, 60, 74-75, 75-76, 78, 85, 87-88, 90; and McCoy, Issac, 58, 59, 60, 62, 81, 85, 90; and ministry, viii, 146, 148, 150-151;——, in Georgia and Tennessee, 5, 6, 7, 10, 15-16, 18, 24;——, in Illinois, 30, 56, 60, 88, 89; ——, Texas, 111, 123, 125, 135; and *A Public Address*, 41, 61, 84; and slavery, 154, 155; ——, in Illinois, 40, 41, 42, 43, 44-45, 50, 54, 71, 86, 87; ——, in Texas, 101, 103-104, 121, 122-123, 124, 125; as a Texas House representative, 51, 111; and the Texas Revolution, 108, 109; and the Third General Assembly, 31, 39, 40; and Two-Seedism, viii, 56, 73, 75, 87, 89, 123, 136, 150-151, 153; *v. Kitchell, Wickliff,* 46-47, 48-49, 50-51, 53, 71-72; *v. Polke, William*, 63, 66, 67, 85, 90; *v. Peck, Jason Mason*, 58, 65, 71, 84, 85, 87, 90; and *Views on Two Seeds,* 72, 73, 74, 75; and Wabash District Association, 41, 61, 69-70, 71, 79-80, 85, 87;
Parker, Daniel, Jr., 106
Parker, Dickerson, 92, 106, 129, 140
Parker, Isaac, 30, 97, 98, 111, 115, 122, 125, 134, 142
Parker, James W., 22, 30, 39, 46, 59, 93, 94, 97, 108, 119, 122, 130, 142
Parker, John, 1, 2, 5, 6, 7, 8, 22, 23, 70, 81, 97, 108, 122
Parker, Joseph A., 22, 47, 93, 95, 97, 105, 106, 111, 118
Parker, Nathaniel, 10, 52, 119, 142
Parker, Patsey Dickerson, 2, 6, 8, 142
Parker, Rachel, 92
Parker, Sally, 7
Parker, Sarah White, 2
Parker, Silas Mercer, 5, 97, 99, 106, 107, 108
Parker v. Kitchell, 49, 50, 52
Particular Baptists, 12, 13, 14, 16
Party System in Cumberland County, North Carolina, xiv
Patoka Church, 66
Paxton, Thomas, 136
Peck, John Mason, 15, 44, 58, 65, 66, 67, 71, 72, 79, 80, 84, 85, 87, 90, 149
Perry, William, 103
Peters, William Smalling, 117
Phillips, Joseph B., 33, 36, 40
Pilgrim Baptist Church, 97, 106, 109, 122, 131, 133, 134, 135, 139, 142, 152
Pilgrim Predestinarian Regular Baptist Church, vii, 95, 129-130, 144
Piper, Edward H., 36, 68
Plain Truth, x, 68, 84
Polke, Charles, 62
Polke, Christiana, 58
Polke, Robert, 72
Polke, William, 58, 60, 61, 62, 63, 65, 66, 67, 68, 70, 72, 85, 86, 87, 90, 157, 158, 160
Pope, Nathaniel, 32
Pound, Thomas, 70
Prairie Creek Baptist Church, 58, 67
Pre-Revolutionary American Baptists, xv-xvi

Presbyterians, vii, 2, 4, 11, 14, 57, 129, 138, 144
Prevo, Samuel, 53
Primitive Baptist Church, 136, 149, 152
Primitive Baptist Library, v
Primitivism, xv
Protestantism, xiv, 17, 88, 129, 131, 132, 156
Providence Meeting House, 95
Provisional Government, 100, 120, 137
Public Address, A, ix, 41, 61, 62, 63, 84, 148, 153
Puncheon Camp Baptist Church, 22
Puritans, xv

Quakers, 39, 40

Red River Association, 15, 61
Red River Herald, 98
Reed, Isaac, 127, 133, 139, 157, 158
Regular Baptists, 17
Remini, Robert V., xiv
Republic of Texas, xviii, 132
Republicans, xii
Reynolds, John, 45
Rice, Luther, 17, 18, 19, 25, 65, 83, 157
Robinson, James W., 99
Roman Catholic church, 97, 127, 128
Rose, Martin, 86, 87
Ross, Reuben, 15
Rueg, Henry, 100, 101, 107
Runaway Scrape, 106, 132
Rutersville College, 138
Ryan, William, 30, 72

Sabine Association, 71, 95, 138, 139, 142
Salem Baptist Church, 21, 22
San Jacinto Church, 140
Santa Anna, Antonio López de, 97, 98, 107, 120
Schlesinger, Arthur M., Jr., xiv
Scott, Lorine Maud, ix
Second Great Awakening, viii, 3, 4, 57, 146, 147
Sellers, Charles, xiv
Separate Baptists, xvi, 13, 16, 133
Shakers, xiv, 88, 89
Shaw, James, 47
Shaw, John, 43

Short Hint, A, x
Sign of the Times, 136
Sloo, Thomas, 45
Smith, Henry, 100, 104, 105, 106
Smith, Joseph, xvii, 89
Smith, Theophilus W., 42, 43
Southern Baptist Convention, 143, 149
Southern Baptist Historical Commission, v
Sparks, William, 133
Sparks' Settlement, 133
Stephens, Ray A., 110, 141
Stephenson, Henry, 129
Stephenson, William, 131
Stone, Barton Warren, 3, 147
Stone's River Association, 151
Straughton, Dr. William, 68, 69

Taylor, John, 148, 149, 156
Tennessee Gazette, 21
Tennessee Methodist Conference, 11
Tennessee State Archives and Library, v
Testament Baptist Church, v, 14, 15, 16, 22
Texas Army, 106
Texas Baptist Home Mission Society, 138
Texas Congress, 118, 120, 121, 138
Texas Constitution, 111, 112
Texas Declaration, 120
Texas Revolution, 91
Texas State Archives and Library, v
Texas Tech University, v
Texas Union Association of Regular Predestinarian Baptists, 152
Third General Assembly, 31, 39, 40, 44
Thomas, Jessie Burgess, 33, 36, 38
Thoughts on Missions, 148
Thrall, Homer S., 96
Tilman, George, 18, 20
Tingley, Donald F., x
Tippecanoe, Battle of, 62
Triennial Convention, 63, 69
Trott, Samuel, 136, 137, 157
Turman's Creek Baptist Church, 67
Turnbull Baptist Church, 6, 22
Two Seedism, viii, ix, xvi, xvii, 56, 73, 74, 75, 76, 77, 79, 81, 87, 89, 123, 135, 136, 137, 150, 151, 152, 157, 158, 160

Union Association of Regular Predestinarian Baptists, 122, 135, 139
Union Baptist Association, 71, 78, 86, 87, 134, 138, 139, 140, 144
Union Baptist Church, 67, 133
Unitarianism, 73, 146, 147
University of Chicago, ix

Views on the Two Seeds, ix, 72, 73, 74, 76, 136, 151, 153
Volunteer State Baptists, 150

Wabash Baptist Church, 67, 72, 86
Wabash District Association, 41, 57, 60, 61, 62, 63, 64, 66, 67, 68, 69, 70, 71, 72, 77, 78, 79, 80, 81, 83, 85-86, 87, 88, 95, 122, 150
War of 1812, vii, xii, xiii, xvii, 26, 31, 81, 155

Watson, Harry L., xiv
Watson, John M., 151
Webb, Robert Louis, v
Welch, James E., 65
Wesleyan College, 138
Western Baptist, The, 79
Western Predestinarian Baptist, The, 135, 137
Whig, 51, 52, 55
White River Association, 71, 87
Whitefield, George, 2
Whitsitt, James, 7, 19, 20, 21, 22
William's Creek Baptist Church, 5
Wimberly, LaMarsha Kay, v
Wiseman, John, 18, 19, 20, 21, 22
Wolf Creek Church, 140
Wood, Gordon S., xv
Woolcott, Ziba H., 46

Young, Thomas, 31

www.ingramcontent.com/pod-product-compliance
Lightning Source LLC
Chambersburg PA
CBHW061256110426
42742CB00012BA/1934